INDIGENOUS PEOPLES
AND GLOBALIZATION

INDIGENOUS PEOPLES AND GLOBALIZATION

RESISTANCE AND REVITALIZATION

Thomas D. Hall
and
James V. Fenelon

Paradigm Publishers
Boulder • London

Paradigm Publishers is committed to preserving ancient forests and natural resources. We elected to print this title on 30% post consumer recycled paper, processed chlorine free. As a result, for this printing, we have saved:

3 Trees (40' tall and 6-8" diameter)
1,236 Gallons of Wastewater
2 Million BTU's of Total Energy
159 Pounds of Solid Waste
298 Pounds of Greenhouse Gases

Paradigm Publishers made this paper choice because our printer, Thomson-Shore, Inc., is a member of Green Press Initiative, a nonprofit program dedicated to supporting authors, publishers, and suppliers in their efforts to reduce their use of fiber obtained from endangered forests.

For more information, visit www.greenpressinitiative.org

Environmental impact estimates were made using the Environmental Defense Paper Calculator. For more information visit: www.papercalculator.org.

Copyright © 2009 by Paradigm Publishers

Published in the United States by Paradigm Publishers, 3360 Mitchell Lane, Suite E, Boulder, CO 80301 USA.

Paradigm Publishers is the trade name of Birkenkamp & Company, LLC, Dean Birkenkamp, President and Publisher.

Library of Congress Cataloging-in-Publication Data

Hall, Thomas D., 1946–
  Indigenous peoples and globalization : resistance and revitalization / Thomas D. Hall and James V. Fenelon.
    p. cm.
  Includes bibliographical references and index.
  ISBN 978-1-59451-657-3 (hardcover : alk. paper)
  ISBN 978-1-59451-658-0 (paperback : alk. paper)
    1. Indigenous peoples—Politics and government. 2. Indigenous peoples—Land tenure. 3. Indigenous peoples—Social conditions. 4. Globalization—Political aspects. 5. Culture and globalization. I. Fenelon, James V. II. Title.
  JF1061.H35 2009
  305.8—dc22

                                                                              2009000979

Printed and bound in the United States of America on acid-free paper that meets the standards of the American National Standard for Permanence of Paper for Printed Library Materials.

Designed and Typeset by Straight Creek Bookmakers.

13 12 11 10 09   1 2 3 4 5

*To our fathers who passed on to the spirit world,
Vincent E. Fenelon and Harry T. Hall, and to all
indigenous peoples who remember and survive.*

Contents

Foreword

GLOBALIZATION THEORY HAS MADE a considerable impact on understanding Western history and the development of contemporary capitalism. Some experts have taken the argument of globalization and addressed more local "world-systems" in differing historical periods and local microcosms of trade and economic exchange. Generally the arguments of globalization and world-systems have focused on the rise of capitalism and its global reach and effects on core, semiperipheral, and peripheral economies and peoples. Globalization research tends to look at market systems, or nation-states, sometimes old civilizations, and the impact of emerging and extending global or regional market or trade relations.

In the social sciences, relatively little attention is given to the historical and contemporary conditions of indigenous peoples. Modernization, and generally most contemporary theoretical viewpoints, and Eurocentric histories often saw indigenous peoples on the far periphery and doomed for destruction in the face of advancing market systems and nation-states. The continued persistence and continuity of indigenous peoples throughout the world have defied such theoretical viewpoints as too simplistic and not broad enough to account for the contemporary world, where indigenous peoples around the world refuse to disappear according to theoretical predictions. Contemporary theories need to reconcile with the empirical counterpoint that indigenous peoples will continue as social, cultural, and political peoples in the contemporary world and into the future. Any theory that predicts the cultural, political, and economic disappearance of indigenous peoples will need to revise its basic assumptions and provide an accounting of the continuity of indigenous peoples, societies, cultures, and nations.

According to the United Nations, there are at least 375 million indigenous people in the world. These peoples have for many years worked in international diplomatic channels and are organized into numerous internationally recognized nongovernmental organizations; they also are recognized within the United Nations as the UN Permanent Forum on Indigenous Issues. After centuries of silent resistance and continuity, indigenous peoples have found more visible voices in the contemporary international context of human rights established as a reaction to the Nazi horrors of World War II. Indigenous peoples are composed of thousands of languages, cultures, social and political histories, and conditions. The experiences and histories of indigenous peoples vary by international political relations, local and world globalization, the features of and relations to their surrounding nation-states, as well as their own diverse social, cultural, and political organization and histories.

Most contemporary theory does not conceptualize the existence or presence of indigenous peoples, let alone offer a theory or conceptualization of the cultural, political, social, and territorial continuity of contemporary indigenous peoples and nations. Truly powerful and ecumenical theories of social change must account systematically for the inclusion of indigenous peoples and their experiences in history, present-day life, and in the future. Any theory of social change or society that cannot include the fundamental issues of indigenous peoples must be considered incomplete—not fully capable of explaining or even describing the range of human experience, history, or processes of change. Contemporary theory should not, and cannot, continue to reflect the interpretations of colonial or even modernization positions that abstract past the continued presence of indigenous peoples and their ways of life. The need to include indigenous peoples in contemporary theory is not a claim on rights or a mode of civil rights inclusion, but rather the beginning of theories that provide more complete understanding and explanatory range about the diversity of human societies and their histories and cultures. Any future understanding of human groups must include the full range of human experience, and not systematically exclude some human groups based on beliefs and understandings that the world is moving toward a singular view of the good life, of the good society, or the most appropriate culture. Our theories need to understand diversity of historical experience, patterns of change, multiple cultural and community paths to the future, and in the end provide some semblance of explanation or understanding of the patterns of human experience and future possibilities.

This book makes a significant step in developing a theory and perspective that provides greater appreciation of the diversity and possibilities of human societies and peoples. Hall and Fenelon take the tradition of globalization theory while adapting it to provide greater understanding of indigenous peoples in historical and contemporary contexts. The major goal of the work is to make an argument that globalization is a significant context for understanding social, cultural, and political action in indigenous communities. The actions of indigenous communities are conditioned by the position and changing relations of globalization. The authors propose several patterns of change and use case studies to illustrate their arguments. The work is original in the sense that research on world-systems and their effects on indigenous nations is relatively spare. Hall is a major contributor to the world-system and indigenous peoples literature. The current book extends the theory and empirical range of the existing literature on globalization and its effects and patterns of resistance or accommodation among indigenous peoples around the world. The book builds on earlier works by the authors, and it proposes new hypotheses and empirical case studies about the global political, economic, and cultural effects on indigenous social and political processes. The contributions are plausible, and they reveal the need for more empirical work and theorizing. The authors include case studies to illustrate points and theories, although they are quick to temporize about both the empirical case material and the theory. The book is a good example of applying globalization theory to analyze indigenous patterns of resistance and change; it should be useful to many scholars, as well as extending world-systems analysis into areas where it has made limited theoretical and empirical headway.

    In particular, the authors discuss implications of the recent passage of the Declaration on the Rights of Indigenous Peoples by the United Nations Assembly. This is a major international event that needs reconciliation within the world-systems theory approach. Even though some world-systems works have studied the marginalization of indigenous peoples and have provided many powerful insights, the indigenous peoples are often seen as passive victims of economic history. Clearly powerful economic forces of globalization are at play and have had powerful effects on the lives and economic fortunes of indigenous peoples. The globalization approach is generally now recognized as creating both constraints and opportunities for peripheral and semiperipheral groups and nations. Too often, however, peripheral groups are seen as marginalized but also as homogenous and powerless. The cultural and political countermovements conducted by indigenous peoples show considerable amounts of cultural, political, and territorial preference and choices. Despite perhaps often extreme forms of cultural, political, economic, and territorial marginalization, many indigenous individuals, groups, or nations continue to express identity, community, and an articulated rights argument in similarity to contemporary human rights expressions. Indigenous peoples express their own culturally informed social action, and they want to develop solutions to globalizations that create economic well-being but within their own cultural and political understandings and goals. Most contemporary theories—and in this number I include modernization theory, postmodernization theory, and even postcolonial theories—are often given to marginalized conceptions of indigenous peoples and therefore have great difficulty accounting for the social action and cultural continuity that are expressed by indigenous peoples in the contemporary world and throughout their histories. The present book on globalization goes a long way in making indigenous peoples the primary center of empirical analysis and seeking to provide more sophisticated and advanced arguments for understanding the indigenous experience. This endeavor is intended by the authors not as a glorification of indigenous ethnicity, but as a direct challenge to the existing globalization theories, with their tendency to homogenize peripheral groups and diversity, and an effort to develop analytical tools that will better understand the processes of international economic and political globalization on human groups throughout the world. The empirical and cultural relations and experiences of indigenous peoples are quite diverse, but they all face the issues of globalization on various political, cultural, and economic levels. The people of the world face the common issue of globalization, and the ways that indigenous peoples will want to face globalization dynamics will differ greatly among indigenous peoples as well as among other cultures, nation-states, and cultures of the world.

This book provides considerable empirical detail in case studies that are helpful and illustrative. The argument builds through the chapters. The book covers theoretical insights that all students in the sociology and American Indian studies fields should be aware of and should take into consideration when analyzing policy, history, and current events among indigenous peoples. Students and scholars in globalization studies will also learn from the book, since no theory of globalization will be complete without analysis and explanation of the patterns of persistence and change among the world's indigenous peoples. The book does not require extensive previous expertise in world-systems analysis. There are a few technical terms, but the authors define them suitably. Fenelon and Hall are clear about the tentative character of both their theorizing and empirical results. The work does not pretend to do more than offer new and systematic proposals in world-systems theorizing, and the empirical cases often are tempered with comments about the current absence of sufficient data. Nevertheless, the book presents a consistent world-systems argument applied to the historical context and political issues confronting indigenous peoples—all of which is worthy of consideration and discussion. The authors make an argument for the significance of cultural, political, and economic globalization on the conditions and contexts of change among indigenous peoples. Their book has a good grasp of this argument, encouraging more theorizing and more empirical works that will systematically consider the effects of the world-system on the past, present, and future of indigenous peoples.

—Duane Champagne

Preface

YOU MIGHT READILY ASK, Who are these authors who write about indigenous movements, and what motivates them? We will try to answer those questions here.

We come at this project from different approaches, though we have been working together since the early 1990s.

Tom Hall's interest in contemporary indigenous peoples was sparked when he taught anthropology at Navajo Community College, from 1971 through 1973, in Many Farms, Arizona. Jim Fenelon's interests are more familial and personal. He grew up hearing stories from and visiting Dakota and Lakota relatives at Standing Rock, North Dakota, and elsewhere in the United States, especially during the tumultuous 1970s, and later in colleges and universities.

We begin by sketching our own backgrounds and interests, then turn to how this specific project grew out of them. For readability, each of us has written a section of what follows in the first person.

TOM HALL

I observed that despite the historical "fact" that Spaniards brought sheep and silver to the Navajo region, wool weaving and silversmithing were thoroughly "Navajo-ized," that is, fully integrated into Navajo culture. I was deeply impressed by the vitality and adaptability of Navajo people and their ability to resist myriad attempts to transform them into middle-class Americans. Not long after I left Navajo Community College, OPEC raised the price of oil to then unprecedented levels—but cheap by 2009 prices—generating intense political debate within the Navajo Nation as evidenced in elections for chapter representatives (something like a county commissioner or township trustee). The clear power and influence of historical and global interactions on local social and political processes led to my interest in world-systems theory analysis.

What continues to interest me about this analysis is that it is a major sociological approach to the modern world that insists that analysts take history and intersocietal interconnections seriously. Although vitally important, these factors and this approach are only a necessary, but far from sufficient, component in understanding all sorts of local social processes.

Over the course of writing many papers I found I had to explain why what I studied was, indeed, sociology, and not "just" anthropology, history, or geography. Actually it is all of these.

I also began to understand that ignoring peripheral areas, peoples, or processes led to "bad," that is incorrect, theorizing about social processes because key processes were omitted from consideration.

Jim Fenelon

I had been impressed with the retelling of the repulse of Custer and the U.S. invasion of Lakota-Sioux homelands, and even more so with intimate knowledge of the SunDance and the Ghost Dance of the 1890s leading to the conflict at Wounded Knee. Activist struggles including the American Indian Movement consumed many of my relatives, while others rose to political prominence, such as Pat "Wambli Topa" McLaughlin. These struggles were often fought over in academic circles, and gradually the rise of authentic indigenous voices tempered an often condescending and assuming dominant discourse. Interacting with and learning from traditional elders such as Chauncey Dupree from Cheyenne River and Mary Louise Defender from Standing Rock, or the late great Vine Deloria Jr., showed me that an indigenous perspective was indeed possible.

Today, my research and personal interests have expanded to indigenous struggles across the world, and I have been lucky enough to interact with and learn from peoples from New Zealand, India, Mexico, the Middle East, Central and South America, and of course the ongoing struggles over sovereignty and autonomous relationships among Native Nations from North America.

Over the course of these studies, ranging from Indian Education to Indigenous Social Movements, I began to observe the centrality of an origin place philosophy, tempered by a focus on community and leadership, all of which came under duress by invasive cultural domination by states. As I came into professional contact with scholars such as Tom Hall, I saw that a frame of world-systems analysis would help to break down these processes, leading to richer theorizing that acknowledged the indigene contribution.

Over many conversations both of us came to see that the study of indigenous peoples offered a unique lens into contemporary global processes and deeper insights into how people strive, often with a modicum of success, to retain some degree of local autonomy in the face of the onslaught of global, neoliberal capitalism. We also came to see that indigenous peoples offer suggestions, and occasionally models, for how other groups might also maintain some degree of local autonomy. Thus, our analysis proceeds at two levels simultaneously: (1) to learn from indigenous peoples ways by which other groups might resist global neoliberalism; and (2) to expand social theorizing about such processes by including these often neglected groups in our thinking.

We are not, however, trying to construct a "how-to" manual for indigenous peoples—they are doing quite well without our input. Nor are we constructing a "how-to" manual for other globalization activists. Rather, we seek to present some observations and theoretical musing for others to ponder in their own theoretical considerations and offer globalization activists some ways to "think outside the box" in their activities.

Because of these goals we did not try, nor do we claim, to present a complete inventory of indigenous movements. Our goal is more modest. We have used those movements that we know, or have learned about, to illustrate our arguments. We invite readers to consider other cases.

Finally, we do not see our account as a final word. Rather, it is a contribution to continuing conversations about indigenous peoples, about social theorizing, about globalization processes, and about ways in which humans might work to make those processes more humane.

Thus, what follows is a discussion that is in reality a freeze-frame of our continually evolving thinking on these matters. If at times it appears to be a forced fit, this reflects that we have frozen a continuous process of thinking and rethinking to get it down on paper. For this reason we also include a brief epilogue that suggests how we might think about events and processes that have occurred during the final writing of this book.

We do not expect readers to agree with us. We do want readers, however, to take our arguments seriously, and when presenting counter- or alternative arguments to bring to bear additional empirical evidence, or different indigenous perspectives.

We can observe some of this contrast in how the late John Mohawk titled his book—*Utopian Legacies* (1999); or the late Vine Deloria Jr. titles—*Custer Died for Your Sins* (1988), *God Is Red* (1994), and *Red Earth, White Lies* (1997). Even better, to paraphrase the late Andre Gunder Frank, let the debate—and the struggle—continue.

T. D. H. and J. V. F., October 2008

Acknowledgments

IRST, WE MUST ACKNOWLEDGE the many indigenous peoples and Native Nations who have shared their perspectives and struggles, and who have persevered to tell their stories.

As is always the case with writing a book, there are a large number of people to thank. These are people who have, in one way or another, influenced our writing for the better, though some may not even be aware that they did so. That we did not always heed sage advice is no one's fault but our own. And as is ever the case, there will be some individuals we have failed to name here, for which we apologize.

In alphabetical order we thank Manley Begay, Fred Block, Duane Champagne, Christopher Chase-Dunn, Mary Louise Defender-Wilson, Vine Deloria Jr., Robert Denemark, Wilma A. Dunaway, Gustavo Esteva, Joe R. Feagin, Andre Gunder Frank, Barry K. Gills, Ramón Grosfoguel, Peter Horsley, Jordan Kerber, P. Nick Kardulias, Smitu Kothari, Glen D. Kuecker, Darrell La Lone, Agustin Lao-Montes, Pat Lauderdale, Walter D. Mignolo, Joya Misra, Mary Moran, Salvador Murguia, Joane Nagel, Kathleen Pickering, Bruce Podobnik, Anibal Quijano, Thomas E. Reifer, Richard W. Slatta, Henry Tom, Immanuel Wallerstein, Charles Willie, and Franke Wilmer.

We also wish to acknowledge the panel organizers, panelists, discussants, and audiences at the many conferences where we have taken some of our ideas out for a test drive. We especially thank the attendees of several Political Economy of the World-System annual meetings and the many anonymous reviewers who commented on our articles and chapters.

We also wish to thank various sources of institutional support. At DePauw University these include the John and Janice Fisher Fund for Faculty Development, the Faculty Development Committee, and the Arthur Vining Davis Foundation Faculty Fellowship 2001–2004 (for Hall). At California State University at San Bernardino we thank the International Institute and the Dean of the College of Social and Behavioral Sciences.

✪

Deep thanks to the International Honors Program run by Joan Tiffany and the many country coordinators carrying on a tradition of experiential learning, especially those with the first Indigenous Perspectives Program. We thank the Dancers and Singers at Green Grass (Cheyenne River Reservation) and all other indigenous traditionalists who teach and keep these ways alive.

We also acknowledge debts than can never be repaid that we owe our spouses, Jean A. Poland and Sandra Luz Fenelon, and Jim's boys Mikhael Joaquin and James Dean, for putting up with his long absences. Our families are our futures.

Finally, we must thank Ann Hopman, Dean Birkenkamp, and all the folks at Paradigm Pubishers for their help, tolerance, and unflagging enthusiasm for this project.

Figures and Tables

CHAPTER I

Globalization and Indigenous Survival

Plate 1.1. Indigenous mask in Mexico City museum. (Photo courtesy of James V. Fenelon)

INDIGENOUS PEOPLES NUMBER OVER 350 MILLION around the globe, and possibly many more, depending on how one defines *indigenous*. This number is comprised of more individuals than the entire population of the United States, or about the equivalent of the European Union. It includes on the order of 5,000 different cultures. Thus, indigenous peoples constitute about 4 percent of the world's population—but more significantly, they account for as much as 95 percent of the world's cultural diversity.[1] Still, many writers have predicted the demise of indigenous peoples, especially for native nations in North America. For instance, in the late nineteenth century, Thomas Jefferson Morgan, the commissioner of Indian Affairs, claimed, "The great body of Indians will become merged in the indistinguishable mass of our population" (quoted in Iverson 1999, 16–17; see also Cadwalader and Deloria 1984 on envisioned disappearance). However,

1

Native Americans are not only "still here" but also one of the fastest-growing segments of the U.S. population (Snipp 1986, 1989, 1992; Nagel 1996). This is also true for indigenous peoples in much of the rest of the world.

Confrontations and conflicts between states and indigenous peoples are as old as states themselves (Chase-Dunn and Hall 1997). Clearly, states have been unilaterally successful in displacing, absorbing, incorporating, assimilating, or destroying indigenous peoples over the past 5,000 years. Yet, despite myriad dire predictions—and, more importantly, repeated military and social actions directed against them by states—many indigenous peoples have resisted steadfastly and survived attempts at total annihilation.[2] Certainly, one might respond, "Not yet, but soon!" But "soon" is now many centuries old. Thus, the question remains as to how or why indigenous peoples have survived the onslaughts against them. In particular, how have they survived into the early twenty-first century when there are no more regions outside the reach of global capitalism, and no regions that are not claimed by one or more states?

We begin by sketching a few of the ways indigenous peoples have survived. The examples will illustrate, among many other things, the need to increase the precision of concepts we use to discuss indigenous survival. This, in turn, requires reexamination of theoretical issues including not only indigenous peoples but also questions about the origin and processes of globalization (Berger and Huntington 2002; Chase-Dunn 1999, 2006; Chase-Dunn et al. 2000; Featherstone 1990; Featherstone et al. 1995; Gills 2000; Holton 2005; King 1997; Manning 1999; Podobnik 2005; Robertson 1992; Robinson 2004; Sklair 2002, 2006; Smith and Johnston 2002). Our exploration of the puzzle of how people without massive resources, numbers, or weapons can resist the transformative and often destructive effects of globalization will shed some light on the general processes of globalization and resistance to it.

The subject of indigenous peoples in a global context is a very large and very complex topic. Actually it is a set of discussions fraught with controversies and contentions, including over the basic concepts and terminologies used. Many scholars use a common gloss for indigenous peoples: American Indians or peoples like them. There are myriad problems in this limited gloss that arose from some of the social sciences themselves. Yet this gloss, however problematic, does permit the beginnings of a conversation. We will refine this description as we proceed in this chapter, to be more comprehensive of the international and global nature of indigenous peoples, as based on the examples we examine in this book.

Defining *globalization* is arguably as complex. Again, many scholars use a common gloss: the intense speeding up of communication, travel, commerce, and interconnections across the planet Earth in the late twentieth and early twenty-first centuries, primarily built on capitalist systems in rich countries that exploit market structures. Given this reference to the capitalist mode of production, it may be more instructive to think of globalization as divided into three general categories of economic, political, and cultural patterns that are involved in a close and complex process of interaction. The same could be said for any period of modern capitalism; however, the differences lie in the distinction between a world economy and a global economy: whereas the former economic pattern occurred on an international scale where production, exchange, and consumption took place between states, in the latter economic pattern production, exchange, and consumption take place on a transnational scale.

In this economic pattern of globalization there is a fundamental notion of expansion, but it is not the type of expansion that occurred during the rise of the international economy. Robinson (2004) describes this expansion as twofold: the first is "extensive enlargement," where the "commodification of social relations" reached locations that were once beyond the structure of "commodity production"; the second is "intensive enlargement," where this commodification of social relations is becoming increasingly privatized (pp. 6–7). As global capitalism has reached into all regions of the world, "extensive enlargement" has grown less apparent. According to Robinson, late-twentieth-century capitalism's expansion is intensive, with a "deepening rather than the enlarging of the system's domain invading and commodifying all those public and private spheres that previously remained outside its reach" (2004, 7).

One example of this "intensive enlargement" is the privatization of education.[3] Based upon neoliberal ideologies, multilateral agencies such as the International Monetary Fund and the World Bank often impose structural adjustment programs that compromise the autonomy of local communities. Operating on guidelines of "conditionality," these structural adjustment programs can mean direct cutbacks to education (Holton 2005). As an already deficient, deteriorating, and neglected institution in much of the developing world, education cannot withstand such privatization, especially at the expense of indigenous traditions of instruction that have already been marginalized within a larger modern context.[4]

One example that is particularly significant to our discussion of indigeneity, resistance, and revitalization in an era of globalization is the 2003 case of the natural gas exploitation in Bolivia.[5] Civil society unraveled when the neoliberal administration of former president Gonzalo Sanchez de Lozada proposed the building of a gas pipeline to transport Bolivian natural gas through Chile and on to Mexico and the United States. In this instance indigenous Aymara communities joined forces with miners, teachers, students, and peasants in a show of an "unlikely alliance" to resist the effects of global capitalism in the form of natural resource exploitations, dependence on Chilean access to shipping ports, and U.S. influence over the region (Postero 2005, 74–76). Encompassing one of the largest indigenous populations on earth, Bolivia is a prime example of how native peoples can resist unjust invasions of global capitalism.

Within recent political patterns of globalization, no single event has done more to alter world sentiment and recognition toward the broader sense of indigenous peoples than the election of Evo Morales in 2005. As the first indigenous president of Bolivia to assume office, Morales's victory exemplifies the changing sociopolitical scenes in countries where indigenous movements have effectively taken hold. It not only demonstrates the global importance of these successes but also adds to a pattern of resistance in opposition to global neoliberal hegemony. Moreover, the acceptance of indigenous politics into a broader movement of resistance to global capitalism is demonstrated by the establishment of close ties with other Latin American leaders.

Cultural patterns of globalization are perhaps the most subjective of the three categories. In a telling description about cultural globalization, Leonor Amarante (1986) captured a scenario indicative of this subjectivity when she reported on the use of video production among the Kayapo Indians of Brazil. By using video-technology in an attempt to document and preserve this culture, a Kayapo leader remarked, "Given that the white man has little interest in us, we have to act on our own" (Amarante 1986, 6). A paradox arises here: on the one hand, the influences of modern technology can be seen as altering traditional customs of cultural preservation; and, on the other, there appears to be at least some notion of agency provided by the availability of this mediating product. Nonetheless, in order to be true to the phenomenon at hand, the interaction of culture on a global level is occurring and must be interpreted as such.

Peter Berger (1997) outlined what he described as "four distinct processes of cultural globalization," including the "Davos" culture, which illustrates behavior attuned to global business and entrepreneurship; the "Faculty Club International" culture, which describes the expansion of Western knowledge; the "McWorld" culture, which encompasses a westernization of popular culture; and the culture of "Evangelical Protestantism," embodied in an explosion of religious proselytizing (pp. 23–29).[6] In addition to these processes, Berger also makes reference to the following four potential adaptations that occur when indigenous cultures[7] are faced with these encroaching globalizations: (1) the replacement of local culture, (2) coexistence between global and local cultures, (3) synthesis of global and local cultures, and (4) rejection of global culture by local cultures (Hsiao 2002, 50) or indigenous nations.

Evidence of these and of even more adaptations within the global cultural communities of indigenous peoples is quite prevalent. Since the end of the fifteenth century there has been no shortage of instances where forces motivated by capitalist accumulation through exploitation have replaced or tried to eliminate local cultures in the Americas.[8] Likewise, the concerted effort to coexist can be seen in the late-twentieth-century attempt to create a democratic plural state in Ecuador (Selverston 1998). The adaptation of synthesis also can be found in the agro-industrial production and marketing of ancient Andean foods (Healy 2004)—especially in contrast to trends in the proliferation of fast foods influenced by the rigid rationalization from the West. And finally, the adaptation of rejecting various cultural patterns of globalization is demonstrated by the Kalimantan Dayaks of Indonesia and their struggle to protect their forests from investors who attempt to profit from the demand for natural resources within the global economy (Fried 2003). It is this adaptation of rejection and the subsequent cases of resistance on the part of indigenous peoples around the world that contribute to the focus of this book.

Globalization as we discuss it accompanies the expansion of the modern world-system and therefore the spread and diffusion of capitalism around the globe. Andre Gunder Frank (1978, 1992), Immanuel Wallerstein (1974, 2004), and others have identified much of this as emerging at the same time and in tandem with colonialism, and they have further identified much of what others have called *underdevelopment* as a purposeful way of constructing and controlling world markets. Frank (1966) uses the term "the development of under-development," whereas others (e.g., Wallerstein 2004) call this "neo-imperialism by core states."

This understanding is essential to analyzing indigenous peoples for two reasons. First, the American Indian nations and other indigenous peoples in the Western Hemisphere—especially in North America—are subsumed in this process of "development" in terms of conquest, coercive assimilation, and nation-building. Second, those who survive these processes are further oppressed and marginalized through forms of internal colonialism. These populations are relatively small in core states such as the United States and Canada, and relatively large but diffuse in Latin American states, where they also are typically less "developed." Recent conflicts in Mexico, Nicaragua, Guatemala, Ecuador, Chile, Peru, and especially Bolivia underscore these relationships of indigenous peoples, resistance, and the larger globalization processes.

Perhaps the most compelling observation is that even in core states with capitalism, social movements by indigenous peoples, such as the American Indian Movement and many sovereignty movements, suggest parallels to other processes of historical domination and injustice. These movements then and now seek to maintain closeness to the land, to retain if not revitalize traditional cultures, and to oppose capitalist social structures. These parallels are found in the Latin American social movements as well and bear remarkable similarity to indigenous peoples' struggles around the globe.

This is one reason why we use specific, landed examples and discussions of indigenous peoples in the following chapters. It is important to note that social systems of governance, community, local economy, and land tenure become arenas of conflict within individual states. They are often sites of resistance to capitalist domination and the imposition of private property, and profit-driven value systems. Besides developing new consumptive patterns, globalization attempts to privatize and corporatize all the social systems it dominates. Examples of such resistance include the remote areas of Chiapas, Mexico, that gave rise to the Zapatistas, Aymara coca-leaf growers in the Bolivian highlands collectivizing and organizing with unions, the Inuit in Nunavut, the Mohawk in Quebec, the Navajo in the U.S. Southwest, and the Lakota in the northern U.S. plains states reorganizing under collective systems that strive to maintain traditional lifestyles. These are all cases where globalization comes into conflict with indigenous peoples in the Americas, with powerful congruence over even longer periods among the Adevasi in India or the Māori in New Zealand.

Globalization is usually referred to as a system that produces "dependency" and "underdevelopment" in developing economies common in Latin America and where corporate profits go to other countries, usually in core areas (Dello Buono and Lara 2007). For indigenous peoples this means socioeconomic depression and continuing cultural repression. Several processes within the larger phenomenon of globalization include significant components of oppression and cultural domination—at times overt and intentional, at others covert and less intentional, and many times unforeseen. Furthermore, many critics of globalization admit it is something of a mixed bag, causing what many see as "positive" changes even while it creates other problems. Clearly, globalization needs further analysis in relation to indigenous peoples.

SOME EXAMPLES OF INDIGENOUS RESISTANCE
TO GLOBALIZATION

What do we mean by resistance to globalization? Indigenous resistance to global capitalism is worldwide, diverse, and loosely interconnected.[9] Many forms of resistance are covert, echoing Scott's concept of "weapons of the weak" (1985); they often transmute and/or masquerade as something else. Other forms, while appearing classically revolutionary, defy any easy description. For instance, the events in Chiapas have sometimes been seen as part of a regional, or a peasant (and hence a class), or a *caudillo*-driven rebellion. They are less often discussed as an indigenous Mayan rebellion.[10] Movements in the United States, such as the American Indian Movement, are often seen solely in terms of localized ethnic, urban, or racial rebellions. Indigenous resisters are often connected via international nongovernmental organizations (INGOs), the United Nations, a large variety of their own organizations, and the Internet (Langman et al. 2003; Smith and Ward 2000).

In other cases traditional culture and organization itself is a resource that facilitates resistance and survival (Calliou 2005; Champagne 1989, 1992, 2005, 2007; Fenelon 1998). Indigenous resistance struggles are occurring all over the world, even in Europe as, for example, among the Saami (Eidheim 1969).[11] Kurdish activities in West Asia and Miskito resistance in Nicaragua have long been noted as indigenous movements (Harff and Gurr 2004). Gurr's (1993, 2000) *Minorities at Risk* is a catalog of such movements, and Linda Smith's (1999) *Decolonizing Methodologies* is itself an act of resistance against the hegemony of European-rooted social science concepts. Her work is rooted in her Māori community and her academic experiences.

These movements are so diverse, so fluid in organization, goals, and methods, they all but defy summary. Probably the most salient difference for indigenous movements is the emphasis on local community, identity politics, land claims, and rights to a variety of traditional practices. The latter include alternative family organizations such as extended kinship, matrilineality and/ or polygyny, communal ownership of resources such as land, the use of land for sacred ceremonies, less or nonhierarchical decision making, cultural membership in community, and indigenous knowledge that may include use of plant-life for medicine and psychic treatment. Many of these practices contradict, challenge, or threaten deeply held values in state-based systems. The most fundamental challenge to capitalism, though, comes from communal ownership of resources because it denies the overarching dominance of private property rights. Contrary to what many early explorers, missionaries, and colonizers thought, and unfortunately many so-called development experts today continue to think, it is not that indigenous people do not understand individual ownership. Rather, they have long recognized what many environmental movements are beginning to force capitalists to accept: most resources are partially, if not wholly, "public goods" (to use the terminology of economists) and are thereby sites of political, economic, or social contestation. The interactions of environmentalists and indigenous peoples have been something of a mixed bag, although in the first decade of the twenty-first century, alliances have become more common.[12]

Another form of resistance has been overt, conscious efforts to maintain "traditional culture." We think of traditional culture not as static and unchanging but rather as evolving according to the desires of group members resisting domination, rather than in accord with desires or directions of outsiders. That is, traditional culture, like all other social forms and structures, evolves and changes continuously, if sporadically and unevenly (Fenelon 1998, 27–30, 72; Smith and Ward 2000). We have observed these processes in North America taking place over some 500 years, ranging from Inuit to Lakota to Zapotecs. They are even older in other parts of the world, such as among the Adevasi in India, who have kept traditional cultures and languages alive for thousands of years.

Culture-building can be another form of resistance. For instance, there are nearly three dozen tribal colleges in the United States (American Indian Higher Education Consortium 2008; Boyer 1997).[13] These are institutions of higher education, typically equivalents of community colleges, run by various Native American groups. They differ from the typical U.S. community college in that many courses promote traditional culture, language, crafts, and customs. In some cases, language programs have been aimed at reviving or reinvigorating a language that has fallen into disuse.[14] Indeed, language education is often a primary mission of these colleges. Thus, tribal colleges are an institutional means of preserving and enhancing "traditional cultures." Some inroads have recently been made in colleges and universities around the world, although these institutions continue to remain purveyors of hegemonic ideologies and history (Champagne and Abu-Saad 2003; Wolf 1982).

Resistance can also take the form of building other localized institutions that conform to traditional cultural values. The Diné (Navajo) have several such institutions. The tribal police force, while acting much like any other rural police force in the United States, is also culturally sensitive to Navajo traditions and works within them. More direct are the "peacemaker courts," which avoid adversarial techniques of Anglo courts by pursuing resolution of disputes among Navajos through means that are in accord with Navajo concepts of harmony.[15] We now see new social forms arise among indigenous resistance, such as the "*junta del buen gobierno*" local justice of the Zapatistas, the coca growers in Bolivia with Evo Morales, or even the autonomous yet Islamic justice of the Kurds.

Other forms of resistance are less institutionalized but nonetheless important. Ward et al. (2000; and Baird-Olsen and Ward 2000) analyze how women among the northern Cheyenne have adapted conventional 12-step programs that address alcohol abuse or spouse abuse to Cheyenne culture, promoting Cheyenne family values. Another common institution among Native Americans in the United States is maintenance of matrilineal family systems, especially through the ownership of property. This often comes at a great price, as missionaries and bureaucratic functionaries have repeatedly attacked matrilineality as "barbaric," "unchristian," or chaotic. Native American feminists often organize in ways that oppose more mainstream feminist movements. Typically, indigenous feminists focus on issues of identity and cultural preservation prior to more narrowly focused feminist concerns (Chiste 1994; Jaimes and Halsey 1992; Marcos 2005; Miller 1994; Shoemaker 1995). Rigobertu Menchu (1984) has documented the oppression and resistance by Mayan women and families in Guatemala, as Gloria Muñoz Ramírez (2003) has done for Zapatista women.

Religion can be yet another form of resistance (e.g., Champagne 2003b). Maintenance of religious practices despite massive attempts to destroy them asserts an entirely different way of approaching the supernatural and the sacred. Among the most critical of these practices are lands that are sacred and necessary for religious ceremonies. This leads to conflicts over use of the land for sacred functions versus "productive" and/or "recreational" use (McLeod 2001). Today as "New Agers" have practiced various forms of shamanism, Indian groups have protested attempts to appropriate native traditions (Fenelon 1998, 295–301; Rose 1992). Native scholars see these multifarious intrusions into traditional culture as a last arena of conflict, where the holistic knowledge of indigenous peoples could once again be exploited by western markets that have a different orientation toward people and land, and of knowledge itself (Deloria 1994).

The revival of older traditions, such as the SunDance (see for example, Jorgensen 1972; Fenelon 1998, 114, 288–294), can be another form of religious resistance. These revivals hark back to many revitalization movements: the Longhouse religion of the Iroquois (Wallace 1969), the Ghost Dance movement (Brown 1976; Champagne 1983; DeMallie 1982; Landsman 1979; Thornton 1986, 1987), and the Native American Church (La Barre 1964; Aberle 1982; Stewart 1987), to name a few. These movements, all of which are somewhat syncretic, preserve many traditional values and have met with some success in combating the destructiveness of incorporation into the capitalist world-system. The Longhouse religion has been a source of strength among Iroquois. Russell Thornton (1986) argues persuasively that adoption of the Ghost Dance religion helped many small groups that had suffered severe demographic losses due to disease to recover both demographically and culturally. More recently the Native American Church (NAC, also known as the peyote religion) has been very successful in helping individuals recover from alcoholism. NAC has won several court battles that allow members to use peyote (Iverson 1999, 181–182).

All of these religious traditions are vastly different from the various monotheisms found in the states of the modern world-system. Their survival and growth are important forms of resistance to the ideologies of the modern world-system and to pressures for increasing homogeneity of culture due to various globalization processes. Duane Champagne argues, "Natives do not see the world as one where only humans have agency or soul. The Native world is full of forces that have agency, soul or spirit. Humans have a role to play in the Cosmic drama, but not necessarily a central role or an exclusive role" (2005, 6). Thus, many indigenous religions not only oppose capitalist philosophies but also challenge the underpinnings of enlightenment philosophy. Indeed, this challenge is the basis of ambivalent relations with ecologists: "Land is given as a sacred gift and a sacred stewardship. People do not own land, but must care for the land as part of their sacred task within the purpose and direction of the cosmic order" (Champagne 2005, 7). These core values are inseparable from traditional culture and are often a very important component of continuing resistance to hegemonic domination.

Some of the most significant forms of resistance are the various ways that resources are managed collectively, for collective good. Phrased alternatively, there are various ways of pursuing collective rationality. Here one must be careful not to read this solely as conventional "public goods" administration. This goes much further, in collective ownership of goods—land and livestock most commonly—that are typically individually, privately owned commodities in the capitalist world-system. As Champagne suggests, many indigenous peoples see their roles primarily as stewards who are a part of nature, not as its controllers or owners.

One of the more dramatic examples of such resistance is the continuing effort of Lakota peoples to regain control of the Black Hills. Several court decisions, including one by the U.S. Supreme Court, have determined that the territory of the Black Hills (in what is now South Dakota) was illegally taken from the Lakota peoples (Lazarus 1991; Iverson 1999, 117; Churchill 1996, 69–80). In accord with capitalist values and U.S. jurisprudence, the settlement of this claim has been monetary. The Lakota peoples, however, have steadfastly refused such commodified settlements and have insisted on the return of the land that they consider sacred. The intensity of this commitment is underscored by the relative poverty of Lakota people. Shannon County, where the Pine Ridge Reservation is located (the reservation closest to the Black Hills), has been, since 1980, the poorest county in the United States. Despite the temptation to take the cash settlement, the Lakotas have continued to reject such a settlement and to struggle for the return of their land.

Running through all these discussions concerning indigenous peoples in the United States has been the issue of sovereignty. Because of initial treaty agreements, indigenous peoples in the United States have a special relationship directly with the U.S. federal government (Deloria and Wilkins 1999; Fenelon

2002). It is on this legal status that many actions of Native American groups rest. Indeed, sovereignty issues are often the basis of challenges to states around the world and cut to the heart of the interstate system built on the 1648 Peace of Westphalia (Wilmer 1993, 2002).

Although native peoples have met with some success in maintaining sovereignty, they have had to fight on European grounds—within European law (for detailed examples from northern New Spain, see Cutter 1995a, 1995b). We will discuss the sovereignty issue in more detail later. Recently, one of the more outstanding successes has been to use the doctrine of sovereignty to build various gaming operations (Mullis and Kamper 2000; Fenelon 2006). By exploiting the contradictory desires for access to gambling and a desire to forbid it, American Indians have begun to turn considerable profits. But for some other groups, such as the Choctaw, this success is fragile and volatile and subject to federal redefinition (Faiman-Silva 1997).

The question remains, How much have they had to give up to win these victories? By fighting European civilization on its own turf, indigenous peoples have had to accept some of the premises of that turf. Thomas Biolsi argues that the law is "a fundamental constituting axis of modern social life—not just a political resource or an institution but a constituent of all social relations of domination" (Biolsi 1995, 543). Thus, courts have been a leading institutional means of commodifying everything, especially land (Biolsi 1995, 2001). Still, indigenous peoples continue to use legal systems to resist incorporation and global capitalism when they are available with direct access. Here we must note an important difference between indigenous struggles in the core or "first" world or global north and those in the "third world" or peripheral areas or global south. The rule of law carries much more force in the first world and so is a more useful tool there. Although this is generally the case, there are exceptions in both directions.

There have been many forms of symbolic resistance. For instance, political pressure has led to several national and/or state parks reserving some areas for traditional Native American ceremonies, such as Bear Butte, Devil's Postpile, and Medicine Wheel (McLeod 2001), although these have been limited in scope. Another example has been the movement against the use of Native American images as sports mascots (Fenelon 1999), along with national movements to remove the injurious term *squaw* from many place names. The expansion of the powwow circuit is also a vital form of asserting Indian-ness that both reinforces Indian identity and presents Indian culture to a general audience (Mattern 1996; Lassiter 1997).

In recent decades there have been indigenous movements that have challenged globalizing capitalism (Wilmer 1993; Champagne 2003a). Among these movements are those by INGOs such as Cultural Survival, the International Work Group on Indigenous Affairs, the Center for World Indigenous Studies, and the United Nations Working Group on Indigenous Populations. There are also several indigenous organizations (see Wilmer 1993, 227–229; Smith and Ward 2000). Most of these movements and organizations represent indigenous peoples on both the social group level and collectively, with great variation in their approaches toward issues, the nature of resistance, and the amount of their participation in political spheres.

The Zapatista movement—Ejército Zapatista de Liberación Nacional, or the Zapatista Army of National Liberation (EZLN), centered in Chiapas—has been one of the most dramatic. The Zapatista ideology contradicts the logic of capitalism; so too do some Zapatista practices. Members reject modernization and so-called development (Ross 1995; Katzenberger 1995; Collier and Quaratiello 1999; Mattiace 2003). Mignolo (2002) argues that the Zapatista movement constitutes an alternative to Greco-Roman legacies of state-making. The Zapatistas seek to maintain traditional lifeways in the face of overwhelming pressure to assimilate into the capitalist culture and practice and are thus opposed to the North American Free Trade Agreement (NAFTA) and the Free Trade in the Americas Agreement (FTAA). The march to Mexico City and the demonstrations in the Zocalo (March 13, 2001) accompanied by a huge outpouring of civil society in support of the Zapatistas are some indication of the growing impact of such movements. We discuss the Zapatistas in more detail in Chapter 3. (See the photo on the back cover.)

Although this catalog of indigenous resistances, overt or implicit, to global capitalism and to the international state system is large, it is but a small sample of such movements. We argue that these movements are more than oppositions to the states within which various indigenous groups are embedded. They are all claims to a continued right to exist as separate entities, a claim to have the right to preserve their own cultures as they see fit. In short, they are claims to autonomy: from the state and from the many forms of globalization. The latter claim, for some degree of autonomy from globalization, is what links indigenous movements to other social movements.[16] It is also why these quintessentially local movements are simultaneously part of a global process.

But why do we insist on a global approach?

A GLOBAL APPROACH

It is important that we be clear about what we are trying to do in this book, and what we are not trying to do. In the briefest terms, our argument is that indigenous peoples and their myriad reactions to globalization must be understood from global perspectives as well as from local, regional, and national perspectives. To do this we use and modify world-systems analysis. We do *not* claim that a world-systems analytic approach is the only approach or even the most important approach to a global examination of indigenous peoples. Rather, we advance a more modest claim that it is a useful tool, but one that must be modified and honed for these purposes. What we *do* argue vigorously is that any examination of indigenous peoples is incomplete if it does not include one or more global perspectives.[17]

Beyond these simple issues we seek to address several additional issues. One is to combat the too frequent, but mostly erroneous, critique that world-systems analysis is top-down and economically driven.[18] To be sure, in some hands, and quite often in brief articles, it appears to be so. However, the best examples, typically books, focus on the back-and-forth, the dialectic, between local actors, forces, and conditions and global actors, forces, and conditions. In short, it is the interplay between the local and the global that is critical. Although global conditions and forces shape local processes, it is equally the case that local conditions and processes construct global or world-system forces and conditions (see Hall 2000a, 2002 for further discussion).[19] The key point is the *interaction* of the two (or more) levels. Asserting primacy, for any level, only makes sense for certain limited topics. We also seek to use our analyses here to address and, we hope, begin to remedy these critiques.

Wilma Dunaway (2001) and Kathryn Ward (1993) charge that world-systems analysis has paid too little attention to indigenous peoples and to gender. In both instances the issue is not that world-systems analysis cannot in principle deal with gender or indigeneity, but that it has not. For both indigenous peoples and for gender, this is not primarily a matter of "political correctness" or "inclusiveness." Rather, it is an issue of defective theorizing. Some processes occur mostly, if not exclusively, in strongly indigenous and/or strongly gendered settings. To ignore them leads to development of bad theories. Thus, while using world-systems analysis, we seek to develop it further and to begin to fill some of these gaps.

Second, we pursue these theoretical goals by working from the bottom up in unraveling these complex interactions. We seek to do so by detailed examination of a few cases from around the world. We supplement these with much briefer discussions of many other indigenous peoples. We do not seek to present a catalog of all indigenous peoples and movements, nor even a representative sample. Even a sample would require a series of books, not one slender volume. Rather, we are seeking to probe limits, discover commonalities, suggest patterns, and model how such a global approach might be used. We hope that our efforts stimulate further research and help facilitate further dialog among scholars and activists who focus on local, national, or regional approaches.

A third issue is that the colonial legacy of the social sciences has often led to the pigeonholing of indigenous peoples in ethnography, so that they seldom are discussed in sociology or political science or international relations. The last lack is particularly glaring in that relations with indigenous peoples are always, at some, if not all, stages matters of international relations (see for example Wilmer 1993, or Fenelon 1998, 2002). This is a situation much like what happens when a large number of people witness a crime, everyone thinks that someone else reported it, and in fact no one did (Latané and Darley 1970). Similarly, many disciplines and subdisciplines assume that some other set of scholars has studied indigenous peoples when they have not. The result is theorizing that is at best highly circumscribed, and at worst simply wrong. We seek to open wider the communications among these sets of scholars.

Finally, we note with some satisfaction that activists, in particular indigenous activists, are often far ahead of the scholars who study them. More and more studies on movements against globalization report that indigenous issues are an important topic. Often they are barely mentioned, such as the Adevasi in India, but some, such as the Mayan-descent Zapatistas in Chiapas, Mexico, are closely examined. Movement leaders exchange views and insights widely and readily. Scholars and activists already report on the links between the indigenous movements leading to the election of Evo Morales in Bolivia and other organizations and peoples throughout broader Latin America. Indeed, this is one of the key avenues by which indigenous peoples have been influencing global movements locally, regionally, nationally, and globally. It is precisely these effects that led us to this project.

CONCEPTUAL REFINEMENTS

Clearly these are complex topics. Discussions of them are often hindered by imprecise or—worse—conflicting concepts. Here we begin refining our concepts, a process that will continue throughout this book.

The category "indigenous peoples" itself is a gross simplification of an immense variety of types of social organizations, with as many as 5,000 distinct cultures (Rainforestweb; Champagne 1999a, 2005; Stavenhagen 1990; Wolf 1999). This diversity is arguably greater than the diversity of types of state organizations found throughout a 500-year history of the "modern world-system," or even a 5,000-year history of states (Chase-Dunn and Hall 1997, 1998; Frank and Gills 1993; Hall 1989b, ch. 3; Smith 1999).

The United Nations working definition of indigenous peoples, written by José Martinez Cobo (1986), is worth quoting in detail:

> Indigenous communities, peoples and nations are those which, having a historical continuity with pre-invasion and pre-colonial societies that developed on their territories, consider themselves distinct from other sectors of the societies now prevailing in those territories, or parts of them. They form at present nondominant sectors of society and are determined to preserve, develop and transmit to future generations their ancestral territories, and their ethnic identity, as the basis of their continued existence as peoples, in accordance with their own cultural patterns, social institutions and legal systems.

Cobo notes that several additional factors are relevant to this definition:

> A historical continuity may consist of the continuation, for an extended period reaching into the present, of one or more of the following factors: (1) Occupation of ancestral lands, or at least of part of them; (2) Common ancestry with the original occupants of these lands; (3) Culture in general, or in specific manifestations, (4) Language; (5) Residence in certain parts of the country, or in certain regions of the world; (6) Other relevant factors. (J. Martínez Cobo 1986)[20]

Terms like *indigenous peoples, non-state societies, first nations,* and *first peoples* lump these highly diverse groups into an overly broad category that emphasizes their differences from states, but little else. Yet, these differences are very important. First, these are *not* state-based organizations. This, however, does not mean that they did not have identities and political structures. Nor is this to deny that there were indigenous states in North and South America prior to European contact—there were: Aztecs, Maya, Inka, and so on (Chase-Dunn and Hall 1998; La Lone 2000). Furthermore, some indigenous societies took on, and sometimes lost, state-like qualities, including the Cahokia (Forbes 1998; O'Brien 1992) and the Haudenosaunee peoples (Iroquois; see Snow 1994). The point is, differences in social organization are crucial, but they are avowedly *not* assertions about claims to rights or international status, which we will discuss later. Second, all these forms of social organization are noncapitalist, a term often glossed as "precapitalist." The latter term has two unfortunate connotations. On the one hand, it refers to organizations that preceded the advent of capitalism as a global system a few centuries ago. Another, dysfunctional connotation is that such organizations are precursors of capitalism. In this view they are seen at best as "primitive" forms of social organization, and at worst as outmoded and outdated. Our point is that such views are blatantly wrong. Rather, these forms of organization are fundamentally rooted in modes of organization, production, and accumulation that have little to do with capitalist accumulation of capital, and thus resist assimilation into those kinds of systems.[21]

That said, it is critical to recognize, as Eric Wolf argued so persuasively (1982), that these peoples have histories separate and distinct from those of European states and, indeed, all states (Chase-Dunn and Hall 1997, 1998). Furthermore, indigenous peoples have been forced to deal with waves of European expansion and the increasing globalization of capitalism over the past 500 years. Many peoples have been incorporated into the capitalist world-system, but far from completely. Many have resisted incorporation heroically, and untold numbers have died doing so.[22]

A key aspect of this argument is that indigenous peoples who struggle to preserve much, or some, of their noncapitalist roots—for example, communally held property rights—constitute, by virtue of their continuing existence, a form of anticapitalist resistance to incorporation into the world-system, and a challenge to the assumption of the state as the basic political unit of human social organization. Their claims for autonomy are a challenge to those globalizers who argue that "there is no alternative." Their continued existence and their struggle for autonomy underscore that not only is there an alternative to global capitalism, there are literally thousands of alternatives. This is yet another way in which the claim to sovereignty by indigenous peoples, especially in the United States and Mexico, is a challenge to the capitalist conception of states. However, the challenge is not only political-economic, but also cultural.

Culture and identity politics have become very highly contested issues in recent decades. Within these debates, the names of indigenous peoples are particularly contested.[23] Thus, it is useful to explain why we use some terms and eschew others. Such things can become especially insidious when their roots are lost. In order to avoid both reading the past into the present and the present into the past requires distinctions that enable us to describe changes with some precision. On the one hand, some argue that to label chiefdoms "nations" confounds a profoundly modern form of social organization with a much older and very different form of social organization. On the other hand, others argue that variations among "nations" are sufficiently distinct from the concept of state or "nation-state."[24]

It may be useful to rearticulate some basic terms that are too often used as synonyms, when in fact they refer to different yet overlapping entities. First is the *state,* by which we mean a formal, bureaucratically organized form of government. States were first developed some 5,000 years ago with the formation of Ur in Mesopotamia. Second is the *nation,* by which we mean a body or group of people with a shared identity that recognize themselves as a more-or-less united group. Third is the *nation-state,* by which we mean a state characterized by a population with a shared identity. Unfortunately, this term is tossed about too easily. There are two salient points about nation-states: the first is that nation-states are very rare, even today. Most states are multiethnic; the United States is not particularly exceptional in its diversity (see Laczko 2000). The second point is that we should question why people ever came to hold the nation-state as an ideal (see McNeill 1986; Hall 1998a). *Country,* by which we mean the territory of a state, is another term to consider. Following this are entities like tribes, chiefdoms, bands, and so on—terms for various types of nonstate organizations. They are often also nations, but they are *not* states.

As we will see in detail in subsequent chapters, these terms have become politicized in complex ways. Often these terms are used for political ends to deny right to treaty making. Sometimes, too, they are seen as an evolutionary sequence. If the sequence is seen as a general pattern with many exceptions and reversals, then this is reasonable. However, too often it is seen as some sort of lockstep, rigid sequence moving from "primitive" [bad] to "modern" [good], which is simply wrong. Such an understanding belies a fundamental misunderstanding of how societies change (see Chase-Dunn and Hall 1997, or Sanderson and Alderson 2005).

We also note that all of these social structures have, themselves, evolved over considerable time. They transform from one thing to another. An indigenous group that continues to exist today is *not* a "living fossil." Rather, it too has evolved, often having changed and adapted to a context in which it has been surrounded by one or more typically hostile states (Smith and Ward 2000). Indeed, one of the powerful insights from world-system theory is that the fundamental entity evolving is the system itself and that the evolution of any component of it—state, nation, nation-state, or indigenous group—must be understood within the context of system evolution. That is, they are part of feedback processes through which the world-system at any specific time limits the possibilities for its components while simultaneously these components constitute the system (see Chase-Dunn and Hall 1997, and Hall and Chase-Dunn 2006, for further details). The salient context in the twenty-first century is that it is a capitalist world-system that is continuing to change.

These issues and concepts shape our presentation and organization.

ORGANIZATION OF PRESENTATION

The next chapter focuses on models of revitalization and resistance. We briefly discuss several other cases to frame and contextualize the cases examined in other chapters. We then present two models: one of indigenous revitalization, and the other of resistance to the forces of globalization.

In Chapter 3 we will discuss the Māori of New Zealand and their long-term treaty relations, with a minor focus on combined repression and racism in the struggles of Australia's indigenous peoples. In addition we will sketch the historical struggles of the indigenous Adevasi peoples of India, who survived more than 3,000 years of tributary relations, British colonialism, neo-internal-colonialism, and contemporary struggles over forestlands and autonomous governance. Within the singular state structure of India, the Adevasi now constitute the largest number of indigenous peoples in the world.

In Chapter 4 we explore issues of what we mean by indigeneity, resistance, and revitalization in relation to globalization, with specific discussion of Mexico and the Zapatista movement, and general reference to cases in Central and South America, especially Bolivia and Nicaragua.

Chapter 5 focuses on examples from North America, primarily Wampanoag and Lakota peoples, with some discussion of Mohawk, Navajo, Seminole, and California peoples. We review long-term effects of globalization arising from colonialism, treaty-making, and development at the expense of indigenous peoples, in terms of cultural sovereignty.

In Chapter 6 we return to the global and long-term level to explore the contexts and timing of resistance movements. Although these results must be viewed as preliminary, they strongly suggest that relative success is to some extent shaped by world-system context and by place in world-systemic cycles.

In Chapter 7 we draw further conclusions and present a sketch of unanswered questions drawn from the models. We then suggest some speculations about possible answers and their significance for the present century. Each chapter ends with a list of recommended readings and useful websites.

We supplement with a brief epilogue where we note a number of changes that occurred as we were completing the book.

As we discuss indigenous peoples and their relationships to forms of globalization, and their resistance to neoliberalism, we develop four central organizing forms of most indigenous societies in relation to invasive and dominant modalities of capitalism. We ground these models in empirical cases, all discussed in later

Plate 1.2. Mary Louise Defender-Wilson, traditional Dakota and Hidatsa woman, who stresses the importance of language, community, generosity, and leadership for the people. (Photo courtesy of James V. Fenelon)

chapters. We hope these somewhat abstract models are helpful in observing the struggles of indigenous peoples to survive, resist, revitalize, and perhaps thrive in this modern world.

NOTES

1. This information is drawn from the UN Permanent Forum on Indigenous Issues, http://www.un.org/esa/socdev/unpfii/ (accessed December 11, 2008), and from Rainforestweb, http://www.rainforestweb.org/Rainforest_Information/Indigenous_Peoples/?state=more (accessed December 11, 2008). Other sources are Wilmer 1993; Stavenhagen 1990, ch. 8; Smith and Ward 2000; Sponsel 1995a; Bodley 2003; Niezen 2003; and Coates 2004. As our discussion will show, counting indigenous peoples is not a simple process for many reasons. Among those reasons is a desire to avoid contact with state-based agencies. If anything, the figures we provide are an underestimate. Similar problems occur with respect to cultures.

2. Of course, many indigenous peoples have been destroyed, especially well documented in North America, often rising to the level of genocide (Thornton 1986; Stannard 1992).

3. For a thorough assessment of the privatization of education in relation to the Canada-U.S. Free Trade Agreement, see Barlow and Robertson 1996, 60–70.

4. For a discussion on the defense of indigenous schooling traditions and the reaffirmation of legitimacy within such cultural practices in New Zealand, see Kçpa and Manu'atu 2008. Also see Fenelon and LeBeau 2006.

5. This was just three years after the Bechtel Corporation took control of the public water system in Cochabamba—one of the largest cities in Bolivia—and attempted to raise

water rates by more than 200 percent. In the face of massive public unrest, Bechtel ceased its operation.

6. Although the simultaneity and interaction of these four processes are Berger's own observations, he does acknowledge the influences of Benjamin Barber's 1995 *Jihad vs. McWorld* and Samuel Huntington's 1996 book *Clash of Civilizations and the Remaking of World Order*.

7. Berger's term *indigenous cultures* does not explicitly refer to indigenous peoples; however, it certainly *can* be contextualized in that fashion.

8. Fenelon 1998 calls the intentional destruction of local Native cultures "culturicide" as Stavenhagen 1990 and Ortiz 1984 apply "ethnocide" to indigenous cases in Latin America. The main point is that this is a violent, exploitive process.

9. Among key sources are Bodley 1988, 1990; Burger 1987; Gedicks 2001; Perry 1996; Smith and Ward 2002; Sponsel 1995a, 1995b; and Wilmer 1993. The entire Greenwood Press Series on Endangered Peoples is also valuable.

10. Some examples of the latter approach can be found in McMichael 2003; Boswell and Chase-Dunn 2000; Collier and Quaratiello 1999; Katzenberger 1995; Mattiace 2003; Mignolo 2002; and Morton 2000.

11. A useful website is the University of Tromso Center for Sami Studies, http://www.sami.uit.no/indexen.html (accessed December 11, 2008).

12. Gedicks 1993 provides an early view of indigenous and environmental movements in the context of Wisconsin. Gedicks 2001 provides a global summary and clearly shows that the budding movement toward alliances is a global movement, often tied, if at times ambivalently, with antiglobalization movements. Nesper 2002 provides a detailed summary of the fishing controversies in Wisconsin. The main difference between these forces is the primary interest area: the "environment" or indigenous communities.

13. Boyer 1997 reports 31 such colleges. Several others have opened since that report was published. For an up-to-date account, see American Indian Higher Education Consortium, http://www.aihec.org/colleges/TCUroster.cfm (accessed December 11, 2008).

14. The issue of language loss is very complex. McCarty 2003 reviews these programs and finds they are having a modicum of success (see also Goddard 2004). Spolsky 2002 finds, however, that language loss has become very rapid in recent decades. Nettle and Romaine 2000 provide a global survey of the language loss issue; see also American Indian Higher Education Consortium, http://www.aihec.org/ (accessed December 11, 2008).

15. Peacemaker Courts are discussed in more detail in Chapter 4. For more information see the PBS documentary *Winds of Change: A Matter of Promises* (1990); or the National Tribal Justice Resource Center, http://www.tribalresourcecenter.org/personnel/; or the Navajo Nation Peacemaking Program, http://www.navajocourts.org/index5.htm (accessed December 11, 2008).

16. In a wide-ranging essay Kuecker 2004 argues that many indigenous movements are related to many of the "new social movements" that envision new ways of bringing about radical change without violent revolution. Also see Guidry et al. 2000; Smith and Johnston 2002; Hall and Fenelon 2008; and Stahler-Sholk et al. 2008.

17. For further elaboration see Hall 1983, 1986, 1989a, 1989b, 1989c, 2000b, and 2002; or Bodley 1988, 1990, and 2003.

18. See the exchange between Steve Stern (1988a, 1988b) and Immanuel Wallerstein 1988 in *American Historical Review* for an example of this debate. For summaries of world-systems analysis, see Wallerstein 2004; Hall 2002; 2000a, and 2000c; Grimes 2000; and Shannon 1996. The literature on these issues is immense. For a beginner it is better to start with more recent work (e.g., Wallerstein 2004) than try to trace the many debates.

19. Roland Robertson drew the term *glocalization* from the Japanese word *dochakuka,* which roughly means "global localization" (Robertson 1992, 113–174; 1995). Glocalization is a useful descriptor for illustrating the hybridization of the local and the global where the interaction between these regions—whether real or imagined—gives rise to an entirely new product aside from that which was initially intended for production.

20. These quotes were taken from the International Work Group for Indigenous Affairs, Identification of Indigenous Peoples, http://www.iwgia.org/ (accessed December 11, 2008). There are an immense number of papers and discussions on UN websites; see especially UN High Commission on Refugees, http://www.unhcr.org/cgi-bin/texis/vtx/home; and UN Development Program, http://www.undp.org/ (accessed December 11, 2008).

21. *Capital accumulation* refers to amassing wealth in any form, *capitalist accumulation* to "the amassing of wealth by means of the making of profits from commodity production" (Chase-Dunn and Hall 1997, 271). For more elaborate discussions of changes over the past 5,000 years, see Bodley 2003; Chase-Dunn and Hall 1997; and Frank and Gills 1993.

22. For detailed examples of such resistance, see Dunaway 1994, 1996a, 1996b, 1996c, 1997, and 2000; Faiman-Silva 1997; Fenelon 1997 and 1998; Hall 1986, 1987, 1989a, and 1989b; Harris 1990; Himmel 1999; Kardulias 1990; Mathien and McGuire 1986; Meyer 1990, 1991, and 1994; Peregrine 1992 and 1995; Peregrine and Feinman 1996; and Pickering 2000.

23. This discussion draws extensively from Hall and Nagel 2000 and 2006; Chase-Dunn and Hall 1998, 25–27; Cornell 1988; Corntassel 2003; Nagel 1996, xi–xiii, 3–42; Riggs 1998a, 1998b, and 1998c; and Hall 1998a. Other general literature on identity politics includes Anderson 1991; Friedman 1994, 1998, and 1999; Featherstone 1990; Featherstone et al. 1995; King 1997; and Robertson 1992.

24. On the former, see Hall 1998a and 1998b; and Riggs 1994, 1998a, 1998b, and 1998c. On the latter, see Fenelon 1998 and 2002; Deloria and Lytle, 1984; and Deloria and Wilkins 2000.

RECOMMENDED READINGS

Roy, Arundhati. 2004. *An Ordinary Person's Guide to Empire.* Cambridge, MA: South End Press.
  A basic introduction to globalization, empire, and so on.
Deloria, Vine, Jr. 1997. *Red Earth, White Lies: Native Americans and the Myth of Scientific Fact.* New York: Scribner.
  A critique of various "scientific" studies about Native Americans by a leading Native American writer. A controversial yet interesting and useful book.
Mann, Charles C. 2005. *1491: New Revelations of the Americas Before Columbus.* New York: Alfred A. Knopf.
  This account covers North, Central, and South America before the arrival of Europeans and provides summaries of the primary intellectual debates and controversies.
Mohawk, John. 2000. *Utopian Legacies: A History of Conquest and Oppression in the Western World.* Santa Fe, NM: Clear Light Publishers.
  A review of European-Native interactions written by a leading Native American scholar.
Wallerstein, Immanuel. 2004. *World-Systems Analysis: An Introduction.* Durham, NC: Duke University Press.
  A basic introduction from the founder of world-system analysis.

Web Resources

American Indian Higher Education Consortium, http://www.aihec.org/ (accessed December 11, 2008).

Center for World Indigenous Studies (CWIS), http://www.cwis.org/index.php (accessed December 11, 2008).

Cultural Survival, http://www.cs.org/ (accessed December 11, 2008).

Indigenous Peoples and Globalization Program, http://www.ifg.org/programs/indig.htm (accessed December 11, 2008).

International Work Group for Indigenous Affairs (IWGIA), http://www.iwgia.org/ (accessed December 11, 2008).

National Tribal Justice Resource Center, http://www.tribalresourcecenter.org/personnel/ (accessed December 11, 2008).

Rainforestweb, Indigenous Peoples, http://www.rainforestweb.org/ (accessed December 11, 2008).

CHAPTER 2

Indigenous Global Struggles

Models of Revitalization and Resistance

IN THIS CHAPTER WE PROVIDE a foundation for a more unified analysis of cases of indigeneity. Whereas it is quite common to discuss social and political resistance and community-based revitalization on a case-by-case basis, we focus on a holistic understanding of indigeneity in the context of a world-system. We seek to go beyond even common "compare and contrast" analyses and frame the struggles for autonomy and cultural survival within a broader context of globalization. We focus on Lakota and Wampanoag in the United States, Warli and Gond in India, Māori[1] in New Zealand, Zapatista-led Mayan-descent peoples (e.g., Tzotzil) in Chiapas, Mexico, and Zapotecas peoples in Oaxaca, Mexico.

World-systems analysis facilitates discussion of autonomy and cultural systems in relation to the states that have dominated, and continue to dominate, indigenous peoples, and how those relations shift with changing positions of those states within the world-system. We frame our discussion within four sets of issues that illustrate the resistance of indigenous peoples to the forces of globalization, as well as revitalization of their cultural traditions:

1. global historical context;
2. cultural traditions built around community, usually with consensus-driven forms of governance by a collectivity;
3. holistic, undifferentiated spiritual values that tend to embody generosity to group and reciprocity rather than competition and accumulation; and
4. worldviews that positively interact with the earth's environment and land, rather than destroying it through extensive, privatized natural resource exploitation.

These issues appear in most indigenous social systems in one form or another. We then use this analysis to illuminate our case studies. Occasionally we refer to other indigenous peoples, as occurs in the UN Declaration on Rights of Indigenous Peoples, and in the "América Profunda in Mexico" meetings in 2003 in Mexico City.

We also model patterns of resistance and revitalization in relationship to spheres of indigenous activity within dominant states. We then propose some conclusions about these interactions on the global, national, regional, and local levels. Finally, we hope to gain a glimpse of worldviews more beneficial for the future of humanity.

We now turn to a discussion of resistance and revitalization in relation to a world-system that includes states that have historically dominated—and often destroyed—indigenous peoples. We consider the history of colonization, hegemonic expansion, conquest, and contemporary patterns of domination. Many indigenous peoples are acutely aware of these historical relations and how they have been affected by them throughout the ages, especially with regard to identity formation. We note that states have strong investments in these relations, especially with respect to land and the economy.

Two models summarize our discussions: "Four Modes of Resistance and Revitalization" and "Indigenous Peoples' Relationships in Resistance to Globalization and Neo-Liberalism." In the latter we use local "Autonomy" as a means to revitalize decision-making processes, economic relations, land/sea tenure, and local community structures.

RESISTANCE, REVITALIZATION, AND WORLD-SYSTEMS ANALYSIS

Here we expand our discussion of the relevance of world-systems analysis to indigenous peoples begun in Chapter 1 and elaborated further in Chapter 6.[2] First, we argue that even the most localized forms of resistance cannot be understood fully without careful attention to larger systems and global processes. Conversely, we also argue that world-system analysis cannot be used in a "one-size-fits-all" mode. Rather, it is the complex interactions and conjunctures of specific cases that shape the processes of incorporation and resistance to incorporation (Carlson 2001). Further, we argue that too little attention has been paid to events and processes in peripheral areas and how those events and processes have affected core areas. This requires a multitiered analysis that attends to highly local conditions, regional conditions, national or state conditions, and global or world-system conditions, and the interactions among all of these.

In our attempts to search for patterns within these complex interactions, we focus on several levels of social change, often moving in opposite directions.[3] As there have been long-term shifts in the realities and meanings of ethnicity, indigeneity, and nationality, the dynamics of interaction have changed drastically.

Within the past century or so, all of these categories have become far more fluid, while increasingly contested politically, socially, economically, and culturally. Thus, the velocity and patterns of social construction of indigenous and other identities have shifted significantly.

Indigenous peoples are especially problematic and salient to an understanding of world-system social processes because their continued existence poses a major challenge to neoliberal capitalism on the ground, both politically and ideologically. In addition, indigenous peoples offer a variety of models of how societies or groups might participate in the world-system while retaining their distinct identities within it. In this way they may provide suggestions as to how the current system might be transformed into something more humane (Hall and Fenelon 2003, 2004, 2005a, and 2005b).

We note that the struggles of First Nations in the United States and Canada generally revolve around various forms of legal sovereignty. Sovereignty is based on treaty relationships, the development of racialized "minority" groups, and various historical changes. In most of the rest of the Americas and indeed around the world, indigenous peoples live in unrecognized autonomous zones and communities, often surviving at considerable individual and group expense. Some key examples are Miskitos in Nicaragua and Mayan-descent Zapatistas in Mexico. These indigenous peoples are still treated solely as "minority" groups within their states, are quite vulnerable to state-imposed policies, and have often formed resistance groups and/or rebellious movements, such as Communidades Indigenas in Oaxaca. In the epilogue we note some significant changes occurring in many places.

The key issues here are:

1. sovereignty is now often recognized within core states, though these states pursued genocidal policies at various times in the past;
2. minority or conflicted autonomy in Latin American states, although historically *mestizo* states, usually confers neither sovereignty nor clear legal protections for indigenous peoples;[4]
3. both within the Americas and globally these issues need to be studied and then presented and understood comparatively;
4. many movements, perceived as resistance by dominant states but as revitalization by most indigenous peoples, are part of larger global processes.

We begin our discussion of these issues with an overview of indigenous peoples.

INDIGENOUS PEOPLES AND ISSUES

Indigenous peoples differ from other groups in terms of political inclusion, resistance to domination, and cultural survival under domination (cultural, political, social, and economic) by local, regional, and state elites. All of these are subject, in various ways, to globalization processes. Locally, discussion and contention often revolve around internal conflict about assimilation and integration, especially with regard to family structures, religious practices and beliefs, and language retention. Other discussions and contentions focus on educational systems, forms of political representation, forms of justice, understandings of historical processes, and claims for autonomy and sovereignty. Throughout this book we present visual examples of community empowerment, resistance to educational dominance, self-reliant governance, identity conflicts, and resistance to the many forces of globalization.

For instance, Plate 2.1 portrays a "Day of the Dead" poster and celebrations in Oaxaca. These celebrations and artworks are links to pre-Hispanic practices. Layers of domination—500 years and more in Mexico—reveal an "Indian" foundation even as oppression stratifies every aspect of life—cultural, political, economic, and social (Bonfil 1996). Therefore, *indigenous* represents both the foundation of society itself and an "enemy" to be overtaken and destroyed.

We identify four thematic issues among indigenous peoples from our discussion:

1. economic relationships are redistributive, partially or wholly;
2. political relations of "cultural sovereignty" and "community autonomy" predominate;

Plate 2.1. Poster celebrating Day of the Dead in Oaxaca City, showing indigenous roots. (Photo courtesy of James V. Fenelon)

3. environmental relationships tend to be symbiotic, with less destruction to animal and plant life than in capitalist societies; and
4. communities value inclusive relationships that tend toward common goals.

Many indigenous communities attempt to maintain their values and social practices while they adopt and adapt various aspects of modernity. For example, indigenous communities tend to show more respect for women than patriarchal colonialism allowed. Indeed, some forms of indigeneity had considerable recognition for women in their traditional ways before conquest and forced assimilation. These conflicting patterns exemplify how contemporary indigenous governance submits to autonomous communities. Zapatista-run communities in the highlands of Chiapas illustrate these relations well.

Land is central to indigenous peoples, even when they have been removed or relocated (Champagne and Abu-Saad 2003; Champagne et al. 2005). Māori Land Courts, established after sovereignty of the Waitangi treaty was recognized in the 1970s, show how some indigenous peoples have fused traditional, treaty-based, and modern political relationships (Henare 2001). Treaty settlements in the United States and Canada demonstrate arrangements with dominant state power elites (Wilkins 2006).

Spirituality is another contested arena for indigenous peoples, in both the maintenance of traditional forms and adaptation to dominant forms, especially during colonial eras. The Gond in central India are instructive here, since they have maintained iconic imagery, statuary, and prayer practices from their deepest traditions while resisting invasive British Christian missionary efforts. They did, however, adopt and adapt some practices and deities associated with the Hindu pantheon (Bijoy 2001), which Fenelon observed in the village of Menda Lekha in Maharashtra in 2003.[5]

These social systems are interactive, both with one another and with changing conditions for indigenous peoples in their local and global contexts. The SunDance[6] practiced by the Lakota and other Great Plains peoples also has been critically important to resistance. The resurgence of the SunDance has been important for revitalization, especially in terms of relation to the land, culture, religion, and leadership (Fenelon 1998; Jorgenson 1972).

INDIGENOUS MODELS

The complexity of indigenous issues spans a wide spectrum of social organization, including community empowerment, resistance to educational dominance, self-reliant governance, identity conflicts, and structural reformation against the forces of globalization. We illustrate this with visual examples from field interactions in 2003.

Guillermo Bonfil Batalla (1996), along with many scholars working on indigenous issues in the Americas, identifies other areas of social organization that differ markedly from dominant groups: medicine (p. 34), community service, and Mexican *cargo*[7] systems "simultaneously civil, religious, and moral" (p. 36). We note that it is the collective nature of indigenous life that appears to be at conflict with modern social systems. This collectivity includes the land, distributive economics, shared decision making, and the community itself. The invasive systems take over land, stratify the economy to build a power-elite, centralize political systems into hierarchies, and relate social issues to ever-larger urban areas that dominate in all arenas of the surrounding communities.

At the América Profunda Mexico City meetings in 2003 scholars and indigenous leaders from throughout the Americas found that "government, based on its monopoly of violence ... was a hierarchical power structure." They identified an indigenous equivalent of *autoridad* (authority) with a "communal authority [that] is the whole community in its assembly," including elders and others sharing in decision making. The governance panel found that "the central idea is to maintain harmony within the community" (América Profunda 2003). They concluded that it was a "process of formation, at the grassroots, a *Consensus of the Peoples*" (América Profunda initial findings 2003) building at that time.

Felipe Quispe speaks of movements of shared struggles throughout "Indian" Latin America that are based on a diversity of indigenous peoples and states. While each is reconstructing traditions unique to its own culture, and often relative to the specific lands they inhabit, they are also finding commonalities across many fronts—notably in opposition to cultural domination and corporate expansion over their lands (see Fenelon 2006b). Even as the essence of a community, economic cooperatives, shared decision making, and land tenure relations vary, indigenous peoples rely on these foundations to resist in their individual situations, and increasingly in global networks (Muñoz Ramírez 2003).

We have used these observations to develop models of contemporary community struggles for or against inclusion, within regional, state, and global indigenous movements (see Figure 2.1). Essentially, these are opposed to, or in contrast to, the capitalist domination and social repression by dominant societies in control of modern states.

The cultural practices and social formations of indigenous peoples are also complicated by their specific geographic and political locations, even with the few cases we present here. Nonetheless, we can identify certain aspects of indigeneity that appear to be consistent across these cases, presented in Figure 2.1. We hypothesize why these seem more powerful explanations for what is occurring on a global level (Hall 2002b) in two general theoretical models: (1) Four Modes of Indigenous Resistance and Revitalization (see Figure 2.2); and (2) Model of Indigenous People's Relationships in Resistance to Globalization and Neoliberalism (see Figure 2.3), which we discuss below, in ideal typic form.[8]

We represent these components of indigenous struggles as four organizational structures:

Figure 2.1
Indigeneity and Autonomy in Conflict with Dominant Society Model of Indigenous Relations in Four Categories of Leadership or Decision Making, Economy, Community, and Land or Environment, in Conflict with Dominant Society, Found in Modern States

Indigeneity and autonomy in conflict with dominant society was first developed as a model of indigenous relations by Fenelon on-site while with the International Honors Program in 2003 and was first presented at the Latinos in the World-System meetings at the University of California, Berkeley, by Fenelon and Hall (2004).

- The first is decision making, or political systems, where a spokesperson is designated by a council of elders to disseminate decisions. It is important to note that this spokesperson often acts in place of any formal leader or leadership.
- The second structure is the economy, which is redistributive on the communal level. This allows for sharing with all members while focusing on familial and communal property. Members value social prestige as success rather than personal profit.
- Land tenure is a third structure, encompassing cultural and historical ties as well as group control. Similar to the economy, land tenure usually operates as a kind of collectivity, often without private ownership, sometimes sacred, and rarely if ever sold to outsiders, although dominant groups may simply "take" land.
- Community cohesion representative of autonomy and self-determination is our fourth structure, with a primary focus on harmonious relationships, based on strong kinship ties and emphasis on a greater group good that individuals submit to.

The ideal-type model "Four Modes of Indigenous Resistance and Revitalization" (Figure 2.2) demonstrates interactive components of indigenous struggles within four "image" spheres,[9] with consensual decision-making systems providing

Figure 2.2
Indigenous-Oriented Model, with Focus on Revitalizing "Modern" Communities, Resisting Ongoing Cultural Domination, and Rebuilding Traditional Social Systems

Four Modes of Indigenous Resistance and Revitalization

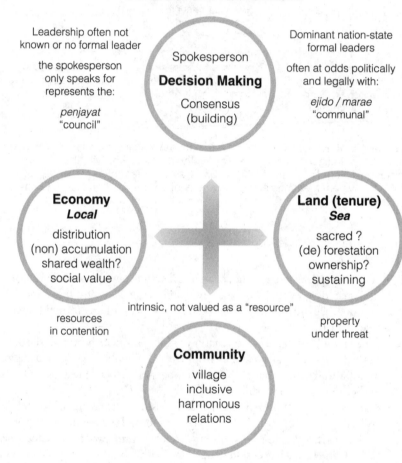

Leadership often not known or no formal leader

the spokesperson only speaks for represents the:

penjayat "council"

Spokesperson

Decision Making

Consensus (building)

Dominant nation-state formal leaders

often at odds politically and legally with:

ejido / marae "communal"

Economy
Local

distribution (non) accumulation shared wealth? social value

Land (tenure)
Sea

sacred ? (de) forestation ownership? sustaining

resources in contention

intrinsic, not valued as a "resource"

property under threat

Community

village inclusive harmonious relations

Indigenous

United States: **Wampanoag**
India: **Warli / Gond**
New Zealand: **Māori**

United States: **Lakota/Dakota**
Mexico: **Zapotec/Tzotzil**
Org.: **Zapatistas**

We use the term "spokesperson" advisedly here, since many words such as "chief" were not traditional, holding no formal role in nearly all American Indian societies, and the terms of "leader" were similarly rejected by Adevasi tribal communities in India and are resisted heavily among the Zapatistas, although some Pueblos Indigenas do accept such terms in Mexico and other Latin American countries.

**Figure 2.3
Indigenous People's Relationships in Resistance
to Globalization and Neoliberalism**

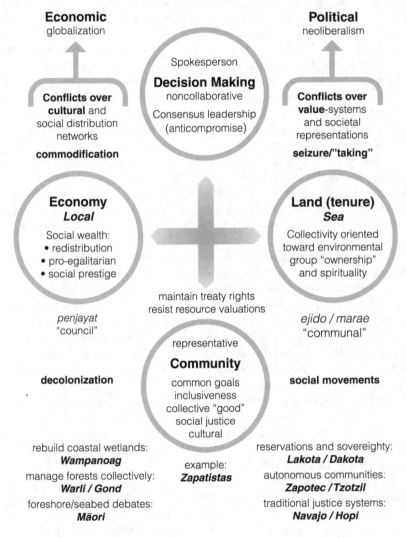

Dominant Society, Capitalism, and State System

Economic
globalization

Political
neoliberalism

**Spokesperson
Decision Making**
noncollaborative
Consensus leadership
(anticompromise)

**Conflicts over
cultural** and
social distribution
networks

commodification

**Conflicts over
value**-systems
and societal
representations

seizure/"taking"

Economy
Local
Social wealth:
• redistribution
• pro-egalitarian
• social prestige

Land (tenure)
Sea
Collectivity oriented
toward environmental
group "ownership"
and spirituality

maintain treaty rights
resist resource valuations

penjayat
"council"

ejido / marae
"communal"

representative
Community
common goals
inclusiveness
collective "good"
social justice
cultural

decolonization

social movements

rebuild coastal wetlands:
Wampanoag
manage forests collectively:
Warli / Gond
foreshore/seabed debates:
Māori

example:
Zapatistas

reservations and sovereighty:
Lakota / Dakota
autonomous communities:
Zapotec / Tzotzil
traditional justice systems:
Navajo / Hopi

the prime conduit to the dominant society and its power formation. It is quite possible that the relationships and systems, taken as a whole, are alternatives to competitive capitalistic societies (Sklair 2002).

The model "Indigenous People's Relationships in Resistance to Globalization and Neoliberalism" (see Figure 2.3) demonstrates interactive components of indigenous struggles within these four spheres, with consensual decision-making the prime conduit to the dominant society and its power formation. We hypothesize that these social practices, which are essentially noncapitalist, survived as alternatives to globalization. Indeed, they are less destructive and less violent in each of the four major spheres of interaction—the political, the economic, environmental, and with community. As nondominant options, they meet the criteria for alternatives to neoliberal capitalistic societies as suggested by Sklair (2002) or Boswell and Chase-Dunn (2000).

For instance, traditional Lakota peoples had a position for every community, referred to as *Eyapaha,* that acted somewhat as a Traditional Speaker for the Council or societies to make announcements and communicate various decisions or directions. Though there would be other positions of leadership, usually with an *Itancan* (literally "leader") to administer the council's findings or the society's decisions, they were always reflected by established organizations that depended on a rough consensus or at least an appropriate cultural basis to decision making. These leaders and speakers had special rights to speak in council, or in emergency meetings, but had no overarching authority. In fact, every *tiwaye* (household or tipi family) or *tiospaye* (extended relatives) could pull out of some decision or direction with which they disagreed, all the way to breaking camp and moving elsewhere. This was an incredibly democratic form of interactive governance, which was intentionally destroyed by a combination of U.S. military and civilian authorities and, to some extent at a later date, by Western scholars and social scientists who had need to identify a "chief" and thereby call the collective a "chiefdom."

One kind of resistance is to restore these positions or traditional relationships, within modern contexts, and usually against neocolonialism and/or neoliberal globalization. Lakota and many other native nations have recently called for great gatherings around Bear Butte near Sturgis, South Dakota, to protest the building of huge entertainment bars, which profit from what the native nations see as "debauchery" by the many biker groups frequenting the bars, and thereby debasing the "sacred" mountains during prayer times. That traditionalist protest takes many forms, posting on the Internet[10] and appointing one longtime activist, Carter Camp, as its *Eyapaha* for the more than thirty native nations.[11]

Similarly, when faculty and students from an educational program met with Gond leaders at Mendha Lekha, in Maharashtra, India, the primary speaker or communicator identified himself as a village "spokesperson." He said he represented the elders sitting directly behind him and actively rejected the "leader" label the students associated with him.[12] These Gond villagers had found strength in having a council of elders make decisions because regional government forces were constantly trying to co-opt any known leaders. These conflicts had come to a head when these Gond reconstituted the Ghotul in defiance of government bans and periodic raids to destroy their Ghotul (see Chapter 3, note 15) fenced-in areas, massively rebuilding across communities so numerous that security forces could not fully respond. Like the SunDance revitalizing the Lakota, this community-building celebration restores important familial relationships, kinship respect, and stewardship of the environment and is a time when the councils guide youth and select future leaders and spokespersons.

As these examples illustrate, economic and leadership components of our model interact with communal organization and land tenure relationships to form cohesive communities. Knowledge of the destructive relationships arising from commodification and capitalism, and resistance to them, is often found in indigenous communities. The patented seeds from corporate farming disrupt centuries-old practices by the Mixtec and Zapotecs in Oaxaca, leading to conflict between indigenous farmers and corporate distributors (Esteva 2002). Gond and Warli Adevasi in India are resisting biopiracy of medicinal plants and similar seed patenting by pharmaceutical companies to the extent of making legal claims to UN legislative bodies.[13]

Struggles over forest management practices, usually against timber industries, often entail all four sectors of our model, with Gond Adevasi actually setting up roving guards, and the Warli regrowing entire teak forests on contested lands worth millions of dollars. Some Zapotec communities have succumbed to clear-cutting while others have resisted and kept diversified land-use strategies. Mapuche resistance in southern Chile has included the selective burning of timber company holdings and of absentee landowners' homes around their traditional lands. The coastal wetlands of the Aquinnah Wampanoag, valuable to elite real estate developers, have been restored with new growth maintenance, even as coastal Zapotecs have an *eijido* (communal lands) with both seashore resources and tourist business. Perhaps most powerful are the Foreshore Seabed debates of the Māori against the Crown, with Pakeha (white) landowners literally up in arms and in denial of the Waitangi treaty. These kinds of struggles are found in the lower left-hand section of Figure 2.2 and are anticommodification and decolonization actions in order to preserve traditional community, or to rebuild new communities with some traditional underpinnings.

Each of these examples involves social movements, such as the sovereignty struggles over reservation lands and the Black Hills by the Lakota (Lazarus 1991; Fenelon 1998; Gonzalez and Cook-Lynn 1999). Indigenous peoples are rebuilding autonomous communities, as the Zapotec in Oaxaca or the Tzotzil in Chiapas, and traditional justice systems, such as Navajo and Hopi are doing within Arizona (shown in the lower right quadrant of Figure 2.3), exemplifying indigenous resistance and revitalization. Some of these indigenous peoples had negotiated treaties—historical or contemporary—whereby insistence on the treaty conditions is viewed as resistance to the dominant states. Lakota in the United States, Māori with New Zealand (Crown), and many other nations—especially those in the treaty-making states of Canada, the United States, and New Zealand—have near-constant presence in the highest courts simply trying to meet the original agreement. Many people, such as the Gond ("Tribals" in India) and the Zapatistas (San Andres Accords), have renegotiated treaty-like instruments that put them at odds with the dominant state, especially in respect to the privatization of group property and any collectively held land.

Quasi-indigenous people like the Iraqi Kurds positioned themselves in complicated laws and agreements in attempts to practice some level of autonomy, for which they have been struggling for more than 600 years, in more than three countries including Iran, Turkey, and Syria. Miskito in Nicaragua found themselves separated from their kin in Honduras because of U.S.-led contra wars against the Sandinistas, as Aymara and other Quechuan peoples in Bolivia, Ecuador, and Peru are caught up in transborder conflicts.

The next model (see Figure 2.3) demonstrates the same conceptual categories in relation to a dominant global society. Again, it is hypothesized that these surviving—essentially noncapitalist—forms are alternatives to neoliberal globalization.[14] Indigenous social systems are less environmentally destructive and less violent in each of these four spheres of social interaction, until they come into contact with colonial invaders and begin to resist the resulting domination of state political-economic structures.

The most important links between indigenous struggles and world-systems processes are the connections that movements seek with other indigenous peoples. For Zapatistas this has meant making invitations referred to as the international Encuentros and Inter-Continentals, illustrated in the mural of four fisted hands united from four directions painted on the headquarters building in Oventik, Chiapas.

The mural includes the words *Democracia* (democracy), *Libertad* (liberty), *Justicia* (justice), and *Paz* (peace) written over the fisted hands. The image is a medicine wheel design with the surrounding words "*Unidad y Victoria*" (unity and victory). The colors used in this mural are identical to the colors used in some Lakota traditions (Maya colors differ although the design is nearly the same), while the use of a Four Directions medicine wheel adds to a remarkable symmetry of indigenous depictions that have been documented globally. Thus, a relatively direct illustration of two very different indigenous traditions and their social movements appears connected in their vision and their sense of struggle.

From this analytic discussion we identify some methodological issues in Africa, draw some conclusions, and make a few speculations about indigenous peoples and their movements. We will then discuss applications of these models to specific peoples and cases.

METHODS ISSUES FROM OUR STUDIES AND INDIGENOUS AFRICA

Representations of these struggles in contemporary art forms illustrate how oral tradition history by indigenous peoples is different and often more informative than the dominant or hegemonic version. In Plate 2.2, the Lakota repulse at Medicine Tail Coulee (Battle of the Little Big Horn in 1876)[15] is presented by a Lakota artist (Troy Fairbanks) demonstrating the fight as a defense of "community" against an armed military invasion. Painted on a buffalo bull skin, the work allows the "indigenous perspective" to be told more than a century later.

Plate 2.2. Buffalo hide painting of the repulse of Custer's force at the Battle of the Little Big Horn, demonstrating indigenous memory and oral history of the invasion. (Photo courtesy of James V. Fenelon)

Indigenous peoples in Africa, usually referred to as "tribals" throughout the rest of the world, pose particularly thorny methodological problems for our analysis, especially in relation to long-term colonialism (Kopytoff 1987). Along with inclusion into governing structures after independence there are additional issues of race and racism arising from some 300 years of "formation," including Western imperialism, racialized colonization, and natural resource extraction.

The peoples referred to as Zulu are instructive here, as their many divisions have provided great resistance to the peculiar dual strand of "settlement" and "colonialism" in South Africa, starting with the Dutch, some Voor-trekkers, and later the Boers, speaking Afrikaans and keeping the indigenous Zulu down while fending off British imperialism, sometimes in nasty wars. The rise of the Boers as dominant in Kwazulu-Natal and their subsequent sharing of local hegemony created layers of both ethnic and racial dominance. After apartheid was created, being "black" carried as much or more stigma, with some "tribes" managing to maintain a rough autonomy, or even rougher sovereignty, as in Lesotho or Swaziland, and in cultural revitalization practices (see Plate 2.3).

Identity and connectedness take various forms over these periods (see Macharia 2003). For instance, Nelson Mandela wore "tribal" clothing during his early trials to establish indigenous resistance to colonial/racial domination. He did this before being imprisoned in Robben Island, which had been first used to isolate the chief leaders of tribal nations opposing the colonial forces. The country became formally stratified along racial lines—majority black on the bottom, "colored" in the middle, and minority white on top—blurring indigenous "tribal" issues with racial issues (Daniel, Habib, and Southall 2004).

After the now-famous insurrections and bloody protests finally brought down the apartheid system, the African National Congress and many other black leaders made provisions with the white elite not to topple the neoliberal reforms that ran the country's effective economy. This ensured reproduction of systemic

Plate 2.3. Zulu youth program, mostly orphans of AIDS victims, celebrating indigenous culture out-side the western gate, Kruger National Park, South Africa. (Photo courtesy of James V. Fenelon)

inequality (Alexander 2002) along racial/tribal lines, which further subordinated indigenous (Zulu) languages and cultural histories. Neoliberalism continues to be dominant throughout South Africa today, with a tiny fraction of elected black and tribal leaders unable or unwilling to tackle the massive suppression of black and indigenous peoples across the country (Bond 2006).

CONCLUSIONS

Indigenous peoples are conscientiously organizing throughout the world, compar-ing their situations and the sociopolitical relations with dominant elites in the states encapsulating them, noting where each of their struggles converge. Because indigenous peoples in general had established habitation prior to present-day dominant elites—a key aspect of indigeneity—they are then the hosts, not the hosted, within the states in which they find themselves embedded. Yet, as we will see throughout the case studies, those dominant states see themselves as "hosts" who tolerate these surviving indigenous peoples.

These alliances have not only proven to be more effective in terms of re-sistance and cultural survival but also are producing new forms of indigeneity that influence existing indigenous peoples. These issues range in importance from the UN's Indigenous People's Working Group to how local indigenes may frame their struggle, any claims to sovereignty and the land, or social justice is-

Plate 2.4. Powwow in Little Eagle, South Dakota (Standing Rock in the 1980s), demonstrating both community and panethnic celebration. (Photo courtesy of James V. Fenelon)

sues, according to their perceptions. Thus, there is a complexity with regard to interaction among indigenous peoples throughout the world, which may shape future practices in many ways.

The efforts of indigenous peoples for rights and autonomy differ in key ways from similar efforts of many other societies (Hall and Fenelon 2008). These differences include their historical depth; their community bases; their decision-making processes; their direct and spiritual ties to the land and sea; their traditional economic distribution networks, which are generally oriented toward egalitarian sharing; and their particular group characteristics, reflected in all of these differences.

Area case studies demonstrate regional differences, such as the Kurds in the Middle East moving into modern national autonomous zones, or possibly the Pashtun in Afghanistan crossing over with ancient understandings to their relatives in the Pakistani mountains. Cases from Africa (see Hodgson 2002) include the Maasai independence movements and the Zulu homelands in South Africa torn asunder by apartheid. Our two models, one indigenous revitalization, another resistance to states and globalization forces, make for an applied analysis to such diverse cases as the Saami in Scandinavia, the Ainu in Japan, the Orang Asli in Malaysia, the Siberian Inuit, or even peoples in Chechnya.

Some are pursuing accommodationist strategies while others are in more direct conflicts.

Struggles over sovereignty and autonomy are important conflict points for indigenous peoples to work out their continuing relationships with the dominant states in which they reside. Historical settlements and documents, especially any treaties made with colonial and contemporary governments, deeply influence relations with current political systems.

Indigenous resistance, ranging from cultural maintenance to violent revolution, continues in all parts of the world and is a vital part of many types and levels of cultural and political survival. Localized community empowerment has a complicated relationship with such resistance, often supporting long-term social change rooted in a collective memory necessary in the face of domination and destruction.

The Wampanoag and Lakota peoples in the United States, the Warli and Gond peoples in India, the Māori peoples in New Zealand, and the Zapotec and Zapatista-led Tzotzil peoples in Mexico have diverse and different backgrounds and yet share some basic characteristics as indigenous peoples in resistance and survival modalities. These sets of social systems are represented in the models presented in this work.[16]

Indigenous peoples are sharing their respective histories and situations in many global networks. Such networks have given rise to the production of new sites of resistance, new forms of cultural survival, new types of indigeneity, and continued social change.

This is evident in political struggles, including those in Latin America, southern Asia, North America, and the southern Pacific. Remarkable as the resistance and survival of indigeneity have been around the world, future directions may depend on how well we understand problems and promises that indigenous peoples experience in our increasingly globalized societies.

Although we will illustrate in the following case studies many broad similarities among indigenous peoples and their struggles for survival, questions still remain. Key among these are, Considering that indigenous peoples have so little in conventional terms of power (i.e., money, resources, weapons, and demographic numbers), why have they been able to resist globalization? A closely related question is, Why is this a concern now? Though these struggles are old—centuries in the Americas and millennia in South Asia—they receive more popular attention today with the onset of advancements in information technologies. New communications and travel capacities have made it vastly easier for widely disparate peoples, both as groups and as individuals, to interact intensively. But these are at best partial explanations. In the upcoming chapters we will return to explicit examination of world-system context, specifically in terms of world-system time. In world-system time, we find periods within various world-systemic processes and cycles that sometimes are more propitious for such movements, while others are less so.

We now turn to our discussion of Māoris and Adevasis.

NOTES

1. The name for this group is often spelled Maori, but their own preference is for Māori, more closely reflecting their own name, so we follow the latter.

2. Our discussion draws on Hall and Fenelon 2003, 2004, 2005a, 2005b, and 2008; and Fenelon and Hall 2005 and 2008.

3. Many of these long-term shifts in "nationality" and indigeneity have been almost glacial changes.

4. While the "legal" and constitutional protections in Mexico appear to do this, in reality few if any such cases ever move through the courts.

5. Fenelon was acting as an "Indigenous Perspectives" faculty consultant with the International Honors Program (IHP) then administered through Boston University, meeting with indigenous leaders during September 2003.

6. SunDance, without a space, is the convention among Lakota for this ceremony. While historically related to SunDances practiced further west, the practice among Lakotas is distinct.

7. Briefly *cargo* means "burden" and refers to obligation to hold civic office, usually in concert with a quasi-religious festival. Though many of these festivals are manifestly Christian, they often have underlying precolonial religious components. There are many discussions of the cargo system throughout Meosamerica. Cancien 1965 and Chance and Taylor 1985 provide good accounts.

8. The interactive components of the organizational structures presented in our models are "ideal typic" in that variation of the experience of indigenous peoples is expected and does not draw from the model. For this analysis, we use typologies stressing interaction, what Weber identified as "ideal types" (Weber 1962). Ideal types are not goals to be sought, but rather ideal in the sense that they are models without all the messy details of daily life, so that one may more readily see underlying processes.

9. This methodological approach is a "Simple Model of Social Research" proposed by Ragin 1994 in "Constructing Social Research" (figure 3.1). It fits this model well, because the "Ideas" or "Social Theory" are that of indigenous resistance and revitalization. The deductive process of developing analytical frames occurs before developing the case study, then moves through "Retroduction" to be reframed by "Images" constructed from a "mostly inductive" compilation of "Evidence" or "Data" arising from the case studies.

10. The Defend Bear Butte website can be accessed at http://www.defendbearbutte.org/, accessed July 14, 2008.

11. E-mail from Carter Camp, March 24, 2006: "My name is Carter Camp, I'm a Ponca Indian and I have been chosen to be the 'Eyapaha' or 'Traditional Speaker' for the Inter-Tribal Coalition to Defend Bear Butte (www.defendbearbutte.org). As such, I would like to announce a major effort by over thirty (30) Sovereign Indian Nations in America to stop the obscene developments which are being built all around the Mountain each of our Nations hold sacred and inviolable."

12. Faculty and students were with the first Indigenous Perspectives Program of the IHP International Honors Program, on-site in Menda Lekha, India, in September 2003.

13. Linda T. Smith (1999) discusses biopiracy explicitly as an important "de-colonization" strategy.

14. It is important to note again that the "ideal types" (Weber 1962) and "research images" (Ragin 1994) used in this model are neither always "true" or particularly "good" or ideal, but are simply analytical tools.

15. The repulse at Medicine Tail Coulee of attacking U.S. forces at the 1876 Battle of the Little Big Horn is called "Fight at the Greasy Grass" by the Lakota and "Custer's Last Stand" by many mainstream accounts, reflecting opposite historical perspectives.

16. We take all responsibility for any discussion of indigenous peoples, either as individual studies or as collectively represented, and for all models in this book, errors and biases included. Even so, we acknowledge that elders and knowledgeable people have provided information and ideas that are valuable and important, and that certain programs helped to provide experiences to develop this work, including the International Honors Indigenous Perspectives Program run by Boston University, our own universities, and many unnamed academics. We thank everyone through the statement *o-midakuye oyasin* (Lakota for "we are all related" in deed and in respect).

RECOMMENDED READINGS

Bonfil Batalla, Guillermo. 1996. Translated by Phillip A. Dennis. *Mexico Profundo—Reclaiming a Civilization*. Austin: University of Texas Press.
> Bonfil Batalla explores the deep indigenous roots in much of Mexico's social structure. His work and approach were one of the forces behind America Profunda.

Champagne, Duane, Karen Torjesen, and Susan Steiner, eds. 2005. *Indigenous People and the Modern State*. Walnut Creek, CA: AltaMira Press.
> This collection provides many insights into indigenous affairs, with many case examples.

Mander, Jerry, and Victoria Tauli-Corpuz, eds. 2006. *Paradigm Wars: Indigenous Peoples' Resistance to Globalization*. San Francisco: Sierra Club Books.
> An excellent series of short essays, mostly from indigenous authors, that resonates well with this book and even adds relevant cases, such as on biopiracy of indigenous medicine.

Ragin, Charles. 1994. *Constructing Social Research: The Unity and Diversity of Method*. Thousand Oaks, CA: Pine Forge Press.
> A superb introduction to the kinds of strategies that lie behind the work in this book.

Sklair, Lelsie. 2002. *Globalization: Capitalism and Its Alternatives*. 3rd ed. Oxford, UK: Oxford University Press.
> An excellent text on globalization that examines various alternatives carefully.

Smith, Linda Tuwahi. 1999. *Decolonizing Methodologies Research and Indigenous Peoples*. London and Dunedin, New Zealand: Zed Books and University of Otago Press.
> Smith, a Māori, explores how the methods of traditional social science often undermine indigenous causes. She also suggests alternatives. Her work has influenced our approach.

Web Resources

Defend Bear Butte, http://www.defendbearbutte.org/ (accessed December 11, 2008).
Indigenous Peoples Survival Foundation, http://www.indigenouspeople.org/ (accessed December 11, 2008).

CHAPTER 3

Māori in New Zealand (Aotearoa) and Adevasi in South Asia (India)

THIS CHAPTER DISCUSSES THE CONDITIONS of the indigenous peoples from New Zealand, the Māori, as well as the indigenous peoples of South Asia collectively referred to as Adevasi, focusing on the Warli and Gond peoples, with some reference to Aboriginal Australias. The foci of our study, Māori and Adevasi, are emblematic in many ways of the range of indigenous relations and offer contrasts to the peoples and cases discussed in the other chapters on the United States and in Latin America.

The Māori are a rare example of a group whose settlement in what they call Aotearoa (what the rest of the world knows as New Zealand) was very close to a true *terra nullius,* an unoccupied land. Although their early history and arrival in Aotearoa is debated (Belich 1996; Keenan 2002) in contrast to their own origin stories, their conflicts with the early English and French settlers and militaries are well known. They also have treaty-law as a basis for their claim to sovereignty, similar to American Indians in the United States. Also like Native Americans, there was an attempt to suppress and deny these rights in the nineteenth century, which provoked resistance. The British government responded with a racialization strategy,[1] which in turn engendered a revitalization of the treaty in the latter part of the twentieth century and struggles that continue today. The British created a subordinate population, but one that refused to disappear or be unequally assimilated into modern New Zealand society. Although at times the struggles have been violent, they have, in contrast to many other contemporary instances, been more peaceable.

In many ways, advanced Māori analysis of this set of continuing relationships exhibits our orientation in this book, found in the following statement by Maori Marsden (2003, xiv):

> I have deliberately chose [*sic*] a conflict, rather than a pluralist/consensus model (now termed multicultural/bicultural model)—models generally offered as best suited to an analysis of the relationships between the indigenous people and the colonial power. From the historical/economic/political perspective, this model offers a context to accommodate the past experience of the *tangata whenua*[2] ... and as illustrating the contemporary methods by which the Pakeha [the Māori term for early settlers of European origin] in the New Zealand situation utilizes new apparatus and mechanisms of social control to ensure his continued dominance, and abort Maori aspirations in his [s]truggles for social justice and the achievement of authentic being.

The Adevasi in South Asia, in contrast, are emblematic of the *longee dureé* of resistance to expanding states and world-systems. They have been labeled "scheduled tribes" by British and Indian governments. They consist of diverse peoples in many parts of the Indian subcontinent. The Adevasi have struggled over millennia within precolonial India, over some 300 years of British colonial rule, and have continued to resist internal domination (or colonialism) by the Indian government since India's independence. Thus, they have struggled with tributary systems, colonial systems, and national governments.

These cases help us contextualize all indigenous struggles. On the one hand, Māoris are an almost pure case of indigenous resistance to modern European colonialism, less muddied by arguments over who has "first occupier" rights. This eliminates the phony arguments for colonialism that say, "we only did to you what you did to the so-and-so's." On the other hand, Adevasi origins are, in most cases, covered in the mists of time, yet may be the most successful—indeed, heroic—of indigenous peoples who have persisted through thousands of years of occupation. Some dispute their ancient origins and see Adevasi modern identity as a more recently constructed tradition, yet this becomes a self-serving nationalism. We will discuss this issue further in the chapter. For now we will only note that some groups labeled *Adevasi* are ancient peoples with continuity to their pasts, and some others may have been reconstructed more recently.[3] As we will discuss in the concluding chapters, the Adevasi are of great historical and theoretical importance to understanding state-indigenous relations because they show that deleterious impacts on indigenous peoples are not solely due to Europeans, nor solely to capitalism. Rather, the issue has become fundamentally one of states in conflict with nonstate peoples. Although such conflicts date to the formation of the first state, Ur in Mesopotamia some 5,000 years ago, the Adevasi remain vibrantly alive today, continuing their struggle.

We will discuss Māori and Adevasi using our four frameworks—history, resistance, systems of (social) justice, and revitalization. Along the way in this chapter we will make occasional comments and comparisons with other indigenous groups in Asia, Southeast Asia, Indigenous Australia, and Oceania in what is now often referred to as the Pacific Rim countries.

MĀORI HISTORIOGRAPHY

Today there is still some debate about when, how many separate times, and from whence the ancestors of modern Māori arrived in Aotearoa. Through a combination of historical and archaeological research juxtaposed with oral histories, the terms of these debates are narrowing. The first human groups probably arrived in the tenth or eleventh century,[4] most likely from the Bismark Archipelago. Peoples that may have preceded the Māori could have been pushed to outlying islands, but that debate is also unresolved. However, the Māori were the first indigenous peoples who stayed and survived into modern times, and who have constructed a rich cosmology of their origins and journeys to Aotearoa.

There were many oceanic crossings, and probably multiple return voyages. These pioneers brought with them seed foods, dogs, rodents,[5] and cultural customs, primarily from Polynesian peoples who spread throughout the Pacific. There are many similarities with the indigenous peoples later called Polynesian, pointedly with Native Hawaiians, including some of the original voyages of their ancestors, and even shared linguistics, causing these peoples to call themselves relatives of one another. Interestingly, only as of late have mainstream social scientists begun to understand these complex relationships, although both the Māori and other Polynesian peoples have recognized this for eons.[6]

The population spread throughout Aotearoa over several centuries, probably expanding to find new hunting and planting grounds. Populations may have specialized to some extent, but all groups needed both protein sources and vegetable resources, including gourds used for containers. Limited deforestation may have occurred with the population spread. As the moa populations declined, and eventually became extinct, probably before 1600, early societies began to rely more on planted foods and harvests from the oceans. These traditions became mainstays of Māori culture over time and in particular environments.

The Māori people have relations with land, sea, and each other that suggest they transported more than people to the islands. They also brought cosmological relationships that focus on community and an underlying philosophy of oneness with the earth, land, and sky (Henare 2001) that constitute a complex indigenous worldview (Marsden 2003).

Scholars argue that between 1350 and 1600 the various "tribal" groupings we know today formed, though the Māori see their origins as continuous, not unlike Native Americans. As the population expanded, they split and spread out so that by the time that Europeans arrived the Māori were living in all habitable environments in Aotearoa. During this time fishing became more common in the south, and early Māori began complex use of a large number of indigenous plants, many of which require careful planning and timing to be fully effective. This involved more formal movement into horticultural society, along with variegation into social forms with leadership formally identified, and stratification. Gradually Māori society controlled its sustainable resources and began to develop concepts of rights to use specific resources in specific areas, often in specific seasons.

With increasing population, both cooperation and social conflict became more common. Because wars are spectacular and much oral history was compiled in the early nineteenth century when levels of conflict were high, mainstream history portrays the Māori as more violent than was the case, even as various levels of organization emerged. Although rivalry was manifest in both cooperation and conflict, collective identities served to contain the extremes of both. The idealized organization consisted of extended families (*whanau*), combined into clans (*hapu*), which in turn could combine to form tribes (*iwi*), occasionally combining into canoe groups (*waka*). In practice, these categories were fairly fluid and often shifted. Still, the thirty or so "tribes" recognized by Europeans were not fully an arbitrary invention, but more a "snap-freeze" (Belich 1996, 85) of fluid arrangements. This division "neatened, romanticized and Europeanized a more fluid reality," although James Belich (1996, 84) argues that Māori also interpreted trends to their advantage.[7] However, Maori Marsden captures the indigenous perspective over the same conditions in finding "Maori social values are based on social obligations which always entail a measure of self-sacrifice, a commitment not simply to one's family unit but to extended family (*whanau*), to the tribe (*hapu*), and to one's people (*iwi*)" (2003, 43). This bears great similarity to identity constructs among the Lakota (described in Chapter 5), reorienting social sciences in respect to indigenous organization. This is also apparent in how Belich sees rivalry over *mana* (status), whereas Marsden (p. 4) finds that "*mana* means spiritual authority and power as opposed to the purely psychic and natural force of *ihi*."

As found throughout the world, there was conflict between some peoples over lands, inheritance, and political and territorial dominance, with rivalry that could be expressed in feasting, raiding, and occasionally war. Groups could cooperate to build and use large seagoing canoes and large fishing nets. As leaders and communities became powerful they might organize the building of a *pa,* a kind of fortified storage area on high ground that could be easily defended. Once one group built a *pa,* others quickly followed suit, so that they spread rapidly. Men might be killed in battle and women taken captive, yet they could be adopted into the new tribe, and their children were free. Some observers claimed Māori women were treated poorly because of the treatment of captive-wives, but women were generally in better social positions than they were in most of Europe, stemming, in part, from women's recognized roles in activities like weaving. But as agriculture became more important the status of women eroded somewhat, with the greatest reduction in status and rights occurring as Māori peoples came into contact with and then domination by European peoples who operated within rigid systems of patriarchy. In short, colonialism and coercive assimilation maximized both ethnic and gender oppression, making an identification of early Māori society difficult for Europeans, who often ridiculed or rejected the oral tradition and indigenous social structures.

There is some disputed evidence that the French arrived in Aotearoa in 1504, but with little lasting impact. In 1642 a Dutch expedition landed. An ensuing fight seemed to drive them off, with no Europeans returning for 127 years; then, in 1769, the French and English made forays, followed by settlement and wars of resistance. The flow of Europeans to the now-called "New Zealand" was light until around 1840 when the flow accelerated, and became a flood in the 1860s (Belich 1996, 115). Early on the Māori were "racialized" as different from Europeans, probably intensified by English colonization practices elsewhere. Diseases, wars, and religious assimilation were means by which Europeans established their hold. The first colonial settlements were whaling stations set up either as reoutfitting stations for deep sea whalers or processing areas for shore whalers. Both were interested in timber and flax, along with food and water. There was also trade in sealskins, extensive sexual contact, and the first attempts at religious conversions.

The year 1840 was a watershed for conflicts. Resistance included all types and modalities, with struggles over control of land and trade with incoming settler populations (known as Pakeha), sometimes leading to actual wars, and periodically the consolidation of new territories. The Māori language came under duress, much as in other colonies. The infamous Musket Wars arose earlier when unscrupulous traders ignited intertribal conflicts, causing Māori infighting and also skirmishes with settler populations. Māori strategies for dealing with this invasive colonialism varied, with some incredibly wise approaches keeping a connection to the land, as in the north with the development of a "gift" of the Tongariro sacred mountains to the Crown. On South Island, agricultural invasions kept the surviving Māori mostly to the coast. The Waitangi Treaty of 1840 established the sociopolitical relationship between the Māori and the Pakeha (European settlers) of New Zealand, in ways that resemble many treaties and claims to sovereignty of indigenous peoples in North America.

The treaty appears to grant sovereignty over New Zealand to the British Queen, or Crown authority, but also guarantees that Māori would retain "exclusive and undisturbed possession of their Land and Estates, Forests, Fisheries and other properties" under stipulation that land could only be sold to the Crown; otherwise Māori had the same rights as all other British subjects. However, language and interpretation differ, with three key words in the treaty differing in Māori translation: *Kâwanatanga* (most say this means governorship); *Rangatiratanga* (Europeans translate this as chieftainship), retaining power by main chiefs; and *Taonga* (meaning precious things/properties), which guarantees leaders have control over all that is valued, including property rights.[8]

The words *tino rangatiratanga* exemplify the relationships we discuss in this book, for Māori understand this to mean sovereignty by Māori authority over their lands, property, and societies, and moreover it includes notions of "cultural sovereignty" that along with Kâwanatanga means self-determination. Although some European Pakeha analysts insist that Māori did not understand the concepts, many if not all Māori leaders and social analysts interpret the treaty's wording as acknowledging Māori leadership, sovereignty, and authority; therefore, there is no cession to the British Crown except as explicitly stated in the Waitangi Treaty. We see how all four model components (Figure 2.2) are indeed important to understand this situation from an indigenous perspective, and we note how they are in conflict with the dominant state structure (Figure 2.3).[9]

Systems of social justice for the Māori have been impacted across the social institutions of cultural sovereignty "laws" covering the economy, community, leadership, land tenure, and control over natural resources, including the bounty of the sea. Chieftain communities were constructed in order to negotiate away the wealth of these indigenous nations. "First occupier" rights, previously ensconced in Māori oral tradition law, were set aside. Instead, new hierarchical structures based on British colonial culture and on Crown law became dominant in a few short decades.

The processes of colonial domination—ethnic submersion of the indigenous populations, followed by coerced devolution into a minority group forced by the dominant groups—followed patterns similar to the mainland areas of North America. Various revitalization strategies and movements arose, including maintaining of contemporary social structures, political struggles, and cultural adaptation, such as to the loss of many fluent language speakers. Stratification set in, with Māori overrepresented in the prison system. The general idea was that they would soon disappear. However, the Māori population continued to comprise a significant percent of the overall population and maintained its language and cultural knowledge, refusing to be subsumed. Different patterns emerged on the South and North Islands. Māori communities were more numerous and often stronger in the North, but with some surprising developments in the South. During the 1960s and again in subsequent decades, marches on government centers were often powerful motivators and reminders of how Aotearoa survived in New Zealand, leading to an insistence of keeping the Waitangi Treaty rights in place, and the cultural and human rights that Māori were deserving of in customary and Crown law. A tribunal was set up to handle these claims. The Māori language was taught in the schools and bilingually represented in government centers.[10]

Māori in Aotearoa/New Zealand have been battling colonialism and discrimination for some 200 years now. They have maintained a sense of community, as in their *marae* (meetinghouses) and their treaty relations, as in the Waitangi Tribunal, and have adapted communal decision making and quasi-modern redistributive economics (first realized with a few Iwi or Hapu settlements and now in corporate form). Even so, Māori are mostly in the lower stratification levels of society, with significant institutional inequalities in all sectors of the society. Discrimination levels have recently increased over such resource issues as the Foreshore and Seabed Debates, wherein Māori have a constitutional right to control land collectively, whereas the Pakeha and the government want to enforce private

Plate 3.1. Kaikoura marae buildings and grounds. (Photo courtesy of James V. Fenelon)

property and new legislation. This latest conflict reflects continuing struggles over indigenous autonomy for Māori.

Māori leaders and scholars now state that the "Maori have never said we owned the seabed" when debating the Foreshore legislation (Waitangi Tribunal 2003). For Māori, their relationship with the land was one of "belonging to it, not one of owning it." Further, they believe that "*Ranguini,* our sky father ... and *Papatuanuku,* our earth mother" make up Aotearoa, over which they have a "role as *kaitiaki*" or guardians/stewards of the land[11] (Marsden 2003). These views are particularly noteworthy because they locate traditional concepts of the land and sea as very much opposed to monetary values that are established by global capitalism and colonial social structures.

Major revitalization efforts include language maintenance and restoration; creation of the Wananga, similar to tribal colleges in the United States; reconstruction of traditional Iwi and Hapu social structures; reforestation and similar environment projects in the ocean; linkage with mainstream political structures; and, as mentioned, a forceful discussion of the central Waitangi Treaty of 1840 (Moon 2002, 162), now with a separate tribunal and official Office of Treaty Settlements in the government.

Educational efforts from elementary to college level at Otaki are particularly strong. These are illustrated in community coming together to fuse traditional practices, such as the Haka often referred to as a "warrior" rite, with

contemporary educational reform, including language revitalization at their local marae. Potential language loss has been turned into cultural recovery for the
next generation resisting colonization effects (Smith 1999), such as at *Te Whare
Wananga o Raukawa* (Otaki).[12]

Economic efforts combined with sociopolitical representation are equally
impressive, including negotiated settlements at Kaikoura that reinvested monies
with great success, even with contemporary tourist businesses like the popular
Whale Watch tours. Similarly, the Ngai Tahu treaty settlements symbolize resistance leadership and revitalization with land purchases, investment in fisheries,
and even corporate technology businesses (Iwi Tuwharetoa) throughout the South
Island areas, along with the controversy over whether they still retain traditional
Māori value systems.

THE FORESHORE AND SEABED DEBATE IN AOTEAROA: MĀORI RESISTANCE, JUDICIAL INNOVATION, AND STATE CONTROL

Perhaps no better example of these struggles would be the Foreshore and Seabed
Debates, as reported by Peter Horsley of Massey University in New Zealand:

> The recent debate in Aotearoa New Zealand over the foreshore and seabed issue is a
> timely reminder that the forces unleashed by state colonization continue to exist in
> ways that are remarkably reminiscent of the early encounters between indigenous
> peoples and settler governments. (The foreshore is the area of "wet" land between
> the low and high tide marks, and the seabed runs from low tide mark to the 12
> mile limits of the territorial sea.)
>
> The issue had its genesis in a June 2003 ruling from New Zealand's highest
> Court (the Court of Appeal). In Ngati Apa v. Attourney General the Court decided
> that the Crown (i.e., the New Zealand government) did not own the foreshore by
> prerogative right and that the Maori Land Court had jurisdiction for tribes to in-
> vestigate title to foreshore and seabed areas. The immediate response from the Gov-
> ernment was [to] bluntly announce that it would legislate to "reassert" the Crown's
> ownership of New Zealand's seabed and foreshore and to remove the Maori Land
> Court's jurisdiction. In August and December 2003 the Government produced
> policy documents that highlighted guaranteed public access, regulation, protection,
> and certainty for all New Zealanders. Limited rights for Maori in the foreshore and
> seabed were also recognized. These decisions led to claims being lodged with the
> Waitangi Tribunal by Maori. An urgent hearing was held in January 2004, and
> the tribunal released its report a month later. It was highly critical of the Crown's
> approach, noting the discriminatory aspects of the policy framework (it breached
> the constitutional principle of equal treatment under the law), and also ignored
> existing public access agreements between Maori tribes and the Government. The
> Government response was equally sharp and critical. It accused the Waitangi Tribu-
> nal of implicitly rejecting the principle of parliamentary sovereignty. Other events
> then unfolded. On 5 May 2004, one of the largest Maori protests in New Zealand

took place when over 20,000 people marched on Parliament to protest against the foreshore and seabed legislation. A Maori Minister, Tariana Turia, resigned from the Labour Government, forcing a by-election in her seat. This led to the formation of the Maori Party which then contested the 2005 General Election winning 4 Maori seats. In the meantime, Government continued to pass legislation that asserted its position despite concerns from many quarters, and which also set out minor and very complicated concessions for the recognition of customary Maori interests. The issue continues to simmer away and there are active moves by the Maori Party and its political allies to try and repeal the legislation. These concerns will not disappear and are bound to resurface in the years to come. What are the lessons from these events? The state still sees sovereignty as defined by colonial forebears as its exclusive domain. It is unwilling to entertain even limited autonomy for its indigenous people and will not explore innovative legal processes for the sharing of power. The courts, however, continue their recent tradition of challenging their own common law history by restating legal doctrines that recognize indigenous rights. Regrettably, Parliament is supreme in the constitutional arrangements and can override common law decisions. People power and protest continue to be the driving forces for confronting state hegemony. They also provide the backbone for the evolution of new political initiatives. And finally, given available political arrangements (in Aotearoa-NZ, the existence of Maori seats and a proportional representation system for electing MPs), new political responses can emerge. The Maori Party has just completed its first year in the current Parliament and has attracted plaudits for its clear and responsible advocacy of Maori aspirations from a Maori perspective. It continues to build both its constituency and policy program and is in a very strong position to win at least 7 seats in the next election (in 2008). Given the nature of the proportional system of government, it will then become a significant player in the formation of the next government. By cementing its position within the corridors of power, the Party's quest for self determination could, and indeed should, find new and potentially radical expressions of autonomy for Maori. (Fenelon and Murguia 2008, 1659–1660.)

Horsley points out that the dimensions of the Foreshore and Seabed Debate are outgrowths of circumstances initiated through colonialism—circumstances with striking similarities to the way in which the political, economic, social, and cultural forces of globalization have begun to reinstate domination over peoples considered to be expendable. The Māori have established a complex system of resistance that demonstrates the advanced counterhegemonic opposition capable of undermining Western dominance, as seen in the Māori land courts revisiting and renegotiating indigenous land tenure governance (Plate 3.2).[13]

ADEVASI HISTORIOGRAPHY

The Adevasi peoples of India have struggled for over 3,000 years with tributary states, with British colonialism and neocolonialism, and now with India over forestlands and autonomous governance. With such a long history, details must

48   Chapter 3

Plate 3.2. Maori Land Court sign at Turangi (Aotearoa), New Zealand. (Photo courtesy of James V. Fenelon)

perforce remain somewhat sketchy. These peoples, however, raise all the issues we noted in the opening chapters: Who is indigenous? What does indigenous mean in the context of groups of peoples who have been in conflict, with spells of cooperation or peace for millennia? Some scholars argue that political activists created the term *Adevasi* in the 1930s in the Chotanapur area. In Devanâgarî script, *adi* means "beginning," and *vasi* means "resident of" (Bates 1995, 104–105). *Adevasi* has become the preferred term over "tribals" or "scheduled peoples." However, Indian scholars have viewed this attempt to name them as "paternalism." They find instead that there is a rich, though mystified, history of Adevasi people extending from before the early Hindu societies. Some relate the linguistic development as having similarities to the word (ironically) *Indian* or the contemporary use of *indigenous.* In the following statement, Indian social activist-scholar C. R. Bijoy finds that the various layers of domination, including external and internal colonization, have further muddled identity issues, especially with the country of India in denial:

> Of the 5,653 distinct communities in India, 635 are considered to be "tribes" or "Adivasis." Most Adivasi communities are classed under the administrative category of "scheduled tribes" (STs): a category neither comprehensive, nor always sociologically valid. There are 577 ST communities numbering 84.32 million as per 2001 census comprising 8.32% of the total population, making the Indian subcontinent the abode of more than a quarter of the world's 350 million or so indigenous peoples. India is divided into 28 states and seven union territories (UTs). STs are found in all the states/UTs, except Punjab, Haryana, Delhi and the UTs of Pondicherry and Chandigarh. They inhabit in about 15% of the country's geographical area, mainly forests, hills, [and] undulating remote terrain in plateau areas that are rich in natural resources. Numerically these communities vary, with the Great Andamanese numbering only 18 to that of the Gonds numbering over 5,000,000. They are also not evenly distributed. More than half of them are in

the central region, whereas they are largely the majority population in the north eastern region.[14] (Bijoy 2008, 1756)

Some indigenous leaders argue that there are 90 million plus Adevasi within India. Many Western scholars argue for an estimated 50 million Adevasi in something like 400 groups in India. Some peoples claiming to be Adevasi had kingdoms in pre-British times. Crispin Bates (1995, 104) goes so far as to argue, "The *adivasis* may thus be regarded as not so much 'original' inhabitants of South Asia but the very recent creation of colonial anthropology. Paradoxically, they might be seen as an invention rather than a victim of modernity." Bates, however, overstates the case and represents a perfect example of social scientists imposing their previously uninformed analytical models on indigenous peoples rather than relying on the perspective and history of the peoples themselves. These scholars see Adevasis only in relation to their discovery of them. We will continue with C. R. Bijoy's analysis, which is strikingly similar to processes in North American contexts:

> Historically the Adivasis ... are at best perceived as sub-humans to be kept in isolation, or as "primitives" living in remote and backward regions who should be "civilized." None of them have a rational basis. Consequently, the official and popular perception of Adivasis is merely that of forest isolation, tribal dialect, animism, primitive occupation, carnivorous diet, naked or seminaked, nomadic habits, with a love of drinking and dancing. Contrast this with the self-perception of Adivasis as casteless, classless and egalitarian in nature, community-based economic systems, symbiotic with nature, democratic according to the demands of the times, accommodative history and people-oriented art and literature. (Bijoy 2001, 61)

The term *Adevasi* serves much like the terms *Indian, Native American,* or *First Peoples* in the United States: as an umbrella term for peoples who have an-cient nonstate roots. Because of the extreme time-depth of human occupation of South Asia, it is probably pointless to try to establish who was where first. Rather, we should recognize that there are peoples who have historical continuity with ancestors who have been more or less autonomous from various states and who have maintained some degree of cultural independence. All peoples have histories, whether or not they are written, and whether or not they have been recognized by various "civilizations" or empires.

In South Asia the "name game" is more complex because of the "posi-tive discrimination" legacy, that is, laws and regulations developed along with Indian independence in August 1947 to help "Untouchables" and "tribals," who had been severely disadvantaged both under pre-British south Asian states and under British rule. Thus, there is incentive for people who are poor to fit into the scheduled castes or tribes in order to make use of those limited advantages. Yet there is also incentive to avoid labels that associate individuals or groups with low caste, especially so-called Untouchables. To discuss this complex set of issues fully would take a rather long book. Here we will restrict our discussion to two indigenous peoples, the Warli and the Gond.

WARLI AND GOND PEOPLES OF MAHARASHTRA

The Warli indigenous peoples have resisted cultural domination for more than a thousand years, and they still maintain a traditional orientation to their land claims. These struggles included tributary relationships with ancient kingdoms as the Adevasi, colonial relations with the British as "scheduled tribes," and internal colonialism with the current government of India as "tribes" with or without recognition (Bijoy 2001).

Forest meetings of resistance groups are still held, contesting oppressive government policies that officially call Warli and Gond villages "encroachment" on their own lands. Whereas past resistance has colluded with Marxist resistance forces, recent efforts have negotiated stalemate agreements by establishing greater community autonomy, especially over forest control, rare plant uses, and timber practices. Both the Warli and Gond are active in reforestation projects that usually collide with private companies and corrupt government officers, and will probably lead to greater conflicts later as the trees mature in large teak forests.

These practices have continued, with a special focus on cultural destruction or erasure, leading to denial by the government of India at the United Nations that it even had so many indigenous peoples (the largest number in the world). India has even denied legal standing for important social structures, such as the Ghotul for the Gond youth,[15] and land creation stories with the Warli literally calling their origin place "mother earth" (Prabhu 2004). Warli families maintain the practice of allowing animals in the house, not differentiating between humans and other life-forms. Villages north of Dahanu experience near-constant conflict with corrupt "foresters" selling rights to private companies, and with government law calling their villages "encroachment" on their traditional, now timbered forestlands.

Gond peoples in central India, likely the largest cultural grouping of indigenous people, also have experienced continuous conflict with local, regional, and Indian governmental control systems. The Gonds' reestablishment of the Ghotul for their youth and as a form of community empowerment is especially instructive in this regard. Government foresters and police tore down the Ghotul structures in the name of "civilizing" efforts, but the Gond rebuilt them on a massive scale, leading to a contemporary standoff and greater autonomy.

Resistance and revitalization organizations have developed in the rural communities, often intersecting with elementary education efforts and local environmental controls. The Gond are increasingly self-reliant and practicing self-determination, such as establishing community values and cultural cohesion.

Government attempts at repression have of late backfired, and both the communities and the schools are getting stronger and more self-reliant. Warli

Plate 3.3. Warli villagers meeting in reforested lands, north of Dahanu, India. (Photo courtesy of James V. Fenelon)

peoples' relationship with forest trees, potentially valuable plant knowledge, and animal husbandry have all undergone a virtual reconstruction lately (Prabhu 2001). Some of the indigenous Warli and Gond success has come from linkage with existing philosophies, such as at the Ghandi Ashram, calling for equalization and respect in India. Other efforts have connected with the World Health Organization and United Nations efforts to protect indigenous property rights, cultural knowledge, and medicinal plants. Elder Gond stand out in this respect, with strict guidelines on sharing of information.[16]

Both the Warli and Gond peoples, as many other indigenous peoples in this country where "tribals" (Adevasi) make up nearly 9 percent of the population—totaling close to 69 million people—but in contemporary parlance are called "scheduled tribes" (Bijoy 2001), are very complex in their social makeup and political representations, are under near-constant scrutiny by government forces, and have limited power through collectively ignoring select laws. Therefore, resistance takes many forms and modalities, with many struggles becoming violent and others contested in social justice systems that involve the four components of our model—the local economy, community, leadership, and land tenure and control over forest areas viewed as "natural resources" by corporatized national interests of India.

Revitalization strategies always considered the cultural value systems in their selected resistance to contemporary social structures, and in terms of what they hope to achieve. Initially the Adivasi were in what is called a tributary relationship. Then they came under two-stage English colonization as "scheduled tribes," followed by the state of India suppressing rights and collectivities as India encountered increased competition under globalization. C. R. Bijoy develops this analysis in an article titled "Forest Rights Struggle: The Adivasis Now Await a Settlement" (2008).

Bijoy's article draws attention to the 2005 Bill for the Recognition of Forest Rights, as recommended through a report by the Joint Parliamentary Committee on Scheduled Tribes. Bijoy explains how the Adevasi resist governmental interference into indigenous rights to land and cultural autonomy. Despite current actions on the part of the organization of the Campaign for Survival and Dignity, Bijoy highlights the historical resistance to foreign imperialism, indifference to environmental responsibility, state greed, and total lack of consideration for the preservation of indigenous cultures. This narrative begins prior to modern-day globalization, established within a historically grounded understanding of indigenous struggle by identifying the larger trajectory of imperialism, resistance to that imperialism, and the ongoing fight for a just environment.

Bijoy develops this argument by referring to a contemporary legislative bill, stating that

> Adivasis and their homelands—the forests—have been ravaged by both state and nonstate actors at a great loss to the nation of its forests and its peoples. The instrument used—the colonial forest act and forest regime. The Scheduled Tribes (Recognition of Forest Rights) Bill, 2005 emerged at this late hour to rectify this "historic injustice" ... that the "rural poor, especially tribals, had been deprived of their livelihood rights." (2008, 1762)
> ... Forest dwelling Tribal People and forests are inseparable. One cannot survive without the other.... Conservation of ecological resources by forest dwelling tribal communities [has] been referred to in ancient manuscripts and scriptures.... Colonial rule somehow ignored this reality for greater economic gains. (Scheduled Tribes 2005, as cited in Bijoy 2008, 1768)[17]

This historical discussion is clearly global as well, connected with timber and natural resources located on land controlled by indigenous Adevasis, which the government is attempting to appropriate from them. Fields of domination are connected too, with Bijoy commenting on the way in which the Indian government has borrowed an "American fiction" of "wilderness" without people as a form of oppression, stating, "After independence ... we continued with colonial legislations.... The reservation processes for creating wilderness and forest areas for production forestry ... ignored the bonafide interests of the tribal community from the legislative frame" (Scheduled Tribes 2005, as cited in Bijoy 2008, 1768). This shared reality of indigenous land tenure relationships, offset by governmental policies and practices that empower corporate privatization, is becoming an all-too-common story around the globe, well evidenced in the following short discussions of indigenous people (Aboriginals) in Australia and Native Hawaiians.

INDIGENOUS "ABORIGINAL" AUSTRALIANS[18]

The indigenous Australians—called Aboriginals—have experienced the full range of dominant modalities, including genocide, urban relocation, coercive education and forced labor, subordination into a minority status, and discrimination for both racial and native ethnic origins. Although the culture and lifestyle of Aboriginal groups have much in common, diverse Aboriginal communities have different modes of subsistence, cultural practices, languages, and technologies. However, a collective identity, "Indigenous Australians," is recognized and exists along with names from the indigenous languages that are commonly used to identify groups based on regional geography and other affiliations.

Like other indigenous peoples, Aboriginal oral tradition and creation stories differ markedly from Western scholarship, itself not of one mind or perspective. The first Aboriginal settlers colonized what is now Australia between 40,000 and 80,000 years ago. At European contact, population estimates run from 350,000 to 1 million Indigenous Australians.[19] The greatest population density was to be found in the southern and eastern regions of the continent, the Murray River Valley in particular. European settlers with advanced warlike technology arrived around 1788 from England and began violently colonizing the region.

Indigenous Australians view the land as their origin place and have constructed a rich cosmology that makes sense of their societies, called the creative epoch "Dreamtime," stretching back into a remote era in history when the creator ancestors, known as First Peoples, traveled across the great southern land of Bandaiyan (Australia), "dreaming," creating, and naming as they went. Most Aboriginal communities were small in relation to sustenance from the land, around which their philosophies were developed.

British colonization began near Sydney with an immediate consequence—within weeks of the first colonists' arrival: a wave of Old World epidemic diseases. Smallpox alone killed more than half of the Aboriginal population. By the 1870s all the fertile areas of Australia were appropriated, with indigenous communities reduced to impoverished remnants living either on the fringes of Australian communities or on lands considered unsuitable for settlement, usually far in the Outback areas. By 1900, British appropriation of land and water resources and direct violence, combined with disease brought by the new settlers, had reduced the Aboriginal population by an estimated 90 percent.

Tony Barta (1987) calls Australia "a nation founded on genocide" with the concept that "genocide must be seen as a policy" with a "bureaucratic apparatus … (targeting) a race … to remorseless pressures of destruction." He finds that basic patterns from North America were repeated in Australia—"pastoral invasion, resistance, violent victory of the white men, mysterious disappearance of the blacks" (Barta 1987, 242). He also sees genocide against the indigenous peoples as societal rather than a "state" with its clear-cut intentions to "wantonly destroy" the aborigines. However, the impetus for developing the "whole bureaucratic apparatus" leading to "genocidal relations" with the natives is underscored by a sensibility that "everywhere the killing—whether officially sanctioned or not—was understood as necessary to the establishment of the new economic and social order" (p. 244) that would "destroy them ... as independent peoples."

A. Moses also sees the multiple instances as part of a broader pattern of extermination, finding that "Australia had many genocides, perhaps more than any other country" (2000, 93). When indigenous peoples resisted the appropriation of land and the sexual enslavement of their women and children, colonists hunted them down in groups, rationalizing the destruction as a civilizing process (Maybury-Lewis 2002; Moses 2004). Barta (1989, 246) states, "Killing on the frontier, then, had to be of a kind that would destroy the ability of Aborigines to survive as independent peoples, with their own social organization, ethnic separateness, and cultural value system in conflict with the world view and economic interest of the invaders. This was clearly understood at the time, by both sides ... as (to secure right to, or fight for) the possession of the land ... [and the] future." Collin Tatz (2003) adds to contact history—disease, violence, assimilation, and forced removal of children—finding intent over culturicide as well as mass death and destruction (see also Tatz 1999). Thus, the cultural identity of Indigenous Australians was intentionally destroyed.

Using the case of the Yorta Yorta to discuss differences between "customary" law and true indigenous sovereignty, Bruce Buchan (2002) identifies "institutions (such as chieftainship) that were imposed on indigenous people under the rubric of 'native authority'" as a means to "bind the 'native' in invisible chains of dependence" under colonialism. He identifies this as a principal method of undermining sovereignty, through representing "custom" as "passive" and "as subject to their own 'superstitions' and 'beliefs,' and as subject to superior European knowledge and government." These examples also are strong examples of attempted destruction of community and family, identity tied to the land or sea, and, interestingly, of traditional authority or leadership, through promoting dependent chiefdoms, all with a purpose of controlling the economy for appropriation of land, natural resources, and other forms of wealth extraction, along with hegemonic dominance over a national region.[20]

Although many surviving Indigenous Australians succumbed to working as stock hands, laborers, or other dependent livelihoods, small groups maintained some semblance of their traditional lifestyle and knowledge. By 1962, with an Indigenous Australian population of 50,000 to 90,000, Commonwealth legislators felt confident enough to "give" Indigenous Australians the right to vote in elections.[21] By then, existing communities had been forced outward, with an urbanization accompanying the racialization policies of the government. Many children were forced into boarding schools that were terribly oppressive toward culture, with the result of an increased mixed-race population. The last mass killings occurred as late as 1926, but cultural destruction continued unabated into the late decades of the twentieth century, with increased racist referencing to Indigenous Australians as blacks and with supremacist policies attached to that racialization.[22] The European-descent Australians had always followed the racist policies and supremacist ideologies of their forebears. Eugenics played a large part in construction of their discriminatory policies, unlike U.S. policies that sharply segregated racial categories, so families could be torn asunder based on their racial makeup. Only recently have Australians come to terms with the practices of this social destruction, as seen in the film *Rabbit-Proof Fence* (directed by Phillip Noyce and released in 2002) and the literature that spawned the film.[23]

In 1971, the Commonwealth ruled that Australia had been *terra nullius* before British "settlement" and therefore refused recognition of native title under Australian law. However, this was overturned in 1992 in the Mabo case, and more complex law has since developed, moving from "self-determination" to "mutual obligation," especially for the nonurbanized Indigenous Australians living in "settlements" (roughly about 27 percent of the total population), often associated with church missions. Both the remote and urban populations have adverse ratings on most social indicators, including health, education, unemployment, poverty, and crime. Urban Indigenous Australians have adopted some aspects of black Americans and Afro-Caribbean groups, reappropriating the racial terms they had been stereotyped with in earlier years. Although over 70 percent are also Christian, "Dreaming" is still considered to be both the ancient time of creation and a present-day reality. Thus the surviving Indigenous Australians are a complex, diverse population that resists discriminatory treatment by cultural invention and also by maintaining traditional knowledge to the greatest extent possible.

NATIVE HAWAIIANS AND PACIFIC ISLANDERS

Native Hawaiians are Polynesian-descent indigenous peoples of the Hawaiian Islands.[24] Their history is shared with Māori and other trans-Pacific voyagers of early times, including Tahitian and Marquesan ancestors.[25] Native Hawaiians made agreements with British representatives and then with the United States, including claims to sovereignty and a distinct ethno-national cultural autonomy.[26]

Scholars identify four general periods of Hawaiian development: that of Ancient Hawaii, with Polynesian settlers arriving between A.D. 300 and 700 (some estimate earlier);[27] the Kingdom of Hawaii under monarchy, especially Kamehameha the Great (1758–1819); the Territory of Hawaii, formally from 1898 to statehood, but actually from 1893 or earlier; and the State of Hawaii, from 1959 to the present. Colonial and corporate interests began in the nineteenth century, intensified in various revolts and takeovers through 1890, and ultimately were instrumental in U.S. dominance and incorporation into the union.

Hawaiian culture developed differently from its Polynesian roots. Various taboos arose, including gender separation as well as ascendancy to leadership, accompanied by a variety of kinship relation rules. After Captain Cook visited the islands and then died there during a scuffle over these *kapu* cultural rules in 1779, social change set in but did not affect the stratification system or the monarchy that had arisen, except to modify for technology and increased trade.

Kamehameha made military moves to unify the islands around 1795 and finally succeeded in 1810, allowing for a single kingdom. The Spanish helped to introduce coffee and pineapples for trade agriculture in 1813. Kamehameha II abandoned the *kapu* system, and Protestant missionaries arrived in 1820, changing the social structure of Native Hawaiians and starting the cultural domination by Westerners that would envelope the islands until they became a territory. Kamehameha III issued the Hawaiian Declaration of Rights in 1839, and the Constitution for the Hawaiian Islands in 1840, changing Hawaiian governance from absolute monarchy to constitutional monarchy and bringing cultural restrictions based on its new status as a Christian nation.

Native Hawaiians numbered between 250,000 to 800,000 strong around the late 1700s (there has been debate over these estimates), but a great many were wiped out by the new diseases introduced to the islands. By 1900 there were only 40,000 Native Hawaiians.[28] Yet by 2000 the census identified 400,000 Native Hawaiians, although over 60 percent had less than 50 percent Native Hawaiian blood.[29] Because all schooling was in English, use of the Hawaiian language and understanding of native culture quickly declined. During the twentieth century, most demographic growth on the islands was by nonnatives from North America or East Asian countries. The 1898 U.S. takeover, in which Queen Liliuokalani was forced out in an early act of imperialism. gave rise to a diverse territory with compelling agricultural and trade concerns throughout the Pacific region. It also left Native Hawaiians culturally, politically, and in sheer numbers a minority in their own land. Native Hawaiian status has gone through many changes since then, with various laws and movements attempting to maintain and revitalize the Hawaiian language and cultural practices.

The Kamehameha Schools are a particularly good example of Hawaiian revitalization.[30] Requiring that the Hawaiian language be taught and spoken and with preference given to Native Hawaiians, the Kamehameha Schools have had to fight off legal challenges since the 1990s over the trusteeship, land ownership by Native Hawaiians, and admission of non-Hawaiians to the schools. Some litigants claim the policies of the Kamehameha Schools are race-based and discriminatory. Although there are similarities to affirmative action fights on the U.S. mainland, these struggles more closely resemble expressions of dominance over indigenous peoples.

Another compelling set of issues for Native Hawaiians are those arising from sovereignty movements that have been a general mainstay of Hawaiian resistance and revitalization strategies, though very controversial to both scholars and political activists.[31] A premier result of these movements has been an "Apology Resolution" brought by Senators Daniel Inouye and Daniel Akaka and signed by President Bill Clinton in 1993. The resolution apologized "to Native Hawaiians on behalf of the people of the United States for the overthrow of the Kingdom of Hawaii on January 17, 1893 ... and the deprivation of the rights of Native Hawaiians to self-determination." The historical and factual basis of the apology has been criticized by constitutional lawyers, scholars, and some civil rights activists;

however, a bill extending federal recognition to Native Hawaiians as an ancestral group is currently being discussed. If passed, it would allow Native Hawaiians to create an unprecedented governing entity to engage in nation-to-nation negotiations with the U.S. government, similar to Native Nations and American Indian tribes. Some maintain that these provisions would grant recognition to Native Hawaiians without the same qualifications necessary for tribal recognition.

Native Hawaiians transformed from Pacific Island indigenous peoples through various political forms under colonial domination, with their kingdom taken from them by the United States, accompanied by language and cultural devolution. Revitalization has restored some traditional culture even as new laws are being constructed to preserve their cultural sovereignty.

CONCLUSION

Māori are a treaty-based indigenous people living in lands now dominated by the Pakeha, descendants and immigrants of settler populations from Europe. Thus, they share many characteristics with First Nations and American Indians from North America, as a treaty people (Waitangi), and also with other indigenous Polynesian peoples in the Pacific. They struggle over the meaning of sovereignty and face discrimination in everyday life.

Adevasi of India are indigenous peoples with histories encompassing thousands of years, from being a true periphery during the rise of various kingdoms, to being forced toward the bottom during colonial rule by the British, and again experiencing lower-end stratification and suppression by the Indian government and by private corporate forces. They are involved in struggles over land, forests, dams, relocation, and urban issues.

Indigenous Australians have experienced near-genocidal destruction and suppression that emanates from both racial (black) and ethnic (indigenous) discrimination. In this respect they are victims of imperial and colonial conquest, and of globalization forces. Native Hawaiian peoples, having a now-unrecognized

Plate 3.4. S.E.A.R.C.H. medical team consults with Gond villagers about culturally appropriate health practices, Menda, Lekha, India. (Photo courtesy of James V. Fenelon)

treaty and a subsumed population, also are engaged in a struggle over sovereignty, or at the least in autonomy over contested homelands.

These indigenous peoples demonstrate a diversity of indigeneity, the complexity of each history of conquest and domination, and singular attempts at ongoing resistance, cultural revitalization, and struggles over autonomy and sometimes sovereignty. These struggles exist in a world increasingly hostile to collective societies without any state recognition, where globalization is synonymous with sociopolitical submersion and community is the primary hope for revitalization as indigenous peoples.

NOTES

1. In an address to the New Zealand Psychological Society, Donna Awatere-Huata considers "the economic cartel that developed based on race. It's an economic and political cartel that continues today, and dismantling that, deconstructing that cartel is something that I believe concerns all New Zealanders. It's about the Maorification of New Zealand. It's about Pakeha becoming more Maori and not about Maori becoming any more Pakeha." http://www.enzed .com/tw.html, accessed July 14, 2008.

2. *Tangata whenua* means "People of the Land"—the first people to settle in the land of New Zealand (indigenous people). http://www.enzed.com/tw.html, accessed July 14, 2008.

3. The imperial and state history of South Asia have been poorly studied (Sinopoli 2006), and that of nonstate peoples is even more poorly known. Carla Sinopoli's overview makes two points germane here: (1) the dearth of extensive historical and archaeological information; and (2) what is known is often highly politicized in terms of contemporary debates, though most of the politicization focuses on states. China, in contrast, is somewhat better known, but much of the work on nonstate peoples focuses, for obvious reasons, on pastoral nomads (Stark 2006a, 2006b; Allard 2006; Honeychurch and Amartuvshin 2006).

4. "Historic Canoes of the Maori and Moriori People, 925–1350 AD," in Te Rangi Hiroa and Sir Peter Buck, *The Coming of the Maori* (Christchurch, New Zealand: Whitcombe & Tombes Ltd., 1949). Available at http://www.geocities.com/wlorac/mfleet.htm, accessed July 14, 2008.

5. Only the northernmost portions of Aotearoa are frost-free, so few of the tropical plants could provide a steady diet. However, the high density of several species of seals and moas (flightless birds related to the emu) provided an easily available source of protein that allowed rapid population expansion and time to adapt to new conditions.

6. One author was in New Zealand and observed the initial meeting of a Native Hawaiian traveling with his group with the local Māori, who immediately connected on a number of levels—cultural, sociolinguistic, historical—and as indigenous peoples, to the extent of formally recognizing one another as relatives.

7. Belich sees rather three overlapping zones: kin, neighbor, and stranger. Rivalry over *mana* (approximately status) was most important but less bloody in the "kin zone" and the reverse in the "stranger zone." These trends were still flowing when Europeans arrived. Tribal groupings, while mappable, remained fluid, but most people had been in place for centuries.

8. New Zealand History online, http://www.nzhistory.net.nz/category/tid/133, accessed July 14, 2008.

9. Māori beliefs and attitudes about ownership and use of land were different from those prevailing in Britain and Europe. The chiefs saw themselves as *kaitiaki,* or guardians of the land, and would traditionally grant permission for the land to be used for a time for a particular purpose. Some may have thought that they were leasing the land rather than selling it, leading to disputes with the occupant settlers.

10. Te Taura Whiri i te reo Māori (The Māori Language Commission) was set up under the Māori Language Act of 1989 to develop and assist with the implementation of policies and practices designed to give effect to the declaration of Māori as an official language. Te Taura Whiri has specific responsibilities: to promote the Māori language and its use as an ordinary means of communication; and to consider and report to the Minister of Māori Affairs on any matter relating to the Māori language.

11. "Mangapouri Stream Research and Restoration Project," lecture-presentation by Pataka Moore and Caleb Royal, at Te-Wananga-o-Raukawa (college) at Otaki, Aotearoa, New Zealand, October 2003.

12. Te Tauihu o Nga Wananga is the national coordinating body for the three Māori tertiary institutions: Te Whare Wananga o Raukawa (Otaki), Te Whare Wananga o Awanui-a-Rangi, and Te Whare Wananga o Aotearoa (Waikato).

13. Recent developments in these issues are discussed in the epilogue.

14. "'Scheduled Tribes' in India are generally considered to be Adivasis, literally meaning 'indigenous people' or 'original inhabitants,' though the term *Scheduled Tribes* (STs) is not coterminous with the term *Adivasis. Scheduled Tribes* is an administrative term used for purposes of 'administering' certain specific constitutional privileges, protection, and benefits for specific sections of peoples considered historically disadvantaged and 'backward.' ... For practical purposes, the United Nations and multilateral agencies generally consider the STs as 'indigenous peoples'" (Bijoy 2001, 54–61).

15. The Ghotul is a separate living area and an open system of informal education where unmarried male and female youth live together, experiment with social situations, and are permitted sexual activity (although after they emerge as adults these practices stop). Not surprisingly, many outside observers see this as promoting promiscuity (see Gell 1992 for a detailed discussion of the Ghotul among one group), although Gond elders themselves see this open living as experiential learning reinforced by social mores and guidance. The Ghotul has been a central issue in conflicts between Western scholars obsessed with sexual practices and the indigenous concern with socialization of their youth. The Menda Lekha Gond themselves protested its misrepresentation, after a couple of anthropologists made and then lost their careers on early film versions, with India banning their return for sexualizing the "primitive" tribals. The Indian government at times banned it, and the Gond at Menda Lekha reconstituted it, in a variant version, at one time defeating local authority by simply rebuilding an extremely large number of Ghotuls at the same time, making it difficult if not impossible for officials to take them down even with huge security forces. Satish Awate asks, "Ghotul: 100 years behind or 100 years ahead?" online at http://www.cgnet.in/FT/ghotul, accessed July 14, 2008.

16. Personal communications followed by on-site interviews with Gond elders at Menda Lekha, eastern Maharashtra, India, in late September 2003.

17. The stated Objects and Reasons of the Bill itself were that the "Forest dwelling Tribal People and forests are inseparable. One cannot survive without the other.... Conservation of ecological resources by forest dwelling tribal communities have been referred to in ancient manuscripts and scriptures.... Colonial rule somehow ignored this reality for greater economic gains.... After independence ... we continued with colonial legislations.... The reservation processes for creating wilderness and forest areas for production forestry ... ignored the bonafide interests of the tribal community from the legislative frame.... The simplicity of

tribals and their general ignorance of modern regulatory frameworks precluded them from asserting genuine claims.... Modern conservation approaches also advocate exclusion rather than integration. It is only recently that forest management regimes have ... realised that tribal communities, who depend primarily on the forest resources, cannot but be integrated in their designed management processes.... Forests have the best chance to survive if communities participate in its conservation.... Insecurity of tenure and fear of eviction ... are perhaps the biggest reasons why tribal communities feel emotionally as well as physically alienated from forests and forest lands. This historical injustice now needs correction before it is too late to save our forests from becoming the abode of undesirable elements.... Recognition of forest rights enjoyed by the forest dwelling Scheduled Tribes on all kinds of forest lands for generations and which includes both bonafide needs of forest land for sustenance and usufruct from forest ... are the fundamental bases on which the proposed legislation stands. The Bill ... reinforces and utilises the rich conservation ethos ... and cautions against any form of unsustainable or destructive practices; [it] lays down a simple procedure so recognition and vesting of forest rights ... so that rights ... vested in forest dwelling tribal communities, become legally enforceable ... provide for adequate safeguards to avoid any further encroachment of forests ... thereby strengthening the conservation regime by giving a permanent stake to STs dwelling in forests ... in a symbiotic relationship with the entire ecosystem."

18. The word *aboriginal,* appearing in English since at least the seventeenth century and meaning "first or earliest known, indigenous" (from the Latin *ab,* "from," and *origo,* "origin"), has been used in Australia to describe its indigenous peoples as early as 1789. *Aborigine* is the noun, and *aboriginal* the adjectival form; however, the latter is often also employed to stand as a noun. Note that the use of *Aborigine(s)* or *Aboriginal(s)* in this sense, i.e., as a noun, has acquired negative, even derogatory connotations among some sectors of the community, who regard it as insensitive and even offensive. The more acceptable and correct expression is *Aboriginal Australians* or *Aboriginal people,* though even this is sometimes regarded as an expression to be avoided because of its historical associations with colonialism. "Indigenous Australians" has found increasing acceptance, particularly since the 1980s.

19. The general consensus among scholars for the arrival of humans in Australia is placed at 40,000 to 50,000 years ago, with a possible range of up to 70,000 years ago. At the time of first European contact, it is estimated that a minimum of 315,000 and as many as 1 million people lived in Australia. The mode of life and material cultures varied greatly from region to region.

20. The image of indigenous life bound by custom and tradition is one of the most salient features of the colonial attitude to indigenous people. Mahmood Mamdani (2001, 651–664) writes of the way that colonial authorities in Africa "crafted" forms of "traditional" and "customary" law and institutions (such as chieftainship) that were imposed on indigenous people under the rubric of "native authority." Mamdani's approach highlights the implication of colonial (and postcolonial) authorities in the creation of the "customary" as the realm of the "native." "Custom" is expressive of the range of forces, beliefs, and superstitions that bind the "native" in invisible chains of dependence, but "custom" is also an object of outside, European observation, knowledge, and manipulation (Tully 1995, 60). To identify custom as the defining characteristic of the life of a people is thus to represent them as passive in a double sense, as subject to their own "superstitions" and "beliefs," and as subject to superior European knowledge and government. For the Yorta Yorta people in this case, their situation—as represented by Justice Olney—amounts to the most abject possible. They are cast as the descendants of a people either washed away by the "tide of history" or hopelessly and impossibly jumbled together by "force of circumstances." Their current "customs" and "observances" are judged to be nontraditional, even though, in many cases, the indigenous people have had to respond to circumstances beyond the experience of their forebears (Buchan 2002).

21. In the United States, another "genocidal society" with similar reduced numbers, this occurred in 1924. Thus the "First" peoples or nations become the "last" to participate in these "democratic" states.

22. The Europeans always considered Aborigines as racially inferior to them, and it was widely believed that they would simply "die out." This belief was challenged a bit by the number of mixed-race children. In the 1930s, 1940s, and 1950s the government and charitable and church groups moved many mixed-race children into orphanages and some into white families. It was felt that part-white children could be integrated into white society. Most children were taken by force. About 15 percent of all aboriginal children were thought to be removed during this period, giving rise to the term *stolen generation.* Aboriginal activism continued strongly but was splintered by different groups pushing in different directions. Most solutions suggested for the future of the Aborigines were a contradictory mixture of the integrative and curative extremes, and were destined to result in an indefinite reliance on welfare, and hence relative poverty. "Cultural subsidization and Affirmative Action has made [white] people suspicious of any Aboriginal with a job or a qualification, and has created mistrust and resentment from others who feel it has reduced their own opportunities" (http:// www.wikipedia.org 2007, accessed September 1, 2007).

23. Pilkington Garimara 2001.

24. The Hawaiian language is *kânaka 'ôiwi* or *kânaka maoli.*

25. The Polynesians brought with them pigs, dogs, chickens, taro, sweet potatoes, coconut, banana, sugarcane, and much more, in large double-hulled canoes.

26. The U.S. Census Bureau 2000 reported there are 401,162 people who identified themselves as being Native Hawaiian, part Native Hawaiian, or mixed Native Hawaiian. Two-thirds live in the state of Hawaii, and the other one-third is split among mainland states. Almost half of the mainland share of the population is in California.

27. History of Hawaii–Timeline of Hawaii, http://www.hawaiischoolreports.com/history/timeline.htm, accessed July 14, 2008.

28. *Hawaiians* are usually defined as descendants of the indigenous peoples of the Hawaiian Islands, exercising sovereignty in the Hawaiian Islands in 1778, and who have continued to reside in Hawaii (see Russ 1992; for civil rights, see Smith 2008, 1817–1833). *Native Hawaiians* are legally defined as at least one-half descendant of the indigenous peoples from the Hawaiian Islands previous to 1778, extending from the Hawaiian Homes Commission Act in 1920 reenacted in the state constitution of 1959 (for sovereignty, see Smith above), and using a blood quantum definition of the indigenous nations with sovereignty (before 1778 and to 1898) and who continued to reside in Hawaii.

29. That same report by the Office of Hawaiian Affairs and the U.S. Census indicated that only 8,244 pure-blooded Native Hawaiians existed out of the 208,476 total Native Hawaiians surveyed.

30. The Kamehameha Schools were established through the last will and testament of Bernice Pauhi Bishop, a princess of the Kamehameha dynasty.

31. Kamehameha declared that *"Ua mau ke ea o ka 'âina i ka pono"* (The life of the land is perpetuated in righteousness), the motto of the future State of Hawaii.

RECOMMENDED READINGS

Belich, James. 1996. *Making Peoples: A History of the New Zealanders, From Polynesian Settlement to the End of the Nineteenth Century.* Honolulu: University of Hawaii Press. This is one of the better accounts of Māori movement to Aotearoa/New Zealand.

Marsden, Maori. 2003. *The Woven Universe: Selected Writings of Rev. Maori Marsden, Te Ahukaramu*. Edited by Charles Royal. Te Wananga-o-Raukawa, Otaki, New Zealand: Estate of Rev. Marsden.
     This recent work is from an indigenous perspective and is perhaps a bit hard to find.
Smitu Kothari, Imtiaz, and Helmut Reifeld, eds. 2004. *The Value of Nature—Ecological Politics in India*. New Delhi: Rainbow Publishers.

Web Resources

Indigenous Australians (aboriginal Australians) links (from Dropbears), http://www.dropbears.com/l/links/aboriginal.htm (accessed December 11, 2008).
The Māori Party home page (see Foreshore and Seabed debate), http://www.maoriparty.com/index.php?option=com_frontpage&Itemid=1 (accessed December 11, 2008).
Native Hawaiians and the Civil Rights Commission, http://www.nativehawaiians.com/ (accessed December 11, 2008).
Tena koutou, tena koutou, Tena koutou katoa (Welcome [to discussions of Māori issues]), http://www.enzed.com/tw.html (accessed December 11 2008).

CHAPTER 4

Indigenous Mexico

Globalization and Resistance

With Glen David Kuecker

INDIGENOUS PEOPLES IN MEXICO have had continuous relationships with Euro-Americans for half a millennium. The southwestern United States was, in many ways, the northern limit of Latin America until the nineteenth century.

Mexico is the northernmost state of Latin America and home to "Indians" who occupy social positions that are, in most cases, the product of more than 500 years of colonization of indigenous peoples in the Western Hemisphere. Today their struggles for survival are against the spread of global capitalism as it manifests in Mexico—whether such struggle be intentional and overt, or neither. Mexico is often characterized by its difference from the United States, described with such labels as "semiperipheral state," "part of the third world," or a "global south." Given such nominal distinctions, it is not surprising that depictions of indigenous struggles in Mexico have also differed in many ways from those struggles in the neighboring United States. We use our examination of indigenous struggles in Mexico and in other parts of Latin America to develop an encompassing concept of indigeneity[1] and to underscore how different trajectories for states and regions in a changing world-system mutually influence each other.

Mexico is home to one of the most renowned of recent indigenous rebellions: the Zapatista movement centered in Chiapas and widely known as the EZLN (Ejército Zapatista de Liberación Nacional, or the Zapatista Army of National Liberation). However, the EZLN is only one of many indigenous movements in

63

Mexico and throughout Latin America. Although these movements are certainly unique in their own ways, they also share several characteristics that are important to our analysis within a global context. First, according to some social analysts, indigeneity may be viewed as embedded in the ethnic/racial hierarchy of *Indio* and *mestizo,* and historically of *ladino* or contemporary *criollos* (Indian, mixed, Hispanic) permeating Latin America. In contrast, however, many indigenous peoples see themselves as culturally and historically separate, even while they live within the state and global systems. Second, some of these movements are examples of "transnational social movements" or "new social movements."[2] Yet, many indigenous scholars see their struggles as a continuation of resistance and revitalization efforts that address new contexts and often use new techniques to pursue these centuries-old goals, and not as some form of modern social movements (Hall and Fenelon 2008; Valandra 2006). Their struggles derive from centuries of interaction with and struggle against an expanding world-system that originated in Western Europe. These two different perceptions of indigeneity in Latin America—specifically in Mexico—also produce different worldviews, histories, and ideas about political participation and stratification, which we need to address by framing our discussion in particular places and times.

At the outset we underscore a profound difference in understandings of indigeneity, of struggles against forces of change, and of survival between indigenous peoples and mainstream social analyses. Often some social analysts (e.g., Barrett and Kurzman 2004; McAdam, Tarrow, and Tilly 2001; Tilly 2004; Kousis and Tilly 2005[3]) see these movements as "new" when in fact they are as old as first European contact. Indigenous peoples and many other analysts, including ourselves, do not see indigenous movements as a subcategory of some larger set of movements. Rather, they are much older and more complex, though they are related, especially to the new social movements, in important ways. Nonetheless, the historical roots and localized struggles are central features of indigenous movements and peoples. Understanding these different perspectives is critical. We discuss each of these perspectives briefly before discussing the Zapatistas and the EZLN, along with other indigenous movements, in detail. One of our goals is to connect these two perspectives while respecting their differences.

INDIGENEITY AND RACIALIZATION IN LATIN AMERICA

In the region that became Mexico there were several states and empires as well as many smaller groups before the arrival of Hernan Cortez and the *conquista* (Foster and Gorenstein 2000; Blanton, Kowalewski, Feinman, and Finsten 1993; Carmack, Gasco, and Gossen 1996). Among these pre-Cortez organizational structures was the Mayan Empire, whose classic period lasted from 300 c.e. to approximately 900 c.e., leaving many bureaucratic and ceremonial centers in the region located on what is now the Mexican state of Chiapas (there are others in the Yucatan and in Guatemala). Nearly a thousand years later the descendants of early Mayans initiated the Zapatista uprising. In southwestern Mexico, around the state of Oaxaca, the Zapotecs, descendants of another empire, developed after the Mayans but before the widely known Aztec empire. The Aztecs had conquered and incorporated many states and peoples left from cities such as Teotihuacán (see Plate 4.1). At the time of Cortez's invasion, Tenochtitlán (present-day Mexico City) was one of the largest cities in the world. It had on the order of half a million residents and was the administrative center of an empire that included millions of people, roughly equivalent to the population of Texas or Afghanistan today, or England in the late nineteenth century.

Cortez and a small force of conquistadors, supplemented with local allies, managed to take the city, destroy Aztec control, and forever change what would later become Mexico. The conquest led to the deaths of many indigenous peoples, primarily from European diseases (Crosby 1972), and the subordination of those who survived. This, in turn, became a major context for the indigenous peoples who survived until the formation of the Mexican state in the early nineteenth century. Some indigenous peoples were incorporated into the Mexican state and apparently disappeared or melded into modern political structures. Postconquest Mexico developed a culture based in Spain and adopted Spanish as the national

Plate 4.1. Teotihuacán ancient city capital ruins, outside Mexico City. (Photo courtesy of James V. Fenelon)

language, but with significant contributions from its indigenous peoples. An important point is that many residents of Mexico are descendants of one or more indigenous states and other indigenous peoples. There is a wide variation, from much to little, of their traditions that persist in some form or another in Mexico today. Many residents are of some sort of mixed ancestry, again with a great deal of variation. The net result is that there is a much higher proportion of "Indian-ness" in Mexico than in the United States or Canada, albeit often in forms quite different from what they were before the arrival of Europeans. The poorest *Indios* live closest to traditional culture, and the experiences of relocated peoples contrast sharply with those of indigenous peoples—throughout North America—who maintained languages, cultures, and traditional relationships to the land. Similar processes occurred elsewhere in Latin America, but with a great deal of country, regional, and local variations (for examples, see accounts in Guy and Sheridan 1998). Murals painted in the barrio Santo Domingo (in Mexico City), in an indigenous cultural center called La Escuelita, demonstrate a detailed knowledge of these relationships, and historical processes, even among more "urbanized" peoples (see Plate 4.2).

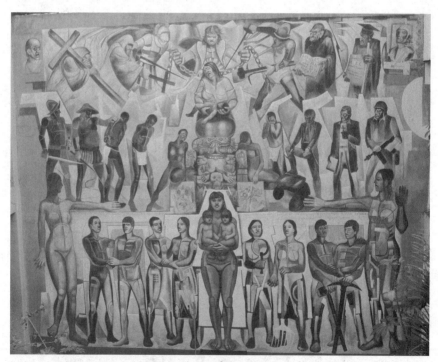

Plate 4.2. Mural of 500 years of history at Escuelita community center, Santo Domingo, Mexico City. (Photo courtesy of James V. Fenelon)

Indigenous struggles have often been over local autonomy, land tenure, community relations, and socioeconomic "development." These struggles usually involve decolonization "resistance" strategies, none more poignantly than Mexico: "The last five hundred years [in the history of Mexico] is the story of permanent confrontation between those attempting to direct the country toward the path of Western civilization and those, rooted in Mesoamerican ways of life, who resist" (Bonfil Batalla 1996, xv).

During this half millennium of struggle, indigeneity became a critical factor in the foundation of many Latin American states built over preceding indigenous groups. Guillermo Bonfil Batalla sees a "historical process through which populations that originally possessed a particular and distinctive identity, based on their own cultures, are forced to renounce that identity, with all the consequent changes in their social organization and culture" (1996, 17). This cultural destruction of individual "Indian" or indigenous communities, nations, cultures, or collectivities[4] was done to promote domination built on deeply racialized concepts of "the Indian." This is a label that characterizes her or him as a generic primitive or "savage." These issues, and similar labels, are quite common for indigenous peoples globally.

In order to explicate what we mean by *racialized,* it is helpful to review some general issues. We begin by noting the general idea in social analysis that "race" is socially constructed, that is, something that is collectively, if unconsciously, decided by humans, as opposed to something that is natural or objective.[5] Such social construction is always embedded in specific flows of history in specific places; hence it is useful to review some general background on this issue.

In recent decades Mexico and much of Latin America have been far less rigid in the way they construct race and ethnicity than the United States has been. Racial categories are seen to be much more permeable and flexible than they are perceived to be in the United States. Indeed, individuals raised in the United States are often quite surprised to learn that "race" is a much more important social factor in the Americas than elsewhere in the world, and that in the Americas the United States is the most rigid in this regard (Russell 1994). Thus, an individual is often able to change his/her "race marker" by changing behaviors of speech, clothing, participation in variations of local cultures, and so on. Furthermore, many Latin American states see themselves as some sort of amalgam of various "races": Spanish, Indian, and occasionally African.

The history of racial distinctions in former colonies of Spain is quite complicated. In the early centuries there was a very elaborate system of *castas,* which might be glossed approximately as "caste" but is not the same as the term typically is used in South Asia (Mörner 1967, 1973, 1983). Some scholars see a conventional trinity of *Indio, mestizo,* and *ladino*[6] that historically approximated a racialized stratification system of lower, middle, and upper classes, but not perfectly, and with many variations throughout Latin America. However, systems in Mexico, and typically throughout Latin America, were in racial formation.

Major populations and colonial stratification in Mexico were changing over time. First there were the classical *conquistadores, ladinos,* and *Indios,* though ladino has fallen out use. Various attempts at bringing black slaves to the Spanish-held lands never really took hold, and thus many *Indios* were exploited for labor, indentured servants, and sometimes enslaved giving rise to caste-like divisions via the *encomienda* system. During this time there were generalized changes to the *peninsulares* (full-blooded Spaniards), *criollos* (Spanish blood born in the Americas), *meztisos* (mixed blood, typically indigenous mother and Spanish father), and the *Indios,* at the bottom of the social stratification. Gradually, the elite and well-educated were more likely to be descendants of the *criollos* and *peninsulares* or associated with more recent immigrants from Europe, all lighter skinned, as the meztiso population surged into the working (urban) and farming (*eijido*) classes (with some converging into a burgeoning middle class). The rural *Indios* population remained at the bottom, increasingly defined culturally and in terms of an origin place (thereby less racially).

Indios are, as the label suggests, Indians or indigenous persons. In many places they are peasants or former peasants, though in parts of Brazil, Mexico, Venezuela, and many other Latin American countries they often follow traditional customs. Typically they do not speak Spanish as a primary language, but rather as a second language. Often they wear forms of clothing different from those of the dominant Hispanic population. They may practice non-Christian religions or overlay their Christianity with pre-Christian practices. Economically they are among the poorest people.

Mestizos, or mixed-race people, are seen as a product of two races, Indian and Spaniard. Typically they speak Spanish, are Catholic Christian, and wear conventional Western clothing. They are clearly part of the national culture and can be part of a regional, if not national, middle class, as well as the backbone of the working class. This is the broadest, and vaguest, of the major categories.

Criollos/ladinos were historically of "pure" Spanish heritage and thus were seen as European. They seldom spoke languages other than Spanish and English, unless they learned them in school to facilitate commerce or education. Most *criollos* were part of the middle class, often the upper middle class. Nearly all of the current elites are drawn from this group or the *peninsulares.*

In popular conception, *Indios* are phenotypically distinctive, as were *ladinos,* while *mestizos* exhibit mixed phenotypical characteristics. However, in practice, they are often not easily distinguishable to an outsider. To be called "Indian" is usually degrading. These labels have, to some extent, migrated to the United States, but they often take different connotations.[7] These differences vary considerably across Latin America, from country to country, and within countries and regions. Often there are different local names for broad categories, and not infrequently there are more distinctions than these.

At one time Mexican intellectuals took this tendency further than in most other Latin American countries. Some argued that Mexico was made up of a new "cosmic race" forged of Indian and Spaniard and that the two were no longer distinct (Russell 1994; MacLachlan and Rodriguez 1980; Ortiz 1985). This conceptualization, referred to as *indigenismo,* was the official doctrine or ideology of the Partido Revolucionario Institucional (Institutionalized Revolutionary Party, or PRI). It originated during the Mexican Revolution, especially in response to the way the political elite subdued rebellious indigenous peoples through cooptation—drastically emphasizing the Spanish heritage over an indigenous one steeped in the reductionism of *mestizo* imagery. *Indigenismo* (according to Bonfil Batalla 1996) constitutes cultural control and is a tool of internal colonialism. Its central feature was paternalism, in which *mestizo,* Westernized Mexico recognizes an intrinsic beauty of the indigenous world but retains a modernizing agenda of de-Indianizing them. *Indigenismo* respected the Indians but sought to "help" them by making them "modern."

Bonfil Batalla (1996) advanced the concept of *Mexico Profundo,* which sought to expose the ills of *indigenismo.* His basic argument is that Mexico is *not* a *mestizo* nation; he rejects the "cosmic race" proposition advanced during the Mexican Revolution. He calls this erroneous conception "imaginary Mexico." It is *not* a rejection of the facticity of biological mixing but rather of the construction of that mixing as a new "race." Bonfil Batalla argues that the construction of the *mestizaje* (mixed-bloodedness) equates to a denial of the Indian portion of the *mestizo* and a privileging of the European portion. A *mestizo* nation is a colonial nation, or really an internal colonial nation, which, in the time of crisis of the early 1980s, needed to be rejected. Bonfil Batalla sought to replace it with the concept of *Mexico Profundo.*

He argued:

> We are not able to construct an imaginary country and it would be insane to insist on doing so. Mexico is what it is, with this population and this history. We cannot persist in the attempt to replace it with something it is not. The task is simpler: to make it better from within, not from without. We must stop denying what it is and, to the contrary, take it for something that can be transformed and developed starting from its own potentialities. We must recognize the Mexico Profundo, once and for all, because without it there is no worthwhile solution. (Bonfil Batalla 1996, 158)

One of the most important aspects of his argument is the proposition that *Mexico Profundo* is not exclusive to indigenous peoples. Instead, it incorporates Mexico's "de-Indianized" people, who may not think of themselves as being Indian, as well as *Indios.* These are mainly Mexico's *campesinos* or peasants. He also includes Mexico's urban poor, a social group that was becoming a major group during the 1970s and 1980s. Effectively, Bonfil Batalla takes Mexico's marginalized people, a huge proportion of the population (40–50 percent), from the "cosmic race"/*mestizo* grouping and incorporates them into the indigenous population. He argues that the marginalized people have retained the cultural trappings of Mesoamerican civilization and that they are more indigenous than those who descend from European immigrants. This argument is, however, problematic, in that it too significantly reconstructs the concept of indigenous peoples in ways that would not be congruent with the ways in which indigenous peoples think of themselves elsewhere in the world. Still, his ideas have had a great impact on Mexican thinking about indigenous peoples, but they are tightly embedded in debates within Mexico over the revolution and the domination of the PRI in Mexican politics.

While the concept of the "cosmic race" might have been useful for building a national identity, it flies in the face of the facts. But these facts, for Mexico, are notoriously difficult to ascertain with precision. Indeed, this ideology led the government to avoid collecting information on "Indians," although it did collect information on language use. More recently the government has begun collecting statistics relating to identity, but there is nothing like the deep historical records found in Canada and the United States. Nevertheless, there are separate groups, *Pueblos Indígenas* (indigenous communities in Mexico), especially in areas where Spanish remains a secondary language. "*La comunalidad Indígena*" is how many indigenous scholars refer to these communities (Maldonaldo 2002). Thus indigeneity for many Mexican *Pueblos Indígenas* stands opposed to historical and current cultural representations of who indigenous peoples are and will be.

With such a long history of labeling and domination and conceptual shifts, it is not surprising that the terminology shifts over time, typically with a great deal of contestation. These layers of domination illustrate Bonfil Batalla's indigenous "Indian" foundation, despite oppression in every aspect of life—cultural, political, economic, and social. This is why *indigenous* represents both the foundation of society itself and an "enemy" to be overtaken and destroyed, or at the least subordinated within lower strata of society. We need to address how indigenous peoples understand their history, in contrast to how it has been presented by dominant groups (see Plate 4.2).

Not surprisingly, many indigenous groups live in areas that straddle twenty-first-century national and provincial borders. This often generates conflicts as such individuals and groups try to ignore these lines, while states and provinces try to enforce them. This is one source of local opposition to the state. Whatever the reason for opposition, any group that opposes the state—whether for land, labor, increased representation, or increased regional autonomy—is often seen as, and labeled as, "revolutionary." During the Cold War (approximately 1945 to 1991) such opposition was often labeled "communist" or "socialist." The two terms seldom carried the same degree of opprobrium that they did, and often still do, in the United States. Since September 11, 2001, such opposition sometimes has been labeled as "terrorist" in a clear attempt to delegitimize and demonize it. Less often, such opposition is recognized as an ethnic movement by indigenous peoples.[8] In recent decades many movements have become more explicitly indigenous.

The Zapotec peoples in Oaxaca and other states of Mexico are an excellent example of indigenous diversity within contemporary Mexico. The Zapotecs arose after the apex of Mayan civilization, but before the rise of the Aztecs. Certainly there were cultural influences going in both directions. The ruins at Monte Alban are very instructive of the many accomplishments of the Zapotec civilization, with large pyramid-like temples constructed at this major ceremonial site located on a butte with views in four directions (Feinman and Nicholas 1991a, 1991b). Although primary institutional social life was in decay by the time of the rise of the Aztec empires, Zapotec communities kept much of their traditional knowledge alive until the strong destructive forces of the conquistador armies arrived. As the central valley became violently incorporated into the new Mexican society, communities and whole regions retained their language and customs, often in distinct ways. Highland communities were especially likely to retain a strong sense of traditional life and indigenous identity, sometimes rising up against the Mexican-imposed *hacienda* system of stratification, although nineteenth-century Sierra de Juárez communities advocated for liberalism, that opposed the elite versions of liberalism that did advocate the hacienda system (McNamara 2007). These insurrections took many forms, resisting any social reorganization that enriched incoming elites and *mestizo* middle classes, and attempted to seize land in addition to imposing their own political, economic, and justice systems.

The Mexican Revolution that began the twentieth century occasionally emphasized this sense of community in opposition to the dominant Mexican society. It also disrupted the colonial *modus vivendi* between indigenous communities and the colonizers that had been more or less stable for several centuries. In many more cases the communities were seeking a restoration of communal rights that had been secured during the colonial period and had been removed by the elite liberal project. Mexico had become part of an increasingly global system that sought deeper exploitation of labor and natural resources. Many of the highland Zapotec communities had thrown out European and Mexican managers and owners during the nineteenth century and had taken limited control of their own resources, sometimes under the *ejido* land tenure systems of Mexico, while others had formed a "popular" liberalism (Mallon 1997).

Thus, the historical memory of these Zapotec communities combined with contemporary resistance struggles, over systems of justice, the economy, local leadership, land tenure, and sociopolitical control. Therefore, when other movements, such as the Zapatistas, arose in recent years, some Zapotec communities were in a position to both resist and to revitalize their indigenous systems in opposition to local elites, regional control centers such as Oaxaca City, the Mexican dominance, and even against growing globalization.[9]

Plate 4.3, a photograph of a banner in Oaxaca City, illustrates these interactive systems. There are indigenous peoples who are still considered or treated solely as "minority" groups within states, and are the most vulnerable, yet they often form resistance movements such as Communidades Indígenas in Oaxaca (Maldonado 2002).

In these examples, we observe how indigenous movements have redefined themselves, renaming themselves in resistance to the imposed dominant typologies and as a form of revitalization that also constitutes decolonization. For instance, the Mexican government refers to people and individuals as *Indios,* used as a

Plate 4.3. Indigenous communities resistance banner at Oaxaca City, Zocalo, Mexico. (Photo courtesy of James V. Fenelon)

degrading term. However, many scholars and some activists referred to these peoples as *Pueblos Indios,* which has more of a sense of community or township. The government recently returned to the term *Pueblos Indígenas,* which may seem to be more respectful but also seems to imply they are peasants. *Communidades Intígenas* is the preferred term by many indigenous movements such as those in Oaxaca. The movement groups are also unafraid to use the term *Resistance and Rebellion,* an outgrowth of the recent struggles in Chiapas and the highland Zapotecs.

Zapotec *Pueblos Indios,* mostly in the state of Oaxaca, Mexico, have used a variety of strategies or tactical approaches toward the incorporating process of the state and its economies, ranging from outright assimilation to relatively direct secessionist autonomy. Yavesia, a Zapotec community in the Sierra Juarez highlands, has formally organized its economy to resist the deforestation that nearby communities have experienced, developed a natural water bottling operation and formalized women's cooperatives, maintains a fishery, and employs computer programs including GIS mapping for its young students to learn about the land and history of their people. Additionally, Yavesia formally receives delegations from other indigenous communities throughout Mexico, and it studies like-minded social movements such as the Zapatistas for applications to its own situation. All decisions are taken in community meetings that include everyone, and they employ *cargo* systems that can demand people return from work in the United States, centering authority in the community, with local and global concerns (Maldonado 2002).

Not all Zapotec communities have been so proactive, especially with respect to globalization. One might expect that deforestation would be a bane for all indigenous peoples. As timber companies have coerced communities into short-term profits from lumber, they became more dependent on outside monies. When their forests were depleted, the result was a weakened social structure, less internal production, and greater dependency. Additionally, the new growth was more vulnerable to fires, flooding, and other natural disasters. Yavesia and some other communities, acknowledging their ancient symbiotic relationships with the land and the forests, banned timbering unless undertaken by community leadership as a whole, for the common good. This is simultaneously resistance and revitalization along ethnic, gender, and class lines (Stephen 2002, 2005).

The focus of the Zapotecs, similar and some would say precedent to the Tzotzil case (Rubin 1997), is representative of large numbers of Mayan-descent peoples in the states near the border with Guatemala. Five centuries of resistance to Euro-American systems of domination have produced constant uprisings, adaptation, assimilation, and cultural regeneration processes interspersed between long periods of quiet yet powerful suppression by elites from the colonial system and emerging states (Campbell 1994). Essentially, descendents of ancient civilizations such as the Zapotecan, Aztec, and Mayan were and continue to be "second-class" citizens in their own lands.

The Tzotzil people, among others, in the even more remote southern state of Chiapas were in a more vulnerable position, with direct suppression of *Pueblos Indios* in the highland areas and clear discrimination in the capital, San Cristobal. These indigenous peoples have retained their languages, customs, and identity from their roots as tributary groups under the Mayan civilization. With each incoming system, they have adapted to new circumstances. However, modern systems have attempted to break up their traditional culture and orientation to the land, including attempts to reduce them to peasant townships whose land could be appropriated for timbering, tourism, and natural resource extraction, under increasing globalization. Formal resistance was less common in the highlands and in the Lacandón jungle region, where relative remoteness and a qualified adaptation to Catholicism insulated the people. After more than a thousand years of living in subordination as a whole people, under Mayan, Aztecan, and Mexican state domination, their survival was threatened by capitalist intrusion and exploitation. They were finally ready to pursue more formal resistance.

The Tzotzil, and every other *Communidades Indígenas* in the highland and Lacandón areas of Chiapas, found their traditional collective orientation to the land, leadership, property distribution system, and often the community itself under duress and targeted for breakup by an increasing police and military function protecting new capital interests. Subsistence itself was in question as they were being forced into peasant labor systems. Resistance groups formed, with some external forces operating in the region as well. Early organization of the Zapatistas began to take place for the decade preceding 1994 (Muñoz Ramírez 2003). Interestingly, many communities had embraced Catholicism so deeply that they maintained a pacifist Christian orientation toward resistance and revitalization. These communities tended to support the Zapatistas philosophically, experiencing the injustice of the civil-military groups operating out of San Cristobal, Tuxtla Gutierrez, and Mexico proper, but were reluctant to take up arms. When EZLN forces mounted an armed rebellion, Tzotzil communities at places such as Nuevo Yibeljoj and Acteal found themselves making an age-old Faustian set of choices—

whether to support traditional autonomous relations or give in to neocolonial military dominance. This is yet another example of the interaction of state globalism with indigeneity. When paramilitaries were supported by the Mexican government, these communities were defenseless. A terrible slaughter occurred at Acteal, supported by the local police (Álvarez Fabela 2000).[10] Similar threats of violence leading to death and rape caused the entire Nuevo Yibeljoj community to leave and spend over two years in refugee camps, barely surviving until its members could relocate to a hillside and start the rebuilding process once again.

Forces of globalization are even more extreme, indifferent to indigenous survival, and use old systems of domination and oppression from the states that in turn were borrowed from earlier colonial practices. Of course, these have led to new forms of resistance, newer adaptations, and even new movements to revitalize and reestablish community. Plate 4.4 shows the San Pedro Polho indigenous community sign just outside Oventik, near the Zapatista regional headquarters. This sign stresses autonomy, *Municipio Autónomo Rebelde Zapatista San Pedro Polho,* subordinating government leaders to the "people," or pueblo. This autonomous rebel community prohibits illegal drugs and its corruption, prohibits selling and buying stolen vehicles, and prohibits trafficking in alcohol. More important, it has revitalized traditional forms of social organization, making leaders respond to and be directed by the peoples themselves, evidenced in the phrase *"Aquí el pueblo manda y el gobierno obedece"* (here the people demand and the government obeys).

ZAPATISTAS: SOCIAL MOVEMENT OF INDIGENOUS PEOPLES

The Zapatista movement is part of a continuous history of indigenous resistance to the colonialism of the Western world (Farris 1984). This resistance movement

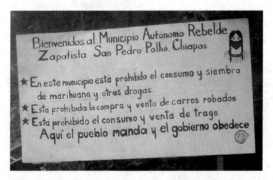

Plate 4.4. *Community sign at San Pedro Polho, Chiapas, noting it as a "municipal autonomous rebel" for the Zapatistas. "Here the people demand and the government obeys." (Photo courtesy of James V. Fenelon)*

originated in the early 1960s and had two central features (Harvey 1998; Collier 1999; Womack 1999). First, it was a product of community organizing peasant groups independent of Mexico's dominant political party, the PRI, which had created peasant unions as a controlling mechanism in its patron-client system. Second, and corresponding to the first, was the important role of liberation theology. Under the guidance of Bishop Samuel Ruíz, a radicalized Catholic Church engaged in the formation of Christian Base Communities with the goal of empowering indigenous people to be full citizens (Meyer 2000; Womack 1999; Krauze 2002). Liberation theology created a new generation of community leaders and set the foundations for "*basta ya*" (enough already) thinking among the indigenous people of Chiapas. These two foundations provided the lived experiences necessary for consciousness formation and radicalization characteristic of new social movements and were precursors to the open rebellion of January 1, 1994 (Kuecker 2004; Harvey 1998; Nash 2001). The state was keenly aware of what was happening in Chiapas, and it used carrot-and-stick tactics of violent repression mixed with rewards for cooperation with PRI domination. One attempt at co-optation was the 1974 Indigenous Congress organized by Bishop Ruíz at the invitation of the PRI. The PRI thought it could "spin" events and the movement toward its favor. Instead, it became a collective radicalization as otherwise divided communities met together for the first time, sharing their stories of injustice and the nature of their struggles.[11]

On October 2, 1968, the Mexican military had killed several hundred citizens protesting in Mexico City's Plaza de Tres Culturas (Plaza of Three Cultures)—to be afterward known as the Tlatelolco Massacre (Poniatowska 1998; Preston and Dillon 2004, 63–93). Later, Marcos was a radical university professor in Mexico City who decided that the only way to change Mexico was by violent revolution.[12] In 1984 he went to Chiapas with the intent of implementing a revolution in which a vanguard of educated middle-class urbanites go to the rural areas to organize a peasant army that is used to take state power.[13] When Marcos and two others arrived in the jungles of Chiapas, they founded the revolutionary army, Ejército Zapatista de Liberación Nacional (Zapatista Army of National Liberation, the EZLN). Quickly, however, they encountered great difficulty and hardship, both in adjusting to the lifestyle of the guerrilla and in working with the indigenous communities. Their Marxist message failed to resonate with indigenous communities that had already begun organizing themselves in the early 1960s. Facing failure, the early members of the EZLN went through a process of critical reflection that led to a readjustment of their strategy and underlying philosophy (Guillermoprieto 2002; Henck 2007).

This ability and effort to reflect critically and to adjust to circumstances became one of the most significant features of the Zapatista movement. This led to a new style of "revolution," defined by the slogan "*mandar obedeciendo*" (govern by obeying). In this style, decisions were to be made by the communities and given to the EZLN command for implementation. This invests power in the communities, not the vanguard elite. Marcos spent much of the 1980s reeducating himself, learning some degree of indigenous languages, as well as the "*normas y costumbres*" (norms and customs) of the communities. He also learned how to become a spokesperson for the indigenous peoples and to serve as a translator between the indigenous world and the Western world—but to do so in a fashion that allowed indigenous people to control the discourse and representation of their growing movement, effectively revitalizing under force of arms (Gossen 1995).

Three important national events took place during the 1980s that set the stage for the Zapatistas to evolve from a movement to open rebellion in 1994. First, Mexico experienced a severe economic crisis, which led to its defaulting on debt payments in 1982. The default opened the door to the imposition of neoliberal economic reforms, a process that eventually led to the North American Free Trade Agreement (NAFTA) in 1994. Implementation of these neoliberal reforms undermined the PRI's credibility among the popular classes. Second, the PRI lost further legitimacy due to its pathetic response to the catastrophic 1985 earthquake. This failure led citizens to build a revitalized civil society.[14] These changes proved crucial to the Zapatistas in the 1990s because they allowed them to tap into a mobilized civil society with grievances against the PRI. Third, in 1988 the opposition ran on an explicitly antineoliberal platform. The PRI nearly lost the presidential election, but for electoral subterfuge. This, in turn undermined the legitimacy of the new president, Carlos Salinas. These three events created a national context favorable for a rebellion (Preston and Dillon 2004).

The January 1, 1994, rebellion was deliberately planned to coincide with the date that NAFTA went into effect. The initial spark occurred in 1992 when President Salinas reformed Article 27 of the Constitution of 1917. Article 27 had allowed the revolutionary state (which became the PRI) to restore communal property through a process of land reform. NAFTA required a standardized land tenure system between Canada, the United States, and Mexico, and Article 27 was a barrier. The 1992 reform allowed for the transfer of communal lands back into private property (De Janvry, Gordillo, and Sadoulet 1997).

The indigenous people in Chiapas clearly saw this as an assault upon their "*normas y costumbres*" since communal land tenure was a key feature of their traditional practices. As we have seen, communal ownership of land is quite common among indigenous peoples throughout the world. It is this clear focus on communal land ownership that makes the Zapatista movement so salient to discussions of indigenous resistance to globalization. According to the Zapatistas, NAFTA was their "death sentence" (El Comité Clandestino Revolucionario Indígena-Comandancia General del EZLN 1994). The 1992 reform coincided with the quincentennial celebrations of the "discovery" of the New World by Christopher Columbus. These celebrations engendered interconnected protests by indigenous groups throughout the hemisphere. Indigenous people in Chiapas were keenly aware of and influenced by the movements in other parts of Latin America, especially Ecuador and Bolivia. Rebellion was the Zapatista response to the neoliberal assault on communal land tenure.

On January 1, 1994, the 3,000 armed soldiers of the EZLN struck violently. They caught the Mexican military by surprise and were able to take control of six towns in the three main geographic areas: *Los Altos* (the highlands), *Las Canedas* (canyon lands), and *La Selva Lacandón* (the Lacandon jungle). They even captured briefly the provincial capital and tourist center of San Cristóbal de Las Casas. President Salinas ordered the Mexican military to counterattack. The army's response lasted ten days, killed at least 145 indigenous people, and touched off national protests against what was seen to be a legitimate indigenous uprising. The Zapatistas used the Internet to gain the attention of international civil society. National mobilization, international protests, and an impending review of NAFTA by the United States Congress made the state's war against the Zapatistas impossible to sustain. President Salinas declared a cease-fire on January 12. A prolonged process of negotiation and stalemate set in.

Negotiations started in February 1994 and reached their apex in February 1996 when both parties signed the San Andreas Accords. The negotiations were sponsored by two mediating bodies. The first, CONAI (National Commission for Intermediation), was organized and directed by Bishop Ruíz, and was perceived by the government as being biased toward the Zapatistas. The second, COCOPA (Legislative Commission of Conciliation and Dignified Peace in Chiapas), was composed of Mexico's leading political figures and was commissioned by the federal congress as part of legislation for finding a just peace in Chiapas. The process was defined by sophisticated political maneuvering, which replaced military conflict with a "war of words and symbols" over the place of indigenous peoples in Mexican society. The Zapatistas used the crisis of legitimacy to outposition and outsmart the Mexican government and to gain the high moral ground in the debates (Couch 2001, 246–248; Bruhn 1999).

For the Mexican ruling class 1994 was a nightmare (Fuentes 1997; Preston and Dillon 2004, 229–256). The Zapatista rebellion merged with an ever-more-aggressive civil society to force latent contradictions within the ruling PRI to the surface. Political violence and assassinations marred electoral politics. Ultimately Ernesto Zedillo took office in December 1994. Within weeks the peso devalued 60 percent, which caused a run on foreign investment and the prospect of total economic collapse. The Clinton administration bailed Mexico out with a $60 billion loan secured by Mexico's future oil revenues. Attached to the bailout were very direct instructions, including a memo from Chase Manhattan Bank for Zedillo to end the Zapatista uprising (Weinberg 2000, 146).[15] Thus, while Zedillo was negotiating with the Zapatistas he was also implementing a military strategy to defeat them. Although the political crisis subsided, these events signified the demise of the PRI's domination of Mexican politics. In July 2000, a conservative opposition party leader, Vicente Fox, won the presidency.

Prolonged, multifaceted negotiations led to the San Andreas Accords. The accord only reached agreement on one of the negotiating points. It formally recognized the cultural rights of indigenous people in Mexico and would constitutionally make Mexico a plural-ethnic state, one where indigenous people would have autonomy to practice their "*normas y costumbres*" within their communities. This would explicitly include recognition of indigenous practices toward land and the use of natural resources, including oil, water, forests, and minerals. Autonomy meant that indigenous peoples had the right to decide how such resources would be utilized (Díaz-Polanco 1997; Navarro and Hererra 1998; Nash 2001; Esteva 1999). This would, in effect, have given Mexican indigenous peoples rights analogous to those held by treaty in the United States—despite Mexico's lack of a tradition of treaties.

The San Andreas Accords was a stunning victory for the Zapatistas: the state had agreed to their demands. Indigenous autonomy, however, was in clear contradiction to Mexico's commitment to neoliberalism, especially the provisions of NAFTA. The San Andreas Accords put President Zedillo in an impossible position. Under pressure from the United States and multinational corporations, he was compelled to betray the agreement his government had signed by subsequent revisions to which he knew the Zapatistas would never agree. This betrayal came in December 1996. It led to a stalemate. The Zapatistas refused to negotiate further until the government implemented the agreement.

During this process the Zapatistas manifested remarkable political ingenuity. First, they built upon the support of national and international civil society in a series of *encuentros* (gatherings or encounters similar to conventions) and plebiscites. The *encuentros* were designed to foster democratic participation in their movement and to highlight the undemocratic nature of the Mexican political system. These were highly successful events that kept the Zapatistas in the headlines and sustained their high moral ground. Second, the Zapatistas also moved to consolidate control over territory gained during the initial 1994 rebellion through the formation of thirty-eight formally autonomous communities independent of the Mexican state. These communities formed five municipal centers called *Aguascalientes* after a town where Mexicans rewrote their constitution during the Mexican Revolution (1910–1920). Third, they continued to utilize the Internet to manipulate media coverage in a propaganda war that kept the Mexican political elite off balance and greatly entertained civil society (Cleaver 1998; Froehling 1997; Hellman 1999; Arquilla and Ronfeldt 2000; Swett 1995).

The Mexican state responded with a strategy of low intensity conflict (LIC). An LIC is a war of attrition designed to demoralize and divide the enemy. Tactics include disrupting community economic production; psychological operations aimed at terrorizing a population into inaction through rumors of invasion, misinformation, and death threats; the use of military maneuvers to harass and intimidate the base of support; economic rewards such as food, health clinics, and new schools for those who turn against the enemy; and the use of paramilitary squads to carry out political violence such as targeted assassinations[16] (Pineda 1996; Marin 1998; Global Exchange 2000).

All told, Zedillo positioned 60,000 troops in Chiapas. These forces were one-third of Mexico's armed forces. They remain in Chiapas today. Between 1998 and 2000 the army expelled at least 150 international observers. This paramilitary violence exploded in December 1997 in the Acteal Massacre, when death squads affiliated with PRI murdered forty-five indigenous people. Despite its sophistication, the LIC strategy failed to defeat the Zapatistas (Centro de Derechos Humanos Fray Bartolomé de Las Casas A.C. 2005).

The election of Vicente Fox from the conservative PAN (National Action Party) in July 2000 followed the PRI loss of the governorship of Chiapas in August of that year, which undermined the local mechanisms of domination and control that had been in existence since the Mexican Revolution. During the presidential campaign Fox boasted that he could solve the Chiapas situation in fifteen minutes. The Zapatistas accepted Fox's offer when he took office in December. They asked for three indications of goodwill to resume negotiations: removal of all military checkpoints, release of all Zapatista political prisoners, and forwarding the San Andreas Accords to Congress. Fox responded by implementing all three—but only partially. Fox's main strategy was to continue the LIC strategy of attrition and to avoid any major event that would give the Zapatistas the political upper hand that they enjoyed with the Zedillo administration.

The Zapatistas' response to Fox's forwarding of the San Andreas Accords to Congress was remarkable. They organized a three-month-long caravan through Mexico's southern, most indigenous states, which climaxed on March 12, 2001, in a rally in the Zocalo, the central plaza in Mexico City, the most politically symbolic place in all of Mexico. The caravan was designed to mobilize civil society in support of making the San Andreas Accords into an indigenous law, which would require amending the constitution of 1917. The caravan met with unprecedented support, especially with *Pueblos Indios* in Oaxaca and many other states. The Zapatistas overshadowed Fox in the national attention. Fox was outfoxed. The Zapatista "leadership" participated in every moment of the caravan, making speeches and enjoying their contact with civil society outside of Chiapas.

They arrived in Mexico City as an armed revolutionary movement seeking to transform Mexico without taking state power. The moment symbolized all that was new and different about the Zapatistas. Their arrival met with no repression because of the immense popular support they enjoyed. The climax came when the Zapatistas were permitted to address Congress. Symbolic of the movement, they selected the lowest person in Mexico's race, class, and gender hierarchy of power, an indigenous woman, Commandante Ramona, to make the speech. Photographs of members of Congress revealed facial expressions of intense disapproval.

The Mexican Congress passed the indigenous law in April 2001, but without the provisions extending autonomy to indigenous peoples. Mexico's indigenous peoples organized in opposition and made a major effort to block the law from becoming part of the constitution. They failed. After the constitution was amended, indigenous peoples attempted multiple court challenges, which the Mexican Supreme Court refused to hear.

The Zapatista response to this defeat took nearly two years to formulate. It came as the Juntas de Buen Gobierno (Good Government Committees) in August 2003. Each of the five *Aguascalientes,* now renamed *Caracoles* (seashells), has a junta. Each member community has a junta member. The junta rotates positions every ten days in order to distribute representation and power. The juntas serve as a municipal administration and act as a conflict-resolution mechanism. The juntas approve or reject all initiatives undertaken within an autonomous community. In essence, they implement the San Andreas Accords within territory controlled by the Zapatistas. The juntas, however, were also a response to the demands of ten years of open rebellion, especially the problem of reproducing resistance in the face of LICs. The Zapatistas were losing members, as some individuals were tempted to accept government handouts, something not allowed within the movement (Stahler-Sholk 2005).

Making the juntas was one way the Zapatistas faced the problem of fence sitting, as some communities were not fully committed to the struggle, yet were clearly benefiting from the Zapastistas' revolution. A major component of solidifying their base also involved the movement's relationship with nongovernmental organizations (NGOs), domestic and international. NGOs have their own agendas, which do not always correspond to those of the Zapatistas despite intent of solidarity. Furthermore, many NGOs have little to no mechanism for accountability, a situation at odds with the fundamentals of autonomy. With formation of the juntas, the Zapatistas redefined the working rules with NGOs by placing each NGO in a position subordinate to the juntas. For many NGOs, this consolidation of power and reworking of the rules of engaging the Zapatistas was a rude awakening.

The juntas enjoy considerable legitimacy. Non-Zapatista communities, for example, often go to them for conflict resolution instead of the Mexican state, because they know the Zapatistas are honest, and they follow indigenous "*normas y costumbres*" in the conflict-resolution process. (Plate 4.5 shows the "Junta de Buen Gobierno" at Oventik, the *Caracole* for *Los Altos* and the "Heart of the Zapatistas and the World" that also respects the Tzotzil language spoken in the community as shown in the picture.) The juntas, in sum, serve as the mechanism for the Zapatistas to endure the stalemate, to reproduce their revolution, and to continue to survive as indigenous people within the ravages of neoliberalism (Stahler-Sholk 2005).

Many observers recognize that the juntas are a risky strategy. If they garner too much power they could, in effect, become a governing vanguard party. Even though their goal is "power to" rather than "power over," if they become too effective they severely undermine the credibility of the Mexican state. They could become an insufferable challenge to the state and bring down its wrath in a "hot war" replacing LIC. At this writing, it is far too early to tell. Whatever the result, they have set a model for how to institutionalize indigenous practices (*normas y costumbres*). In this they are roughly similar to Navajo Peacemaker Courts (see Chapter 1, note 15). In the larger global arena, they demonstrate that there indeed are alternatives to neoliberal globalizations—alternatives that promote democracy and the maintenance of autonomy and a continual evolution of indigenous values and practices. Furthermore, one clear lesson from the Zapatistas is that pursuit of such goals requires autonomous, serious efforts by and in collaboration with local indigenous populations. The Zapatistas are not a boilerplate model for

Plate 4.5. Junta de Buen Gobierno (good government) at Oventik, Chiapas. (Photo courtesy of James V. Fenelon)

how to resist globalization. Rather, they model one kind of process for resisting it. There are other processes, in different situations throughout Latin America and internationally, as we have seen in other chapters (also see Stahler-Sholk, et al. 2005).

INDIGENEITY IN LATIN AMERICA: EXAMPLES FROM CENTRAL AND SOUTH AMERICA

Perhaps the most important observation among the preceding examples is to see how social justice issues are developed and defined by indigenous leaders and peoples when confronting dominant societies and their systems of suppression arising from a colonial past. The Zapatista indigenous resistance and revitalization movement has at times been revolutionary, and it has always been about change that supports autonomous communities. It is one attempt to fuse traditional indigenous social justice with responsive and reflexive forms of "governance." This is also an important example of resistance to neoliberalism and attempts at revitalization of communities for other indigenous struggles.

Zapatista-led communities began to organize in new ways that attempted to respect traditional culture, simultaneously sowing new patterns as well, including equality and involvement for women, direct challenges to local and state authorities, and community self-defense. Conflicts took various forms, forcing struggles with paramilitaries, government officials, military forts, restive localities, peasant organizations, and a depressed economy. The social changes made by the Zapatistas in developing the "Junta del Buen Gobierno" (Muñoz Ramírez 2003) were similar to the restorative justice systems of North American Indian Nations such as the Lakota, which were written into treaties in the nineteenth century (Fenelon 1998, 2002). These exemplify mediating social structures that place community relations as the highest value for indigenous peoples interacting with dominant societies and their states.

Mexico City meetings of scholars and indigenous leaders from throughout the Americas found that "government, based on its monopoly of violence ... was a hierarchical power structure." They identified an indigenous equivalent of authority (*autoridad*) where "communal authority is the whole community in its assembly," including elders and others sharing with decision making: "The central idea is to maintain harmony within the community" (América Profunda 2003). The governance panel at the América Profunda meeting concluded that at the grassroots level a "consensus of the peoples" was in formation (América Profunda initial findings 2003).[17]

Indigenous peoples make up significant population percentages of many Latin American countries, and in some cases, when grouped together, constitute a majority. This is the case in Bolivia, where the Indian movement Pachacuti (led by Felipe Quispe Huanca, an Aymara) initiated protests in Bolivia, connecting with unions and other protest groups, leading to the downfall of a sitting president.

> We believe in the reconstruction of the *Kollasuyu*, our own ancestral laws ... our own philosophy.... We have ... our political heritage [that] can be successful in removing and destroying neoliberalism, capitalism and imperialism.
>
>   It is community-based socialism ... that is what the brothers of our communities hold as a model.... In the Aymara and Quechua areas, primarily in La Paz, we have been working since 1984 on fostering awareness of community-based ideologies. (Felipe Quispe Huanca, *Washington Times*, March 3, 2004)

Quispe Huanca speaks of movements arising throughout "Indian" Latin America, shared struggles that are based on a diversity of indigenous peoples and states. While each is reconstructing traditions unique to its own culture, and often relative to the specific lands they inhabit, they are also finding commonalities across many fronts, notably in opposition to cultural domination and corporate expansion over their lands. Even as the essence of a community, economic cooperatives, shared decision making, and land tenure relations vary, indigenous peoples rely on these foundations to resist in their individual situations, and increasingly within global networks (Muñoz Ramírez 2003).

Miskito people in Nicaragua are an example that shows many of these contentions in reverse. Here a socialist revolutionary government tried to impose conditions, boundaries, and forced removal on an indigenous people. The Sandinistas were, no doubt, responding partly to hegemonic forces that attempted to employ Miskito in Honduras to support the Contras and U.S. interests (Harff and Gurr 2004; Hale 1994). However, the central indigenous concerns were against incursions over a limited but existing sovereignty, for Miskito "autonomy" over their lands and sociopolitical life. Although the majority of indigenous struggle is against neoliberal and state politics, heavily involved with capitalist exploitation and inside increasingly globalized systems, pressures to suppress resistance occur in noncapitalist states as well. There is speculation that these are less explicitly invasive and not as likely to be culturicidal. Nonetheless, these can rise to the level of genocide, and they have done so in the twentieth century.

The Miskito conflict erupted when Sandinista military forces attempted to suppress their Moravian-based religious practices that included their traditional culture and language. Miskito had resisted incorporation into the Nicaraguan and colonial systems preceding the U.S.-backed dictator Somoza, mostly in a live-and-let-live relationship that resembled conditions in Chiapas. Additionally, there had been significant intermarriage with slave-descent African people, interjecting some race and racism into their relations with the dominant *mestizo* groups. When the Sandinistas had successfully led a socialist rebellion, Miskito leaders viewed them as another dominant group in patterns worked out over the past 400 years. Initially, schooling was bilingual and cross-culturally conscious, as were the local politics, and many thought a socialist orientation toward land and property would work out well. However, when political leaders attempted ideological indoctrination combined with party leadership, friction developed. When their traditional culture was suppressed, along with lack of respect for their councils and collective systems, they became more open to forming resistance groups. The Sandinistas, under Cuban and Soviet influence, attempted to relocate villages near the Rio Coco basin bordering with Honduras, and they went into open armed rebellion (Ortiz 1984).

Miskito forces operated in ways similar to the Lakota resistance in the nineteenth century, forming small groups with mobile bases and significant support from the rural villages (Reyes and Wilson 1992). These forces demanded autonomy for their peoples, insisting on traditional land tenure and justice systems. After two years of internecine warfare, the Sandinistas agreed to the Zelaya Norte Autonomous Zone for the Miskito, as long as their military operated small bases to observe Contra activity. When Daniel Ortega and the FMLN (Farabundo Martí National Liberation Front) lost the elections in 1990, this autonomous region again became heavily marginalized, within an economy moving into an economic depression without American support, at least partly because of the breakup of the Soviet Union and containment of the Cuban influences. This demonstrates that globalization can have just as powerfully a negative effect over indigenous peoples involved in struggle with anticapitalist states.

Ecuador is an outstanding example, with recent protests and insurrection rising to levels of revolutionary activity, some of it in concert with mainstream military forces, leading to the Quito accords and ultimately a broken alliance. Indigenous peoples are often in the middle of social unrest and rebellion, especially when there are high numbers and they are well organized. Unfortunately, all too often they are left out of resolutions and agreements arising out of the conflict. This marginalization has been a distinctive feature of indigenous social movements, and when accompanied with cultural suppression and oppression has caused revitalization movements to arise. Usually the dominant society reacts with military pacification reminiscent of the *conquista* hundreds of years ago. Leon Zamosc (1994) finds that in Ecuador, as the Quechuan-speaking peoples made greater alliances, their demands "to redefine citizenship" to recognize Indian rights to cultural and political autonomy were seen "at odds with both the model of liberal democracy being enjoined by political elites and the dominant perceptions of national identity in Latin America" (p. 39).

As Quispe Huanca described earlier and Evo Morales speaks to as the elected head of Bolivia, and as traditionalists throughout the history and the current reality of the United States and Canada's indigenous nations have struggled with, it is the essence of community, economic cooperatives, traditional decision making, and land tenure relations that may sometimes lead to violent uprising or perhaps a more localized economic reorganization. Yet indigenous peoples rely on these foundations to resist in their individual situations and within global networks (Muñoz Ramírez 2003; Sklair 2002). These new movements have collective orientation toward communities that are transparently antiglobalization, and specifically target neoliberalism as modern "evil" for the poor, indigenous, marginalized peasants making up their constituency. Examples such as coca leaf growing in Bolivia—disconnected from U.S. cocaine markets—as indigenous horticultural practices, challenge regional dominance and hegemony operated by corporate economic practices.

As noted earlier (Bonfil Batalla 1996, 88), one of the basic relationships of indigenous peoples is having a relationship to the land. This relationship is often sacred, rarely has direct economic value, and is usually held collectively rather than by individual ownership. Mayan-descent peoples in Guatemala and in the states of Chiapas and Oaxaca, Mexico, are moving away from Liberation Theology to new indigenous "Liberation Philosophy," which is partly based on traditional understandings of culture, land, and community.[18] These are epistemological movements that reject not only the hierarchy of European social orders but also the very nature of their social organization. This orientation to the land is in direct opposition to how modern, capitalistic society approaches land, with direct economic values and individual title: "The larger problem for the Indians was the struggle against breaking up the communal lands. The Liberals made private property sacred.... The communal ownership of land in Indian communities became an obstacle to be removed (Bonfil Batalla 1996, p. 100).

Invasive systems want to take over the land, stratify the economy to build a power elite, centralize political systems into hierarchies they control, and relate all social issues to ever-larger urban areas that dominate in all arenas the surrounding communities. Because indigenous peoples utilize alternative systems of social organization and do not dissolve relationships, they are seen as obstacles, and if they resist, they are seen as "enemy."

In seeing the "Indian as enemy," Bonfil Batalla observes (1996, 103–104) "the radical denial of the imaginary Mexico. The struggle over land involved one side, which wanted free trade and individual property, while the other side protested the land was communal and inalienable." With this we see how the historically developed concepts of the "hostile" against the U.S. conquest or domination are fully realized in many twenty-first-century Latin American conflicts. We also observe how important such racist icons and symbology are in American society, why they are fought over in many universities and social institutions by dominant groups, and how they connect with hegemonic histories and struggles over racialized imagery. Eric Langer (2003, xiii) finds that a "racist ideology" placing indigenous peoples at the bottom of Latin American societies, and by government policy, was accompanied by a greater push to dominate indigenous groups for the consolidation of territory by states. Autonomy movements such as the Zapatistas in southern Mexico and Aymara in Bolivia have become typified as "socialist" or even as "terrorist" in nature, even though they actually represent over 500 years of indigenous struggle in the Americas.

In describing the modern constructs of empire, George Steinmetz describes the early steps in the process: "colonialism entails the seizure of sovereignty from locals and the formation of a separate colonial state apparatus" (2005, 344). But countering that, recently elected Bolivian president Evo Morales (an Aymara "Indian") has stated, "With the unity of the people, we're going to end the colonial state and the neoliberal model." Morales went on to speak for indigenous peoples throughout the Americas: "The time has come to change this terrible history of looting our natural resources, of discrimination, of humiliation, of hate" (Associated Press 2006).[19]

Conclusions, Redefinitions, Speculations, and Questions

Whereas the United States had formal treaties with indigenous peoples until 1871, when they were replaced with agreements, Mexico seldom used either device. Although the U.S. government usually abrogated and degraded treaties and pressured Native Americans to assimilate, treaty rights and sovereignty remained as tools for pursuing collective rights, conditional, of course, on sociopolitical survival. The San Andreas Accords, though derailed, were an attempt to negotiate similar rights to the Zapatistas. It is interesting that the accord would have formalized the right to retain cultural practices, *normas y costumbres,* obviating attempts at forced assimilation and the right to collective land ownership. Thus "self-determination" in the United States and "autonomy" in Mexico are the most recent forms of the continuing struggle to maintain separate political and cultural communities, even while participating in the larger state system. (Plate 4.6, taken outside Toluca not far from Mexico City, shows government leaders being blessed in a local indigenous ceremony, before an important conference on civil rights.) In pursuing this goal, indigenous peoples are pressuring states to become explicitly multiethnic. This is a fundamental assault on the concept of the need for a nation-state and nation-building. With the strong emphasis on collective ownership of land and maintenance of traditions, this is also a reaction

Plate 4.6. Government leaders blessed by indigenous leaders at a congreso outside Toluca, Mexico. (Photo courtesy of James V. Fenelon)

to and an assault on the cultural aspects of globalization, what Sklair (2002) has called the "culture-ideology of consumerism."

Comparison of the Latin American cases with those from the United States further underscores the role of treaties and sovereignty in state-indigenous relations. These examples from Mexico further show the importance of widely divergent colonial histories in the shaping of identities and in engendering different forms of resistance. What begins to emerge is that the immense variety of forms of indigenous activism and resistance to colonization and assimilation is the consequence of complex interactions between the history of colonial relations and the specific forms of local social organization. The underlying unity is a continuous effort by indigenous peoples to maintain some level of autonomy and, where possible, legal sovereignty to manage their own affairs. Their sovereignty is becoming increasingly problematic, not only for indigenous peoples but also for all states in dealing with an increasingly globalized and transnational capitalism (Sklair 2002).

Another obvious and very interesting aspect of these examples is how, in the case of the Zapatistas, armed rebellion against the state has turned both nonviolent and into an effort to implement local control by providing much-needed culturally sensitive mediating services. It remains to be seen whether these efforts will be seen by the state and civil society as attempts at taking responsibility or as attempts to erode the power of the state. Movements have risen and receded over the past 500 years, some successful, others less so, with mixed results. Those indigenous peoples who have survived these conflicts have adapted to changing systems of domination, have resisted in key cultural areas, and usually have attempted to revitalize their sense of indigeneity. These have nearly always included cultural constructs around land tenure, collective distribution, traditional group leadership, and a strong focus on the community. Increasingly this has also meant claims for autonomy of one sort or another, especially in the area of resisting many neoliberal economic forces attempting to penetrate their region, in forms of corporatism and labor consumerism that disrupt the traditions and lifestyles that have sustained them for half a millennium of resistance and revitalization.

We have seen how the Zapatistas have energized indigenous resistance and formation in Mexico and elsewhere in Latin America, comparing that with short discussions of how other *Pueblos Indios* have fared, and some movements have formed. Increasingly, local leadership is making alliances within their states and in regional interactions, as we have identified with Bolivia and Ecuador. The example of Miskitos in Nicaragua indicates that it is not solely capitalism that is at issue, but also modernity per se. In many ways this is the legacy of the Enlightenment and its hubris that European states are somehow the best form of human society—a proposition that indigenous peoples have always rejected. The same example, however, does indicate that governmental forms that are not tightly harnessed to neoliberal globalization may be less adamant in their attempts to transform indigenous peoples.

Last, but far from least, the cases we have presented here underscore how theories of racialization, the social construction of race and ethnicity in general, and indigeneity specifically are severely distorted when they rely solely on the study of processes in the United States. The converse also applies. Theories of social construction of race, ethnicity, and indigeneity based solely on Latin American cases are also distorted. Again we see complex interactions among states, historical processes, and aboriginal indigenous social organizations in the ways these concepts and practices are socially constructed and transformed over time. And again, we see that these differences give rise to different forms of resistance and revitalization. Finally, the underlying unity in all this variation is the continuing struggle for survival and some degree of autonomy on the part of indigenous peoples. The election of Evo Morales on a unity platform explicitly to support indigenous groups in Bolivia is one indication of how these movements have adapted to political realities and changing circumstances in their countries, and are alienated by and struggling against neoliberalism with its notions of private property and corporatization.

With these discussions in mind, we now turn to reexploration of the situations of indigenous peoples in the United States.

NOTES

1. The term *indigeneity* has emerged in addition to, and as a replacement of, other similar terms such as indigenousness, indigenous identities, and indigenous cultures.

2. The use of the term "X social movements," whether X is replaced by "transnational" or "new," is fraught with intellectual land mines. We stated our position in Hall and Fenelon 2008 and in subsequent paragraphs. Glen Kuecker (2004) argues that the expression "new social movements" refers to the changed contexts of contemporary struggles that use new tactics and strategies of resistance. The collection edited by Stahler-Sholk, Vanden, and Kuecker 2008 provides many insightful discussions of movements in Latin America.

3. Tilly often does study much older movements, but not indigenous movements.

4. Described as "culturicide" in Fenelon 1998.

5. Briefly, "race" is in the eye of the beholder, not an objective fact. Cavalli-Sforza and Cavalli-Sforza 1995 via detailed exhaustive biological examination demonstrate that there are no sharp lines between the so-called races, and that each blends into the other through gradual and virtually imperceptible increments. Thus, the demarcation of "races" is socially

determined. This, however, does not mean that they are arbitrary or capricious. There is a loose coupling to phenotypical manifestation, but it is both very loose and quite variable through time and space. For further discussion, see Smedley 1999, Omi and Winant 1994, Nagel 1996, and Hall 2004.

6. Scholars argue as to the exact origin and contemporary usage of the term *ladino,* though most see at least passing reference to the collusion of *La Malinche* with Cortez and the ensuing "mixed-blood" midlevel bureaucrats and administrators who ran the country. Over time, the term came to refer to Europeans, that is, putatively lighter-skinned and Spanish-speaking persons. Most observers do not find it in use today.

7. In New Mexico, in particular, the racialization of Hispanic identity has a long and complex history that is at considerable variance with usage elsewhere in the United States. On New Mexico, see Nostrand (1980, 1984, 1992, 2003); for parallel changes in Texas, see Montejano (1981, 1987); for California see Pitt 1966; Acuña 1988; and Barrera 1979 compares and contrasts all three.

8. See Stahler-Sholk et al. 2008, especially part 4 (pp. 147–211), for further discussions of the roles of race and ethnicity in Latin American social movements.

9. Uprisings in Oaxaca City in the last decade of the twentieth century and first decade of the twenty-first century, and their violent suppression, are near-perfect representations of these ongoing struggles that entail traditionalist indigenous groups, urbanized poor and working class, and social change agents, all challenging an entrenched elite who answer to Mexico City rather than its citizens; see http://www.ccha-assoc.org/oaxaca07/narrative.htm for more details, accessed December 11, 2008.

10. Álvarez Fabela was a university student who went on a civil society caravan to deliver material aid in the highlands. His group arrived a couple of days before the massacre. His book is *the* definitive account of what happened before, during, and after. It carefully documents the events through eyewitness accounts.

11. Two important caveats need to be made here. First is that Bishop Ruíz worked more for indigenous peoples than the government and paid a heavy cost for that, both with the PRI and later the Catholic Church. Also, eventually liberation theology itself underwent a strong reorientation, which local leaders in Chiapas have referred to as "liberation philosophy" (stated in San Cristobal meetings with author Fenelon, December 2003).

12. Marcos started university in 1977 and finished his philosophy degree in 1980. He started teaching at UAM (Universidad Autonoma Metropolitana) in 1979 and left for Chiapas in 1984. The Post Tlatelolco setting was when the left in Mexico went underground and turned to armed revolutionary movements and guerrilla warfare because the path of democratic change was completely shut down in 1968. Marcos gained his political education in this radicalized setting and was heavily influenced by the theoretical developments of poststructuralism as it pertained to the strategy and tactic of revolutionary change (Henck 2007). Marcos said, "I'm definitely post-'68, but not the core of '68 ... I was a little kid. But, I do come from everything that followed" (Henck 2007, 14).

13. This is often called the Guevarrista model after Argentine revolutionary Ché Guevarra (Childs 1995; Johnston 2000). Chirot (1977, 1986) argues that the most radical socialist revolutions in the twentieth century grew out of an alliance between what he calls "western-ized intellectuals" (local people either educated in Western universities or their outposts in the West) and rural peasants. This is a common world-systems explanation for such revolutions and in part accounts for the popularity of the Guevarrista model.

14. *Civil society* is a term referring to a situation in which citizens act politically but in-dependent of state or party structures. For a fuller discussion, see http://pages.britishlibrary .net/blwww3/3way/civilsoc.htm, accessed December 11, 2008.

15. The text of this memo is as follows:

"It is difficult to imagine that the current environment will yield a peaceful solution. Moreover, to the degree that the monetary crisis limits the resources available to the government for social and economic reforms, it may be difficult to win popular support for the Zedillo administration's plans for Chiapas. More relevant, Marcos and his supporters may decide to embarrass the government with an increase in local violence and force the administration to cede to Zapatista demands and accept an embarrassing political defeat. The alternative is a military offensive to defeat the insurgency which would create an international outcry over the use of violence and the suppression of indigenous rights.... While Chiapas, in our opinion, does not pose a fundamental threat to Mexican political stability, it is perceived to be so by many in the investment community. The government will need to eliminate the Zapatistas to demonstrate their effective control of the national territory and of security policy" (Weinberg 2000, 146).

16. The Chiapas LIC was implemented by large numbers of Mexican special forces who had trained at the School of the Americas at Fort Benning, Georgia, after January 1, 1994, paid for with the money of U.S. taxpayers (Weinberg 2000, 172–174).

17. "Consensus of the Peoples" (América Profunda 2003) includes the headings Radical Pluralism, Personal Dignity, Autonomy, New Political Regime, Subordinate the Economy, Radical Democracy, Conviviality, Communality, Create a New World, Autonomy in Exchange, Socialization, and Service and Reciprocity (defined in document).

18. This was reported to author Fenelon in 2003 meetings in San Cristobal, Chiapas, by an anonymous representative of the local leaders in support of social change and struggle by the Zapatistas.

19. Also in Forero and Rohter 2006.

RECOMMENDED READINGS

Barrera, Mario. 1979. *Race and Class in the Southwest: A Theory of Racial Inequality.* Notre Dame, IN: University of Notre Dame Press.
  A classical treatment of the legacies of colonial Hispanic concepts of race and ethnicity as manifested in the southwestern United States.
Farris, Nancy M. 1984. *Maya Society Under Colonial Rule: The Collective Enterprise of Survival.* Princeton, NJ: Princeton University Press.
  This is a detailed account of how Mayans have resisted and survived through centuries of colonial rule.
Guy, Donna J., and Thomas E. Sheridan, eds. 1998. *Contested Ground: Comparative Frontiers on the Northern and Southern Edges of the Spanish Empire.* Tucson: University of Arizona Press.
  This edited collection compares and contrasts colonial processes under Spanish, and some Portuguese, colonization between New Spain and the "southern cone" of South America, that is, what is now Argentina and Chile, and parts of neighboring countries.
Hale, Charles. 1994. *Resistance and Contradiction: Miskitu Indians and the Nicaraguan State, 1894-1987.* Stanford, CA: Stanford University Press.
  This is one of the most thorough and authoritative histories of the Miskito Indians.
Henck, Nick. 2007. *Subcommander Marcos: The Man and the Mask.* Durham, NC: Duke University Press.
  A recent, excellent biography of Marcos.

Muñoz Ramírez, Gloria. 2008. *The Fire and the Word: A History of the Zapatista Movement.* San Francisco: City Lights.
  Reports the struggles of the Zapatistas in Chiapas from their own perspective, a revised version of the Ramírez 2003 cited in the text.

Web Resources

Global Exchange: The San Andrés Accords, http://www.globalexchange.org/countries/americas/mexico/SanAndres.html (accessed December 11, 2008).
Zapatista Network, http://www.zapatistas.org/ (accessed December 11, 2008).

CHAPTER 5

American Indian Survival and Revitalization

Native Nations in the United States

IN THIS CHAPTER we discuss indigenous people's struggles in what has become the United States and Canada. We discuss the Wampanoag and then focus on the Lakota peoples, who together experienced one of the earliest and one of the last conquests by peoples of European ancestry in the history of the United States. We also discuss the Navajo (Diné) and more briefly several California peoples, both to add breadth to our discussion and to present the considerably different experiences of peoples first conquered and absorbed by Spain. This is a very small sample of the well over 500 different "nations" who inhabited the territories that eventually became the United States. Yet, we argue their collective experiences bracket the range of experiences of indigenous peoples with Europeans in the United States. These discussions add to the basis for comparing and contrasting with experiences elsewhere in the world and support our argument for why these processes and experiences require a global, as well as a local, understanding.

For each of these examples, we consider four important analytical perspectives—historicity, resistance modalities of survival, social justice issues, and revitalization. For many people, American Indian peoples have become archetypes of indigenous struggles against colonialization, of limited survival, and of resistance. Some say this has risen to the level of stereotypes. Over the past fifty years or so, American Indians have become emblematic of movements to reestablish their legitimate status as sovereign nations although most of the rest of the world is in sharp conflict over the status of sovereignty, and relations in the United States are as much internal colonies as independent nations. Nonetheless, the devolution of independent

91

native nations under colonialism and later U.S. expansion and incorporation, at times rising to the level of genocidal war, contrasts with a rising rule of law in the twentieth century affirming American Indian nations and leading to a firm sovereignty as "domestic, dependent" status in the United States and as "First Nations" in Canada. This compelling story varies widely by the temporal period of incorporation and the geographic location of the indigenous peoples, making each nation unique even as there are shared aspects. Therefore, we ground our discussion with descriptions of individual Indian nations, beginning with the Wampanoag peoples.

THE EASTERN SEABOARD AND THE WAMPANOAG

Wampanoag peoples have struggled for survival in over 400 years of interactions with peoples from Europe. Here and throughout we use *peoples* to recognize the sometimes complex and often poorly understood divisions and alliances among indigenous nations that have been lumped under the broadly racialized term *Indian* and then too often seen as an undifferentiated mass of people speaking similar languages. Of these, the Mashpee Wampanoag, who assisted the initial Pilgrim colony at what is now known as Plymouth, maintain their traditions and history, but as an "unrecognized" people until recently.[1] Previously, the Aquinnah Wampanoag had won formal recognition in legal battles and were allowed an official reservation land base. Aquinnah people established a "tribal council" that, similar to those of other indigenous peoples, is unwilling to give up any more land. They are replanting beach dunes to their original forms, have reestablished shellfish operations using traditional methods, and have entered into various cooperative ventures, notably on their trust lands with a tourism base. See Plate 5.1 for an example of this revitalization, in this case as the Aquinnah attempt to protect their replanted dunes from further encroachment on Martha's Vineyard island.

Wampanoag peoples existed in developed societies before Europeans came to the Americas, living in homes that included extended families in communities well adapted to their environment, connected to loose confederacies extending over lands throughout present-day Massachusetts. Fishing vessels, "explorers," and slaving ships were the first to make contact in what is now known as the New England coast, leaving disease and social disruption (Peters 1987). When the Pilgrims and Puritans first arrived in 1620, they built a colonial village in the "deserted" Patuxet area, with roughly half dying in the first difficult winter.[2] Wampanoag peoples took pity on them, allowing the multilingual Abenaki leader Samoset to approach them, saying "Hello Englishmen!" followed by Tisquantum (Squanto), who had learned both English and Spanish during his earlier enslavement in Europe. Wampanoag leaders helped the Pilgrims to survive and engaged them in meetings and mutual thanksgiving around harvest festival times, which were to be honored as peaceful relations under their religious traditions, negotiated by the great leader, or Massasoit.[3]

The Pilgrims were reinforced by shiploads of English immigrants and other Europeans who were intolerant of religious beliefs different from their own and

Plate 5.1. Wampanoag (Aquinnah) boundary marker noting coastal revitalization and sovereignty, Martha's Vineyard, Massachusetts. (Photo courtesy of James V. Fenelon)

hungry to take more Indian lands, causing armed conflicts with the Pequot, Narragansetts, and other Native peoples, usually leading to their destruction. Some Wampanoag, fewer in number, were coerced to move to "Praying Towns" where they underwent religious instruction and worked like indentured servants for the English. This phenomenal growth of the English continued until the Massasoit's death more than forty years later. His sons, taking English names, moved into leadership. Wamsutta was murdered during a meeting with the colonists, and Metacom, called Philip, ultimately led an uprising (later called King Philip's War) that was put down almost to a level of genocide, ending with his head and others posted on poles outside Plimoth and his family sold into slavery (Jennings 1975). Wampanoag people survived by going underground for hundreds of years, similar to so many other indigenous nations of the New England region.

On the mainland, Wampanoag people mostly congregated around the Mashpee area, sometimes getting recognition or agreements with the local townspeople. The Aquinnah Wampanoag on Martha's Vineyard also underwent colonial domination, but they managed to negotiate better terms and continued with a rough autonomy into the reservation system developed by the fledgling United States. Ultimately, though all the surviving Wampanoag were eventually recognized by the state of Massachusetts, only the Aquinnah were federally recognized; the Mashpee Wampanoag fought and lost long legal battles where their very existence was questioned, both as indigenous people and as native societies. This example exemplifies how the United States has worked to deny and curtail indigenous recognition, history, and contemporary society, along with any indigenous claims to cultural autonomy.

During the 1960s broad revitalization efforts began to spread across the United States and Canada, along with resistance movements linked by the growing urban population partly developed out of government relocation policies under Congress's Termination Act, which had seriously backfired (Valandra, 2006). Beginning with Civil Rights Movement successes, legal battles were more likely to focus on established law and collective land rights, leading to a series of court cases for the Mashpee Wampanoag. Even so, courts resisted giving recognition to people long since believed to have disappeared, keeping the focus on existing treaties negotiated by the United States. Although the Wampanoag had kept their presence known for over 300 years, the courts only accepted bureaucratic claims. This caused the Wampanoag to experience a basic division—legal acknowledgment of the Aquinnah and nonrecognition of Mashpee—until the latter's federal court case was finally won in 2007.[4]

Despite differential treatment by the U.S. government, indigenous identity has remained strong for all the Wampanoag. Mashpee, Aquinnah, and indeed many other Wampanoag in nearby areas[5] have maintained a sense of community, a relationship to the land, economy, leadership, and a historical legacy of their indigeneity. Similar to indigenous peoples in other parts of the world, the Wampanoag resist full culturicidal incorporation into dominant societies by keeping their main traditions alive and retelling their histories and ancestral lineage.

The Wampanoag have maintained an orientation to the land even though they have been subsumed under colonial and then U.S. legal cultural domination for centuries. The Aquinnah "sacred lands" cliffs, on trust status land on Martha's Vineyard, provide an archetypical case of contested sovereignty. Revitalization in this case includes their continuing struggles for "tribal sovereignty," recognition, maintenance of oral tradition history, and modern economic development that does not run counter to their traditional values (Fenelon 2002).

Education is critical to Wampanoag revitalization, ranging from rewriting their histories, such as the great Massasoit and other leaders in the 1600s, to remembering icons such as the *Mayflower* as a "pirate ship," to schooling of their children in order for knowledge of their traditions and perspectives to be perpetuated, to retellings of how Indian preachers and Praying Towns made sincere attempts to become Christian. Perhaps more important is for the young to get instruction on how the tribal councils work, where land boundaries were in the past and where they are now, and about tribal sovereignty.

THE NORTHERN PLAINS AND THE LAKOTA[6]

We now consider the more contemporary struggles of the northern plains people known as the Lakota. The Lakota (Teton-Sioux) are an excellent example of the multimodal, intertwined issues of indigenous identity in relation to the dominant American society and invasive policies of the United States. Development of separate Sioux (Lakota) Indian reservations during the twentieth century demonstrates an ongoing fractionation of identity by the U.S. Bureau of Indian Affairs. Standing Rock (Sioux) Indian "Reservation," or "Nation," illustrates all of these issues. We begin with an overview of the Lakota peoples.

Prior to the arrival of Euro-American governments, the Lakota viewed themselves as *Oyate*, or "the people," with *Ikce* as native or common together, that could be applied to any substantial grouping, including the largest groups of all— "Sioux" Dakota, Lakota, and Nakota (Powers 1986). Seven major subdivisions, now glossed as "tribal" affiliations, became associated with "Sioux" (Walker 1982): Dakota Oyate of *Mdewakantonwan, Wahpekute, Wahpetonwan,* and *Sisitonwan;* "Dakota speakers" of the *Ihanktonwan* (*Yankton*) and *Ihanktownanna* (*Yanktonai*); and the "Lakota speakers," *Titonwan* (also seven divisions), usually referenced as the "Teton" (see Walker 1982, 14–20) or the Lakota.[7]

In traditional Lakota culture, responsibility toward relatives, sacredness, sovereignty, and homeland extend outward in networks of extended relationships from the household (*tipi*), ultimately reaching the nation (*oyate*).[8] Therefore, Lakota arrange themselves first in a household and then into family-neighbors (villages), followed by extended relatives (associated villages/hamlets or mobile towns with outlying districts), large groups with many allied "camps" such as a "tribe" or "band," and then relatedness alliance on the "nation" level, with *otonwe* (by blood) and *oyate* (common society). Every level commands greater attention to being a "good relative"—so much that Lakota political relations with *oyate unma*, or "other people," follow these same ordering principles. U.S. representatives consistently failed to acknowledge this, until it became to their political advantage to forcibly separate these levels or divisions.

These various national identities of Lakota and Dakota peoples known as Sioux provide an overview of the differences between the Lakota concept of *Oyate* and the concept of sovereignty as used in the United States. The incorporation of Lakotas is typically discussed as struggles over sovereignty and treaty rights leading to formation of the "Sioux Nation" and six separate Lakota-Sioux reservations. External labels range from negative "hostiles" to racialized "Indians" to "citizens." American citizenship implied individuals in the United States and has been viewed as dissolving other memberships.

However, reification of Euro-American social structures as "tribes" versus nations oversimplifies the processes at work (Dunaway 1996; Wolf 1982). The nomenclature used here draws on James Walker's early writings (1917), with primary emphasis on the Lakota. He consistently refers to the overall Teton and Santee (Sioux) people as the Lakota. Yet, most textbooks, nearly all of the major contacts with European derived governments, and most reports from other Indian nations on conflicts with them identify them as Dakota. Thus, Lakota, Dakota, and Sioux are conflated in most linguistic and cultural works.[9] Here we use *traditionalists* to refer to the aforementioned Lakota Oyate versus assimilated "Sioux" U.S. labels. "Nation" primarily means modern political situations.

Over a 200-year period the Lakota Oyate experienced three phases of incorporation[10]: a conquering mode aimed at sociopolitical domination, a profiteering mode aimed at sustained economic exploitation, and a "culturicidal" mode aimed at systemic social domination and erasure of traditional identities. Each mode of domination targeted, manipulated, or deeply influenced forms of indigenous Lakota identity.

Many of these changes in identity were on the ideational level (Berkhofer 1979, 123). These were typically coerced. Dakota and Lakota leaders and scholars responded by invoking "ancestral rights," which were seen to emanate from a close relationship between the people and the land (Standing Bear 1933). Therefore, we distinguish between *external identity* (Green 1995), *internal identity*, and *knowledge-building traditions* (Whitt 1995). These identities changed over time with changes in relations with the United States.

The problems of migration theory are shown in many documents by an overreliance on mainstream and military historians such as Francis Prucha (1975, 1984, 1990), Stanley Vestal (1963), and especially Robert Utley (1984, 1993). Declarations of sovereignty for purposes of controlling riverine trade networks, the land, and later mineral resources were the central political motivation of the United States from 1804 until 1868.

Common scholarly stereotypes such as "white travelers were frightened by the turmoil and commotion caused by intertribal raids" (North Dakota DPI 1995) underscore "tribal" differences rather than alliances based on identity. Thus, "intertribal raiding" served as justification for U.S. intervention after the 1851 treaty (White 1978). However, in reality "treaties" were broken by the U.S. government, military, and civilian forces under pretext of various identity labels, including that of "hostile," usually applied to nonassimilated, resisting Lakota (Wilkins 1997, 95). Thus incorporation was a divisive, violent process,[11] which destroyed internal social systems and traditional relationships. Many "Indian Wars" resulted from armed resistance by Lakota leaders to this political and cultural invasion.

The Louisiana Purchase in 1803, followed by Lewis and Clark's Voyage of Discovery from 1804 to 1806, began the invasion into lands controlled by the Lakota (Fenelon and Defender 2004). With each incursion, friction between incoming militaries and settlers with indigenous nations increased. The United States began to pass laws allowing for its territorial expansion, usually accompanied by armed exploration and claims to have dominating sovereignty. Various small armed conflicts ensued, with the United States entering into negotiations with the "Sioux Nation of Indians" in 1851, and then again in 1868, the latter after two years of warfare wherein Lakota and Cheyenne leaders refused to accept belittling treaty terms and relocation efforts by the United States.

The 1868 Fort Laramie Treaty is especially important for our discussion for many reasons, the most important being that the Lakota leaders insisted on traditional homelands being kept intact, notably the "sacred" Black Hills, and for Lakota social justice to be maintained, as well as economic restitution for land transfers and losing sustenance from their hunting grounds. In this respect, similar to many indigenous peoples' struggles, they demonstrate an acute awareness of the social conditions of their community and their relationship with incoming dominant groups and the incorporating forces of the nation-state system.

The United States invaded the lands anyway, of course, and through a series of land seizures exerted political domination and began initial extraction activities in the valuable Black Hills. Whereas some communities stayed around the newly developed "agencies" and the nearby forts, others became restive and moved to join the armed resistance. This led to another set of famous fights, perhaps the most important being the Little Big Horn Battle, where General Custer and his Seventh Cavalry were destroyed less than two weeks after General Crook was defeated along the Rosebud River. Two other army columns began search-and-destroy missions through the treaty lands, with Crazy Horse leading one group of Lakota into highlands and Gall and Sitting Bull leading most of the others up into Canada.

With most of the armed resistance divided and in exile, the United States took the treaty land and separated the Lakota into reservations around the major agencies, the main ones including Pine Ridge, Rosebud, Cheyenne River, and Standing Rock. When Sitting Bull returned after five years in Canada, he was allowed to live with his people, the Hunkpapa, following two years in military custody. The forces of the United States were unhappy with the arrangements keeping traditional leadership in place and large numbers on Pine Ridge. They started antitraditional strategies including banning religious practices, creating boarding schools, and dividing land allotments to break up the social cohesiveness of the Lakota. Although traditional leaders attempted to make limited adaptations, they also resisted the coercive social destruction of U.S. Bureau of Indian Affairs (BIA) policies. Plate 5.2 shows the installation of Standing Rock Indian reservation with both Lakota traditional leader Sitting Bull and the U.S. Indian agent James McLaughlin, exemplifying these adaptive relationships.

These differences came into sharp conflict when two major events coincided—the United States broke the Dakota Territory into two "states" that were clearly meant to finish incorporating Lakota peoples into subordinated groups, and the Ghost Dance swept onto the 1890 Great Plains from the west (Brown 1970; Mooney 1896; Fenelon 1998). While the United States was attempting to destroy the traditional lifestyles and all sense of indigeneity of Lakota peoples, the Ghost Dance offered a bridge to return respect for the traditional society and history of being indigenous people under a new quasi-Christian, partly pan-Indian set of religious practices, which most social scientists now refer to as a revitalization movement (Wallace 1956).

The American public was alarmed through sensationalist newspaper headings fueled by both military and political leaders interested in "subduing" the Lakota once and for all. After moving vast numbers of troops into the Dakota region, U.S. authorities ordered the arrest of all leaders associated with the Ghost

Plate 5.2. Installation of Standing Rock Indian reservation
(1880s) with Sitting Bull and James McLaughlin (agent),
Fort Yates, North Dakota. (Photograph from the Major James
McLaughlin papers, microfiche roll 36)

Dance, and the suppression of all traditional social practices. The violent conflict
first came to a head on Standing Rock with the killing of Sitting Bull by the
Indian Police dispatched ahead of the army forces. After military threats and a
violent chase across the wintry South Dakota plains, the conflict ended with the
slaughter of more than 300 Lakota people who had already "surrendered" near
Wounded Knee Creek. This act was effectively a death knell to revitalization
and armed resistance.

Bureau of Indian Affairs agents, backed by military forts and armed
militias and supported by a slew of congressional laws and edicts, began the
cultural destruction of the Lakota and other indigenous peoples who had resisted incorporation and subordination. This suppression included attempts to
destroy knowledge systems and the economic, political, and cultural practices
of traditional Lakota society. Land transfers, called "taken land" by indigenous
leaders, increased over the next few decades, when most observers and all political
leaders predicted the complete disappearance of the "Indian" as a social force.
However, the larger reservations stayed intact, partly because the United States
refused to grant citizenship without denial of "tribal" membership, until 1924.
Also, traditionalists took knowledge and practice of their lifeways "underground"
and kept this out of view—some would say entirely secret—from the dominant
society and its invasive bureaucrats.

This led to some of the most compelling forms of resistance to culturicidal
incorporation known to modern American society, and, with the loosening of such
restrictions during the second half of the twentieth century, some very impressive
forms of revitalization. Knowledge and practice of the Lakota SunDance,[12] which
had been integral under Sitting Bull's spiritual leadership in the 1870 conflicts, in
many ways demonstrate this central feature of cultural resistance. These practices
were so secret that, with a few local exceptions, major universities and nearly all
analysts, ethnographic and political, believed them to be eliminated from Lakota

society. However, Lakota and Dakota people continued with their traditional ways when living under duress (Fenelon 1998, 287–294). Thus in the 1930s, during which time the government allowed the 1934 Indian Reorganization Act to restructure tribal governance, indigenous peoples were revitalizing in secret. This continued until well into the 1960s, when the leaders brought some social practices back into the open while maintaining a level of guarded secrecy.

With the reappearance of the SunDance, and American social life after the Civil Rights Movement showing some semblance of openness to histories and cultures of minorities, the next struggles were over indigenous perspectives and the very nature of indigeneity. Traditional Lakota follow oral history and name their origin place as the Black Hills and surrounding points (Goodman 1992).[13] However, many mainstream scholars state their origin as somewhere west of a forest fringe near Minnesota woodlands.[14]

Arvol Looking Horse, a well-versed Lakota traditionalist, uses both of these perspectives. He describes himself as "the nineteenth generation to serve as [sacred] Pipe keeper," given to the Lakota near the Iron Lightning community on Cheyenne River (DeMallie 1987, 67–68). This places Lakotas west of the Missouri River 400 years ago. Looking Horse (DeMallie 1987, 71) also says, "Our people used to be *probably* in the Minnesota area, or eastern South Dakota." This statement reflects a standard migration history from school textbooks, clearly influencing the Lakota attending those schools, and permeating all mainstream accounts, leading to conflicting accounts of the Lakota homelands.

Although Lakotas regularly moved through the eastern portion of the current Dakota states preceding the seventeenth century and the western regions as well, with the advent of the horse and pressure from their Dakota allies in the early 1700s, Lakota encampments reentered more forcefully the central Dakota plains, including the Black Hills. Thus, their historical lands of origin were politically strengthened by allied Lakota groups and by diplomatic relations in the region. Importantly, the Black Hills are noted in the most ancient mythology and may have never fallen out of Lakota control until the U.S. attacks. Besides conflicting history, this indigenous perspective helps to account for strongly held views toward the treaties and understandings of the Lakota with the United States. Other social institutions were similarly involved and are still contested in modern conflicts. Justice systems have been restored in the context of sovereignty and laws as subsets of the dominant society in the United States as well, leading to a more nuanced and less fully indigenous system. Tribal courts run the gamut in terms of structure and approach, yet some are more reflective of the traditional society of the people than others. Perhaps the single most influential set of decisions, and later legislation, dealt with the Lakota, namely conflicts worked out through the courts after the signing of the 1868 Fort Laramie Treaty, granting full sovereignty over vast lands in South Dakota, Wyoming, Montana, and Nebraska, including the Black Hills, which were sacred to many indigenous peoples in the area.

After the separation into reservations and the completely illegal and unilateral "taking" away of the extremely valuable, resource-rich Black Hills region by the United States, Lakota people began to adapt to the new conditions, including changed leadership forms, such as quasi-appointed "chiefs" that replaced elder councils. On the Rosebud Reservation in the 1880s, Spotted Tail took such power and probably abused it, leading the counselors to appoint Crow Dog to restrain him. In an argument, Crow Dog killed Spotted Tail and was later arrested by U.S. marshals and put under trial and certain conviction in Rapid City, the territorial headquarters. The officer in charge allowed Crow Dog to return to Rosebud and let the people and elders make restitution and clear up the matter for the Lakota using restorative justice. The press and townspeople went crazy with criticism yet were amazed when, in the dead of a winter storm, Crow Dog did return to his death sentence.

However, the case was challenged, as treaty law allowed for Lakota justice to be primary. The case was decided in Crow Dog's favor in 1883 (ex parte Crow Dog, 109 U.S. 556). U.S. Supreme Court decisions notwithstanding, Congress quickly enacted the Indian Offences policies banning religious and cultural practices of the Lakota, followed by the Major Crimes Act in 1885 making U.S. federal criminal law dominant, and the Dawes Allotment Act in 1887 allowing for maximal land-takings. These culminated in cultural suppression, outlawing the Ghost Dance, and using these policies to kill Sitting Bull and "legally" slaughter a group of survivors at Wounded Knee in December 1890. Thus traditional social justice systems that were remarkably evenhanded and culturally appropriate were first of all subordinated to, and then destroyed by, the U.S. punitive criminal justice systems.

Tribal courts as Western-based justice and tribal councils as Western-based government were constructed on the reservations and became intermediary and internal colonialist structures for controlling and containing "American Indians" and any sovereignty claims (Deloria and Wilkins 1999). As Indian nations have reestablished internal sovereignty, these existing court and council systems have acted as effective governments for tribes, yet are often opposed by traditional peoples and movement groups as U.S. "puppets." The newly built Standing Rock Nation government building shown in Plate 5.3 now officially represents this constructed governance system.

Thus resistance and revitalization are one and the same, at least after a formal U.S. recognition of American Indian "tribes" and nations. In other respects, gatherings and a shared set of practices that analysts call "pan-ethnic" or "pan-Indian-ism" span North America. Most representative of these practices are the ubiquitous "powwows" that nearly every "Indian" community has, along with many major universities, and regional, national, and even international events drawing thousands of dancers, drummers, and participants. Though such events fly the U.S. flag, they also observe traditional icons of sovereignty, such as eagle staffs representing native nations. In this way, modern social structures have connected a great many indigenous nations in North America in collective practices with the focus on maintaining indigeneity, generically and with cultural particularity. In the past few decades, these have included activists in opening honor songs when veterans are asked to come forward and dance.

Plate 5.3. New government offices for Standing Rock (Nation), exemplifying their sovereign status. (Photo courtesy of James V. Fenelon)

Of course, the dominant society uses flags and other icons to demonstrate its superior position as well, in some cases to mark the taken land as under its sovereign control. For the Lakota, in remembrance of the 1868 Fort Laramie Treaty, the sacred Black Hills symbolize their emergence place and the injustices and breaking of the treaty conditions. The United States carved huge faces of its most famous presidents on the mountainsides, calling them Mount Rushmore, which has become a beacon for immigrants and tourists, supposedly typifying freedom and democracy for the country. Many Lakota refer to it as "the Four Thieves" and instead acknowledge sacred thunder beings on the mountaintops, refusing to accept monetary payments made in unilateral settlements reaching $800 million or more. This contributes greatly to the surrounding county's status of having the lowest income and greatest poverty in the country.[15] Activists remind us not only of the military and government breaking the 1868 treaty but also the billions of dollars that were taken out of the largest gold mine of the nineteenth century—the Homestake, which traditional Lakota referred to as an open sore, a wound in "mother earth's body." Land is central to indigenous value systems, so it interacts with injustices such as broken treaties and outright theft, demonstrating all four spheres of life we identified—community, collective economic systems, leadership/decision making from the people, and land tenure—viewing all life as both holistic and environmentally grounded.

Sacred lands are central to most indigenous peoples, and the Lakota share this respect for places where they are granted visions and guidance, as leaders and traditionalists, shown in Plate 5.4 of Bear Butte (*Mato Paha*). The following statement from one of the most respected traditional Lakota, Frank Fools Crow, demonstrates all four qualities that we have observed—reverence and respect for the land, leadership as speaking for the people, having the collective "community" good in mind, and generosity without greed for self or attachment to material goods—in both holistic and spiritual ways.

FASTING AND PRAYING ON BEAR BUTTE

I want to speak about a sacred hill which we Indians used in our fasting and praying. I have stood at the highest point on this butte, and pray for four days and nights without the necessities of life. During 1959 I was up on Bear Butte fasting on the East side of the Butte. I was inside of the cave without food and water. I received my guidance and visions by the Great Spirit.... This, my beloved people, does not mean that I am a Holy Man or higher than everyone else. I consider myself as a poor man. I am a peaceful man. As the days pass by I humble myself among my people to do the best I can to help my people. Days later, I went to Washington, DC and went inside the President's Fort office and sat down to pray. My people and friends, today I come in peace to this President's office with prayer and to make a short speech. After all this was done, I felt very good. Thank you all and may the Great Spirit guide you all in the special way. (Frank Fools Crow 1976)

Lakota often use the phrase *ikce wicasa* ("common red man") when they undertake many leadership roles, which can be glossed to mean, "I am no better or worse than the people." Herein we observe how resistance to Western and colonial forms of cultural domination, especially personal aggrandizement, is also often linked to revitalization of traditional lifestyles that are further connected to ongoing oppression and injustice, such as treaty rights and lawful or ethical behavior. This is also demonstrated when Frank Fools Crow and another "headsman," Frank Kills Enemy, were selected to represent all the traditional Lakota in terms of monetary "settlement" for treaty-breaking that led to the loss of land. Again, land is perceived spiritually and collectively, just as relations with "the people" are understood to change the behavior and orientation of a person selected to be "leader"—or, more accurately, "spokesperson"—for the councils of elders to represent the people.

Plate 5.4. Bear Butte, sacred mountain area for indigenous peoples near Black Hills, South Dakota. (Photo courtesy of James V. Fenelon)

WE SHALL NEVER SELL OUR SACRED BLACK HILLS

Joint Statement of Chief Frank Fools Crow and Frank Kills Enemy on Behalf of the Traditional Lakota Treaty Council (September, 1976):

Kola [friends] ... I am Frank Fools Crow, Lakota Chief, and I am here today with Frank Kills Enemy, respected headsman and expert on Indian treaty rights....

We have come here from Pine Ridge today to discuss this house bill which permits the tribal councils to get interest on the award given by the Indian Claims Commission.... Our people have been holding meetings on the Black Hills for many years and we have just held such a meeting at Porcupine.... The people authorized us to come to this hearing today and speak for them. *The people unanimously reaffirmed our long-standing position that the Black Hills are not for sale under any circumstances.* We are therefore standing behind the resolution we passed at Fort Yates, reading:

RESOLUTION ON 1868 TREATY[16] (EXCERPT)

I want to repeat that there can never be an acceptance of this bill or the total Black Hills Claim under any circumstances. This is the wish of the people. We have a treaty and it requires ¾ of all adult male members to sign before our land can be sold. I believe that this provision was stuck in the treaty by the whiteman because Lakota do not sell their land. The whiteman claims that he is not bound by the ¾ provision of the treaty.... The treaty was broken by the whiteman before it was even signed by him. But we Lakota are more honorable men. We have signed the treaty and we will try to live by it, and respect it. Even though this treaty may not be binding on the whiteman, it is binding on us until we vote it out. It says that ¾ of Lakota adult male members must sign before land can be sold and the Lakota people can never accept any payment until this provision is fully complied with.

The Black Hills are sacred to the Lakota people. Both the sacred pipe and the Black Hills go hand and hand in our region. The Black Hills is our church, the place where we worship. The Black Hills is our burial grounds. The bones of our grandfathers lie buried in those hills. How can you expect us to sell our church and our cemeteries for a few token whiteman dollars. We will never sell. (Fools Crow 1976)

There are two important points to make from the above passage—first, traditional people are quite sophisticated in their understanding of treaties, lawmaking, and "realistic" objectives; and second, value-systems of indigenous peoples are interconnected with orientations to land, community, and spirituality. This is doubly important in a society undergoing globalization, subordinating all people and communities and societal values to economic determination. It is not just that indigenous peoples are most often at the bottom of this stratification system, but that their very values and beliefs are under attack.

This means that indigenous peoples represent a fundamentally different form of social organization than capitalism or even modern notions of "progress" or "development." These perspectives are often perceived by dominant groups as being a challenge or even threat to the system itself, or at least are used as an excuse to dominate or suppress them. All this leads to further injustice, at least from the indigenous perspective. Perhaps more important, historical representations of these conflicts or struggles usually stereotype and simplify indigenous peoples, especially their forms of resistance and revitalization. Typically, scholars identify one of the major problems of these relationships as being locked into past labels or icons, which contribute to the denial of modern social change, both by indigenous peoples and in their contemporary relations with dominant groups. Fools Crow refers to the Black Hills, Bear Butte, the Pipe, and the traditional people while showing deep awareness of what the 1868 treaty actually represented, but he also demonstrates awareness of contemporary resistance and its relationship to settlements, including calling tribal councils U.S. "puppet governments" when referring to negotiations over the land. In this way, a typification of the past can be as important to contemporary relations as current perspectives of such important issues as "treaty land."

Museums, and many academic disciplines, often present American Indians or indigenous people only in a conflict mode or "noble savage" symbolism, "legitimately" and perhaps somewhat historically accurate, yet without even noting the social change processes they were engaged in in the past, much less currently. The Battle of the Little Big Horn is one of the most discussed, researched, and described military conflicts in the history of the United States, yet it is primarily Lakota who know that the "shirtwearer" function of leadership was in such deep contention by government appointments of "chief" and then unequal rations that spiritual or religious leaders had risen to prominence in trying to resist and revitalize Lakota society. Sitting Bull had called for a great meeting of the peoples throughout the region at a SunDance, where they would seek out a grand vision of where they should go. Also, he had his own vision of many "soldiers falling into camp" (and being defeated), which empowered many of the Lakota military leaders, who saw themselves as defending their communities and families rather than being engaged in a kind of noble warfare (Fenelon 1998, 52–58, 111, 124–128, 140).

This is why museums, scholarly histories, schooling, and public presentations are so important for indigenous relationships. This is most clearly seen in how many indigenous peoples, when the resources are available to them, connect these social realities. One example is an eagle feather headdress on display at Sitting Bull (Standing Rock) College, in its library, next to the books that make up college education (see Plate 5.5), thereby demonstrating traditional values in a modern setting.

Revitalization and resistance go hand in hand with these modern-day images, reflecting American social institutional structures of higher education, even as it is contrasted and enhanced with traditional Lakota value systems. This entire set of constructions—college, Standing Rock reservation as a "nation," indigenous history and knowledge alongside contemporary Western versions of the world, and imagery of respect for Lakota society—exists solely because of sovereignty.

Plate 5.5. Eagle feather headdress displayed at Sitting Bull College on Standing Rock, demonstrating traditional and modern forms of learning and knowledge. (Photo courtesy of James V. Fenelon)

Traditionalists resisted full incorporation for nearly 200 years and maintained Lakota social structures even as they adapted to the dominance of contemporary American society. In this way, cultural and political forms of sovereignty intersect. Without the political recognition, under constant perusal by legal interpretations but ultimately providing constrained claim to limited "tribal sovereignty," there would likely be no Sitting Bull College. But just as true, without the struggle over cultural practices and belief systems, under constant attack by the dominant U.S. society, and with a constant defense by many traditionalists as seen in revitalizing the SunDance, there would likely be no Lakota traditions to honor and show respect, and thus revitalize the Lakota people.

We will now discuss another remarkable struggle of an "Indian nation" or indigenous people in a very different social and geographic setting, and over different time periods, but with similar results.

THE AMERICAN SOUTHWEST AND THE NAVAJO PEOPLES[17]

Navajo, or Diné, people originated hundreds if not thousands of years ago and took part in ancient movements across the Americas; they are related to people in Canada by the same name. They settled in their current lands after living on the central plains of North America and founded the Navajo nation with strong connections to the land, bounded by four sacred mountains. American people became familiar with the Navajos sometime in the nineteenth century, after the Santa Fe Trail opened in 1821, and more so after the Mexican-American War (1846–1848), after which the United States annexed the northern half of Mexico and gained control of what would become Texas, New Mexico, Arizona, California, and parts of Nevada, Utah, Colorado, and Oklahoma (Reséndez 2005). However, by that time Navajos had been in contact with Spanish people for nearly three centuries. Spaniards first entered the region in 1536 when Cabeza de Vaca traversed the territory in a journey to Mexico City after he was shipwrecked somewhere along the Gulf Coast of what is now Texas. Francisco de Coronado explored the region in 1540–1542. Don Juan de Oñate led the first colonizing expedition to what we now know as Santa Fe, New Mexico, in 1598,[18] a decade before the founding of Jamestown and over two decades before Pilgrims landed at Plymouth Rock.

Similar to the colonization of Mexico, "New" Mexico was colonized in the hopes that it would be a source of wealth and labor. When this proved not to be the case, some settlers had to be forced to remain there. In addition to seeking religious converts, the colony was maintained to preempt intrusions by other European states and to provide a large buffer zone between the very lucrative mines in and around Zacatecas.[19] Spanish explorers and colonizers divided the peoples they encountered in the region into two categories: *gente de razon* and *Indios bárbaros.*[20] Both categories grouped together widely diverse peoples and showed deep Spanish ethnocentrism. The term *gente de razon* was applied to the peoples we know today as the Pueblos because they lived in square houses with a central plaza, like "civilized" Spaniards did. The name *Pueblo* itself generates some confusion because in Spanish it can mean either people or village, but in English, when capitalized, refers to any one of several Native American groups. At the time of Coronado and Oñate there were approximately 140 functioning Pueblos; today nineteen remain. Pueblo peoples spoke languages from at least four different major language families, with several different specific languages within each family. Old Oraibi, a Hopi village in northeastern Arizona, is the oldest continuously occupied settlement north of central Mexico. People have lived there for at least a millennium. All other Indians in the region were labeled *Indios bárbaros,* literally as barbaric Indians, or those without reason, or savages, because they did not live in fixed settlements.

Here it is useful to explicate these variations as they are understood today. First, for many of the non-Pueblo groups, kinship was the major form of social organization and government. In this sense their social structure parallels, or is analogous to, that of the Lakota, yet much different in the details. However, this was not the rather truncated kinship used by middle-class citizens of the United States in the twenty-first century. Navajos, for example, reckon kin relations with specific named categories, and specific obligations and duties among the categories to what we contemporary U.S. citizens would label a third cousin thrice removed, or more prosaically, a "stranger." Many, but not all, of these groups traced primary descent through the female line and thus are considered matrilineal.

Second, many of these groups exhibited a degree of nomadism, a term that engenders much misunderstanding. It is sometimes misinterpreted to mean people who wander randomly over the countryside. This is absolutely wrong. All nomadic indigenous peoples have a strong sense of territory, and when mobile follow specific patterns of travel and land use, most of which are dictated by which natural resources are available in specific seasons. This can hold even for the most basic foragers. In the greater Southwest, groups ranged from foragers, to groups that had one or more fixed settlements during one or more seasons, to peoples who moved their settlements every few years, and finally to "Puebolos" with fixed adobe structures, often centuries old. After sheep were obtained from Spanish settlers, many groups, the Navajo among them, became transhumant. That is, they moved their herds into lower elevations in winter and to mountainous areas in summer.

Third, many groups had a sense of shared identity that transcended their forms of organization. Thus, there were many Navajo who shared the self-appellation Diné—which means "the people" in Navajo—but who had no formal relationship to each other. This, too, is typical, but not universal, for indigenous peoples throughout the world.

Fourth, many of these characteristics shifted through time. Some nomadic peoples, as noted, became transhumant, and others became settled either permanently or for part of the year. Especially after they acquired horses from Spaniards, some sedentary groups became more nomadic even while maintaining summer gardens. Some even shifted back and forth several times with changing circumstances. Similarly, modes of organization changed, again often in reaction to changing circumstances. Some groups became more scattered and less centralized as they became highly mobile to avoid attacks and to take advantage of hunting opportunities—especially of buffalo—after acquiring horses. Some peoples became more centralized and developed more complex organizational forms as a matter of defense. Again, some groups changed back and forth more than once.

In some cases this centralization was imposed by Europeans. The most dramatic case of centralization of non-Pueblos was the lasting peace with Comanche bands forged in the 1780s. After a significant military defeat, Spanish officials required Comanches to elect one chief—the first was Ecueracapa—and a secondary chief. A few years after the treaty when weather led to poor hunting, the Spanish residents of Santa Fe took up a collection to feed hungry Comanches. This action, more than any other, cemented peace between Comanches and New Mexican Spaniards. The chieftaincy became institutionalized among Comanches and lasted for some time (Kavanaugh 1996). The peace lasted through Mexican independence (1821) and well into the American era.

In other cases, either on Spanish *establicimientos de paz* (peace establishments, approximately forerunners of reservations in the United States) or subsequently on reservations established by the United States, different groups were forced onto the same territory, sometimes even groups that had recently been hostile to each other. In such cases the new form of organization, imposed by Europeans to be sure, was larger than any one identity group. This reversed the typical precontact situation in which the group with shared identity was significantly larger than any formal political organization (Cornell 1988).

The fluidity of social organization and identity caused considerable confusion among Spanish, later Mexican, then American officials. All were caught up in nation-building sweeping through European countries and their settler colonies from the sixteenth century onward (Bartlett 1993), trying to forge one identity for the entire state, without Indians. They projected their own desired unity and permanence onto various indigenous groups that were much more fluid in their concepts of group and identity.[21]

In the Spanish era, especially during the seventeenth century, the low level of support from the viceroy in Mexico City or from the king in Spain for New Mexico meant that governors had to raise revenues on their own. Various Pueblos were pressed to supply food and blankets for Spaniards. Some governors of New Mexico even consolidated some of the Pueblos, ostensibly for defensive purposes, but often to facilitate Spanish administration and exploitation of Pueblo resources, including labor. Efforts to control Pueblos, including forced conversions to Catholicism, eventuated in the Pueblo Revolt in 1680 (Weber 1999). The Pueblos united briefly under Popé and drove all Spaniards from New Mexico. However, they returned in the early 1690s ostensibly to save the souls of Christianized Indians, but primarily for the same reasons they originally colonized New Mexico. It is important to recall that the region was organized as the province of New Mexico. Texas was not colonized until the early 1700s, and California only in 1769. David Weber describes the region as "the periphery of the periphery" (1982).

The low level of support from the viceroy and the king also pushed Spanish officials in New Mexico to raise funds by forcing Pueblos to pay tribute and by trading with various other indigenous groups. Though indigenous peoples sought horses, sheep, and other Spanish products, they had or produced few goods other than buffalo hides wanted by the Spanish. They could, however, supply captives, or slaves. These were used locally primarily as household servants, but initially many were sold to work in the mines in Zacatecas. Very quickly, every group was forced to participate in the captive trade or face becoming captives themselves. This situation facilitated the spread and use of horses and guns far beyond the region (Blackhawk 2006). It also gave rise to a state of endemic warfare, wherein every group raided every other group to gain revenge for past raids and for captives to trade for horses and guns.

Because they lived on the extreme northwest edges of Spanish-controlled territory, Navajos were more often the victims of raids than the perpetrators. Many Navajo captives became absorbed into other indigenous groups and into Spanish society, albeit at the bottom. But their location also protected them to some extent from intense raiding, missionizing, or Spanish settlements. The net effect was that Navajos were able to absorb new materials and technologies from Spaniards, but adopt them in ways that were consonant with Navajo cultural practices.

After the American conquest in 1848, New Mexico was held at arm's length because of racist attitudes toward both its indigenous and to some extent Hispanic populations.[22] During the Civil War (1861–1864) the geopolitics of Union-Confederate conflict led to the parceling of the territory into Arizona, associated with the Confederacy, and New Mexico, associated with the Union. Because California also was part of the Union, this intentional division made it all but impossible for the Confederacy to gain a land route to the West Coast. Both

Arizona and New Mexico remained territories until 1912, primarily because the majority of residents of each were indigenous or Spanish or Mexican.

After a brief but failed attempt to brutally relocate Navajos to Fort Sumner, New Mexico (1864–1868), called the "Long Walk" to Bosque Redondo,[23] they returned to their homeland and large reservation straddling the New Mexico–Arizona border in 1868. Because the region was largely ignored, Navajos could adopt U.S. practices, goods, and technologies selectively and at their own pace. Often they were able to indigenize them fully. Thus, though horse riding, sheepherding, silversmithing, and blanket weaving were in some sense obtained from Spaniards, by the late nineteenth century they were also fully Navajo.[24] The tribe also grew in population, and more land was added to the reservation.

Even in the twentieth century relative isolation afforded Navajos time to adjust to changing circumstances (Iverson 1981). During the 1920s and 1930s, under the Collier administration of the Bureau of Indian Affairs, concerns over erosion led to an effort to curtail pressure on the environment by reducing the number of sheep grazed by Navajo families. Navajos viewed the destruction of their herds as one of the worst periods in the long history of interaction with Europeans. This engendered a distrust of the BIA and led them to refuse to adopt the boilerplate tribal constitutions that the Bureau of Indian Affairs sought to impose on various American Indian populations. Rather, they developed their own "tribal government," known today as the Navajo Nation.

World War II brought many Navajos into more involvement with U.S. economy and society. Men were drafted and volunteered for service in the military; others, including some women, became more involved in wage labor in areas surrounding the reservation. Navajos in the military became the now-famous code talkers.[25] As happened throughout Indian country, returning veterans brought new ideas and new activism to indigenous peoples. Many veterans went on to become Navajo Nation leaders in the ensuing years. Paved roads to the center of the large Navajo reservation (roughly the size of the state of West Virginia) were finally built. These in turn increased travel, commerce, and tourism, and stimulated Navajo arts and crafts production.[26] Also during this time country-western music and rodeos became popular (Iverson 1994; Iverson and MacCannell 1999).

In 1971 Navajos built the first tribal college in the United States: the Navajo Community College. One of the college's goals was to provide higher education for Navajo students in a culturally sensitive setting on the Navajo Nation. An equal goal was study and enhancement of Navajo culture. The college offered courses in Navajo language, religion, silversmithing, and rug weaving. At the first permanent site in Tsaile, Arizona, a school for religious healers or "medicine men" was established.[27] The museum has the only permanent rendition of a Navajo sand painting, made with special blessing and dispensation by Navajo spiritual leaders to be used for training and preserving the *hatathli* tradition.[28]

Navajos have been creative in the development of legal institutions. As noted in Chapter 1, they have developed "peacemaker courts" that avoid adversarial techniques of Anglo courts by pursuing resolution of disputes among Navajos through means that are in accord with Navajo concepts of harmony. Their foundational principle is *k'e,* or "respect, responsibility and proper relationships among all people." These courts seek a common goal among groups of individuals and assist disputants in the healing process by fostering a mutually beneficial agreement.[29] This is yet another example of how Navajos have taken a foreign institution, a court, and indigenized it.

Also during this time coal, oil, and uranium were mined, initially via contracts with outside companies at bargain-basement rates. Navajos were major players during the 1970s in the formation of the Consortium of Energy Resource Tribes (CERT), a U.S. domestic analogue of the Organization of Petroleum Exporting Countries. CERT, like gaming, has helped some Native Americans, but for the most part has not changed their overall place at the bottom of the U.S. socioeconomic system (Snipp 1988a, 1988b; Mullis and Kamper 2000; Champagne 2003). As part of the actions that led to the formation of CERT, Navajo leaders were able to renegotiate mineral extraction contracts on more favorable terms. Some of the proceeds were used to build Navajo Community College. While Navajos have used their resources, at least through 2007 they had continually voted down gaming operations,[30] when they finally moved to build casinos (see Epilogue).

The Navajo government built a utility authority to electrify the reservation, developed a forest products organization to use timber resources, and built a large and effective tribal police force. The latter has been celebrated in the novels of Tony Hillerman and his two Navajo police heroes, Jim Chee and Joe Leaphorn. The reception of Hillerman's books among Navajos is emblematic of the ambivalence that marks the reception of many influences from outside. Some Navajos appreciate Hillerman's books because of his very positive portrayal of Navajo police and culture. Others strenuously object to an outsider not raised in Navajo culture discussing it in such a public way and for monetary profit.

More problematic during this era has been the erosion of Navajo language, again a problem common to many indigenous peoples. In the early 1970s approximately half of the five-year-olds entering school on the Navajo reservation were monolingual Navajo speakers. Indeed, this situation was a major impetus for building the Rough Rock Demonstration School and other "contract schools" in which the Navajo Nation government contracted with the BIA to build and operate its own schools, staffed with Navajo teachers or by non-Navajos selected by Navajos. A major program of the contract schools was to teach reading and writing in Navajo, then to teach English after the students had mastered the fundamentals of reading and writing. By the turn of the twenty-first century the proportion of monolingual speaking Navajos had dropped drastically (Spolsky 1970, 2002). Ironically, it was not so much the strenuous efforts of BIA boarding schools to stamp out indigenous languages (Adams 1995) but rather increasing media presence and off-reservation employment that undermined traditional languages (Spolsky 2002). This is all the more ironic in that this also was the era of expansion of Navajo language radio, and that a portion of the *Navajo Times* was being published in Navajo. It is interesting however, to note that such programs have had some success in retaining and enhancing the use of indigenous languages.

In these latter issues like language loss and reactions to the Hillerman novels, Navajos find themselves in much the same position of people everywhere who are overwhelmed by changes brought on by globalization (Sklair 2002): they are impacted by changes and processes originating elsewhere and over which they have little or no control or say. But Navajos have a small advantage in years, indeed centuries, of adjusting, adopting, and adapting external processes and changes to Navajo needs. They are masters at participating in a larger world and, so far, have not yet been swallowed up by it.

THE WEST COAST AND CALIFORNIA INDIANS

Among peoples aggregated because of geographical area, none is more representative than California Indians, or indigenous peoples from the region now known as the state of California, who experienced nearly every form of domination and resistance, especially with the California Indians mission system of incorporation.

The diverse groups of peoples collectively called the California Indians illustrate a very different process of incorporation, resistance, and survival in the modern world-system. Some of the indigenous peoples were living in California before the *conquista* had come from Mexico. They lived in medium-sized communities that traded extensively across the region, maintaining cultural autonomy with minor levels of conflict. Some coastal peoples—Chumash around the Santa Barbara area, for instance—had developed complex societies that were well adapted to their respective environment. California was ethnographically complex with a large variety of different groups (Heizer 1978). Some had been expanding their territory—albeit very gradually—at the expense of other groups (Chase-Dunn and Mann 1998).

When the mission system arrived in the late 1700s, conflict arose throughout the California region. Administrators in New Spain and Mexico used this conflict to maximize dominance, similar in many ways to the techniques used on Pueblos and Navajos. Missionaries used Indian labor to build missions and oversee farmland, and broke up traditional patterns of life and indigenous identity. Revolts were common and were usually brutally suppressed. The missions did not extend much beyond the coastal areas and some of the bays such as at San Diego, San Francisco, and Los Angeles, with many interior peoples maintaining some level of resistance and often counterraiding against the invaders.

Gold was discovered in California just as the Mexican-American War ended, unleashing a flood of Anglo immigrants. The Indian communities could not resist the newcomers militarily. Indian communities were increasingly shunted aside into ever smaller *rancherias* as they were overrun first by Spanish, then Mexican, then Anglo, and even later, Chinese immigrants. Conflicts in northern California often erupted into small-scale genocides (Hurtado 1988). Even in the southern regions violent incorporation was far from unusual. The state legislature enacted harsh laws, indenturing Indian labor and even women and children, especially girls (Johnston-Dodds 2002). Murder, genocide, and disease wreaked havoc on many indigenous groups (Cook 1976).

Indigenous identity had been reformulated inside the missions, so when the few treaties and agreements with the United States were made, they were usually with "mission bands of Indians." These groups bore at best a distant resemblance to precontact traditional lands and collectives. The small size of many of the groups of indigenous peoples who survived this violent incorporation led many observers to believe that California Indians had been effectively eliminated. However, when the autonomy and sovereignty movements arose later in the twentieth century, these "nations" resurrected their struggles and attempted a series of revitalization efforts.

The United States had convinced California to become one of the now-infamous PL 280 states that further subordinated many Indian communities to state interests, although they fought to retain autonomy and recognition as indigenous peoples (Goldberg 1999). Indian gaming became a point of conflict, with key Supreme Court decisions such as *Cabazon* (1986) helping to force the Indian Gaming Regulatory Act through Congress. Many American Indians had been coerced into moving to Los Angeles, partly because of the relocation program during the 1950s and 1960s. This significantly complicated the demographics even more than the changes in the eighteenth and nineteenth centuries.

California Indian nations collectively organized in the 1990s to pass a referendum that would support Indian gaming in the state. This subsequently became passed as Proposition 5 and, later, Proposition 1A. These events were unprecedented. They marked the first time when popular mainstream elections in the United States supported pro-Indian policy in more than 200 years of conflict, resistance, survival, and finally revitalization.

This last stage of incorporation of indigenous peoples in California may well prove to be the most complex. Because a majority of California Indians are "urbanized" they are distant from their traditional homelands, often without protection or recognition. Some California Natives have moved into the middle and even upper middle classes, with political and economic power unknown in earlier decades. Whether this produces more internal conflicts or deeper incorporation into capitalist systems that have historically alienated Native peoples remains to be seen. Even so, most California gaming "tribes" support traditional culture and sovereignty movement in the state and thus clearly see their future as being with indigenous peoples and not only as actors on the world scene.

CONCLUSIONS, REDEFINITIONS, SPECULATIONS, AND QUESTIONS

Even with this brief examination of only a few indigenous groups in the United States it is clear that globalization and resistance to it are old, easily datable to at least 1492 c.e. Though natives often are portrayed as reactive or defensive, these accounts should make clear that many American Indian groups have been proactive in defending themselves from outside encroachments and even genocide. It is equally clear that they have used myriad strategies and tactics and that these have varied widely in effectiveness. The accounts presented here may seem overly successful, in that they are accounts of survivors, groups who in some way or another continue to exist as indigenous peoples. What we think should be equally clear is that Native Americans have had to face many obstacles not of their own making. Many of their problems originated elsewhere.

Although we did not go into detail here, many problems faced by indigenous peoples originated in geopolitics, what are often called "reasons of state." One glaring example is the celebrated Four Corners, where Colorado, New Mexico, Arizona, and Utah meet, which splits the Navajo people into three separate states officially, and unofficially into all four. This division was not driven by a geographical imperative—indeed, it flies in the face of any geographical consideration. Rather, it was driven by the politics of the American Civil War and by considerations of international trade with Asia that made possession and development of California particularly desirable. The discovery of gold sped these processes immensely. Similarly, many problems and conflicts arose because of disputes between local officials, regional officials, and national officials, all of whom used indigenous peoples as pawns.

Thus, one key conclusion is that although indigenous survival and resistance are quintessentially localized, they often are shaped by regional, national, and especially global forces and factors. This has been so for over five centuries. To omit any level of these interactions is to distort and fundamentally misunderstand indigenous survival and resistance. Another conclusion is that simple accounts or explanations of indigenous survival and resistance are all fundamentally flawed. Survival and resistance are complex processes with deep historical roots. Furthermore, these roots are often better remembered in indigenous communities than in the general population.

The situation of indigenous peoples in the United States is special, if not unique. Key among these is the sovereignty issue. That Native Americans have been recognized as separate nations, even if later interpreted as "domestic, dependent nations," has contributed to and shaped their histories profoundly. Likewise, the reservation system—a key consequence of sovereignty—has maintained a territorial home base for many Native Americans. This has been important, not only from conventional points of view of having a home base, but from an indigenous point of view because the connection to the land is vital to identity and spiritual well-being. Sovereignty and a reservation base have allowed many groups to preserve and adapt communal landholdings over time. Conversely, those groups who have either been denied sovereignty (or recognition in BIA terms) and/or reservations have had a more difficult time surviving. Yet as both the Mashpee Wampanoags and some California "Mission Bands of Indians" show, they have survived despite recognition.[31]

The importance of homeland is often lost on the general population of the United States since most citizens are descendants of immigrants, many voluntary, many others not. Whether seeking new opportunities or fleeing harsh conditions, most early U.S. citizens voluntarily severed their roots—with the obvious exception of those individuals forcefully removed from Africa. In short, they gave up, or were forced to give up, their connections to their homelands. The long history of indigenous survival and resistance may equip Native Americans to face the winds of change emanating from forces of globalization better than their fellow citizens who have seldom had to resist such forces.

Another peculiarity in the United States is the way in which Indian "racial" identity has been constructed with the concept of blood quantum, as if culture were something carried by DNA (though to be sure this conceptualization precedes any knowledge of DNA). As many observers have noted, the legal requirement of one-quarter blood (i.e., one grandparent) to qualify as an Indian was and remains an effective strategy for minimizing the number of individuals who meet the formal, federal criteria to be recognized as Native American. Though there was, and remains, considerable variation among Native American groups, holding to the culture and beliefs and practices of a group typically meant far more than accidents of birth. One of the asymmetries of Indian-white relations has been that Indians raised in white communities have almost never been accepted as white, whereas very often non-Indians raised as Indians have often been accepted as Indian, whether they came to live with Indians by accident, by capture, or voluntarily.

Finally, although their special status has allowed use of resources and development of intergovernmental relations for such things as gaming and reduced taxes on some goods, the benefits have been rather limited when viewed across the entire indigenous population of the United States. Certainly, a few groups have prospered greatly, and a few others have at least avoided the direst poverty (Snipp 1988b, 1989, 1992).

Navajo experiences show the many ways that indigenous people can, and do, adopt and adjust to the outside world while maintaining their own traditions, or more precisely have considerable autonomy over how and when their traditions will change. No tradition is frozen in time; they all change. The issue is who will control, or have the major impact on, those changes.

The hard-fought struggles over sovereignty and autonomy still render it difficult to adapt foreign institutions to traditional cultures. Among some Pueblo peoples, forms of theocracy are woven into governance and justice, which often conflict with U.S. traditions of separation of church and state. Select Northwest Coast peoples have used ancient systems of partial and/or temporary banishment to isolated areas for juvenile offenders. Navajo Peacemaker Courts stand out as an example of indigenizing an institution. Interestingly, these courts have drawn considerable interest among other Native Americans and nonindigenous groups as a means of resolving their conflicts—very difficult to do within the adversarial tradition of Anglo-American jurisprudence.

Relative isolation has given the Navajo people time to adjust, and the large size of the Navajo population and reservation has also been an advantage. Indeed, an anthropologist even suggested that the Navajo Nation could become the fifty-first state of the United States (Stucki 1971). In addition to size, Navajos, and Native Americans in general, constitute a large portion of the populations of Arizona and New Mexico, affording a little more electoral clout than is typical for Native Americans in most of the United States. Ownership of valuable resources is something of a mixed bag. On one hand, such ownership is a source of revenue; on the other hand, it can attract strong efforts to exploit those resources by outsiders.

Lakota peoples have similar demographic advantages in North Dakota and especially South Dakota. However, that demographic advantage is undercut by the division of the Lakota into six different reservations, each now considered a "nation" with separate governments, and deep salient racism. Lakotas also have not been able to regain control of their sacred lands, the Black Hills, which are rich in resources. However, in those fights over sovereignty, especially the highly contested 1868 treaty, the Lakota and Cheyenne provided the basis for continued struggle with the United States, as seen in twentieth-century legal battles. Resistance by elder councils and revitalization, as through renewals of the SunDance, give hope and sustenance to many other Indian nations and First Nations to persevere. Finally, Lakota treatment by the U.S. government has probably been influenced by their own history. They are the only nation to have twice defeated U.S. armies in battle, and they provided much later armed resistance to U.S. invasion and conquest. Thus, it is all the more ironic that so many Lakotas have served with distinction in the U.S. military in the twentieth and twenty-first centuries.

Conversely, the demographically small base of various Wampanoag groups and for many California groups may have aided their survival in that they were not seen as a significant threat, either militarily in earlier times or politically in recent decades. As genocide survivors, these Native nations have powerful stories to tell about the expansion of the modern world-system and its contemporary struggles with globalization. To that discussion we now turn.

NOTES

1. The Mashpee Wampanoag won federal recognition as a "tribe" or Indian Nation in 2007, after a decades-long court fight of searing irony on indigenous identity, historical continuity, and collective rights. Also, we note that "formal recognition" by the U.S. Bureau of Indian Affairs is entirely different from internal indigeneity, with self-recognition of their history, traditions, and struggles against a denial by a dominant social group.

2. The Pilgrims, who had been living in Holland after persecution by the English, arrived in what would later be Massachusetts in November 1620 (they were to be dropped off for a fee in Virginia) and took up residence in a deserted village of Patuxet that later became the Plimoth Plantation. (Wampanoag people had earlier died in droves after smallpox was transferred to them by traders and slavers roving the eastern coast.)

3. http://plimoth.org/features/homesite.php, accessed December 11, 2008 (Nancy El-dredge, Linda Coombs).

4. The Mashpee Wampanoag have recently won their federal recognition struggles and have persevered for over forty years in the face of courts and townspeople doubting their very existence. Even so, it was negotiated recognition, in that the Mashpee have had to make agreements with non-Indian townspeople of Mashpee and other local townships and are continuing to wait for the final process: recognition from the U.S. Congress.

5. As late as February 2005, a federal appeals court rejected claims of the Seaconke Wampanoag to land in Rhode Island. Although these people had claims extending back to a 1661 deed from the English Crown, the First Circuit Court of Appeals rulings were based on bureaucratic interpretation of 1978 deadlines giving only six months for "other tribes" to file after a decision recognizing the Narragansett people and their land.

6. This synopsis draws on many accounts of the Lakota and "Sioux" peoples. For more extensive details and references, see Fenelon (1997, 1998) and the references therein.

7. There is extensive literature on social organization of the Dakota, often called the Santee Sioux, and the Lakota, known as the Teton Sioux (Walker 1980, 1982, 1983 [1914]; Wissler 1912; Deloria 1933). DeMallie (1987, 1984) describes Lakotas based on Walker's work (1982).

8. Walker: "The Lakota *taku-kiciyapi* (consider-one-another-kindred), because they are all either *owe* (of-one-blood), or *oweya* (considered-of-blood), with ancestors *oyate unma* (other people).... Lakota divide into seven *otonwepi* (i.e., Teton), and seven *ospayepi* (i.e., Oglala).... Oglala divide into seven *ti-ospayepi* (tipi divisions); each *tiyospaye* is composed of one or more *wico-tipi* [camps], and each camp is composed of two or more *ti-ognakapi* [husbanded tipis].... Thus the strength of the relationship of one Lakota to another is in the following order: 1, *ti-ognaka*; 2, *wico-tipi*; 3, *ti-ospaye*; 4, *ospaye*; 5, *otonwe*" (1914, 97–98).

9. In many of the traditional circles, however, *Dakota* refers to a most common-used dialect, including the *Illahanktowan* (Yanktonai) or the Northern Dakota, just as *Lakota* refers to the so-called L-dialect, used exclusively by the *Titonwan* people, commonly referred to as the Lakota. Complicating matters more is the knowledge that other allied peoples used the Nakota language, or N-dialect (*Hohe* speakers). Since these languages are associated with the so-called middle-Sioux, referring to the region between the easterly Santee-Dakota and westerly Teton-Lakota, the Yanktonai and Yankton often find themselves given status as Nakota people.

10. We use the term *incorporation* in its somewhat modified and expanded world-system sense. For fuller discussion of the entire process, especially as it relates to indigenous peoples, see Hall (1986, 1989b, 2006), Carlson (2001, 2002), Dunaway 1996c, and Hollis (2004, 2005); for the incorporation "phases" of the Lakota, see Fenelon (1998).

11. Violence was, of course, not limited to the Lakota and the northern plains but was common all over the western part of the United States; see Blackhawk 2006.

12. Among some Lakota this ceremony has been called SunDance, with no letter-space, although there is no singular convention. Elsewhere in the U.S. West it is called the SunDance, with a space. See Jorgensen 1972.

13. There are many accounts of this history. One standard history is Anderson 1984.

14. Conventionally, the Lakota are divided into seven major groups—the Oglala, Sicangu (Brule), Miniconjou, Oohenumpa (Two Boils Kettle), Itazipco (Sans Arc or No Bow), Si-hasapa (Blackfeet), and the Hunkpapa—that roughly correspond with the reservations in the Dakotas.

15. Fenelon worked at Standing Rock (Sitting Bull) College in Fort Yates in 1987 when the government tried to get three-fourths of the reservation households to agree to a settle-ment of $440 million to quiet the outstanding Black Hills treaty claim that courts note was

broken egregiously by the U.S. Congress. To the credit of the reservation families, in some of the poorest counties in the United States they could not get even close to the number of signatories, so instead the government put the money "in trust" until the Lakota would accept it. The U.S. representatives cannot or refuse to see that it is a matter of values, not money.

16. "Whereas a meeting of all Sioux Tribes concerned with the 1868 Treaty was called by the Standing Rock Sioux and all elected and traditional leaders were invited.... Be It Resolved, the delegates of the eight Sioux Reservations have unanimously agreed that all land involved in the 1868 Treaty is not for sale, and all monies appropriated for such sale will not be accepted by members of the Traditional people of each reservation."

17. *Navaho* with an "h" is an older spelling of *Navajo* with a "j," which is one official spelling today. The Navajo word for themselves, *Diné* (meaning "the people"), is also often used. The history of the Navajo in the American Southwest is rich and complex. We draw heavily from Gutiérrez 1991, Hall (1989b, 1998b), Kessell 2002, and Weber (1982, 1992). See these works for extended bibliographies.

18. Oñate is viewed as heroic and the founder of New Mexico by many Latino and Chicano activists today, perhaps in their minds as counter to the hegemonic Anglo history of the development of "America." Yet, Puebloan and other Native Americans from the region view Oñate as the first of the Hispanic invaders, especially because of his brutal methods of suppressing indigenous resistance, such as cutting off the feet of military-age men and parading the disabled and sometimes dead results to other Pueblo communities. This makes an excellent example of how different histories can view the same set of events.

19. These mines were the richest in the Western Hemisphere, over their existence producing more silver than the celebrated mines in what became Peru, Bolivia, and Ecuador.

20. For an excellent and detailed account of *los Indios bárbaros* throughout Spanish America see Weber 2005.

21. For contrasting accounts see Hall 1989b, which describes in detail how the various groups we know today were forged over centuries of interaction, and Brooks 2002, which describes in considerable detail how individuals were quite fluid in their affiliations, more significantly how individuals, families, or clans maintained close relationships across putative boundaries—even ones that were generally hostile. The point is that though there are broad patterns, they are all quite flexible and vary widely in specific circumstances. Andrés Reséndez (2005) discusses how the various groups shifted their national identities in response to the U.S. conquest of northern Mexico. His account balances general patterns and detailed differences.

22. Note that the racialized construct of "Indians" allowed invading societies to collapse all the native nations together, for potential elimination, and that *Hispanic* became more of an ethnic signifier than race, allowing for limited assimilation as a "minority" group.

23. Many scholars see the Long Walk as genocidal in scope and nature (Thornton 1987; Stannard 1992). For Navajo accounts of the Long Walk, see Roessel 1973. Bosque Redondo is the area where Navajos were relocated. It was intended to become a permanent reservation, but it was only temporary. Many Navajos think of it as more like a concentration camp.

24. Navajos had practiced weaving before European arrival, but they used various plant fibers. When they obtained sheep, they built on these traditions to make much more durable blankets. These blankets eventually became the "Navajo rug" woven for sale to tourists in the late nineteenth and early twentieth centuries.

25. We note that other groups, notably Comanches, also served as code talkers. However, only Navajos actually developed a separate code within the language, which proved unbreakable. Native Americans have volunteered and served with distinction in the U.S. military in every conflict since World War II.

26. For an account of the rise of Navajo sand painting, and tourist art production generally, see Parezo 1983.

27. Most Navajo healers and spiritual leaders, sometimes called chanters or singers, resist or reject the term *medicine men.* They will not allow the sand paintings they use for spiritual healing purposes to be copied, reproduced, or used outside the specific settings or ceremonies for which they were made. Tourist art sand paintings, when using traditional themes, use only a small part of a much larger design, never the entire design.

28. *Hatathli* is the Navajo word often translated as medicine man, or occasionally as shaman. *Shaman* is a Tanguts (Siberian indigenous people) word for their holy person that anthropologists have made into a generic term for religious specialists in many indigenous societies. Like most other features of indigenous societies, the specialists and their practices are highly varied. Typically they involve spirit possession, but not always, and not for all practitioners. The category *shaman* includes elements of what middle-class U.S. culture would call psychiatry, pharmacy, medicine, priesthood, and theology. Classic sources for Navajo religion are Reichard 1950 and Zolbrod 1984, but we must note that Navajo singers and spiritual leaders still reject the "medicine man" label from mainstream scholars.

29. See National Tribal Justice Resource Center, http://www.tribalresourcecenter.org/personnel/, or the Navajo Nation Peacemaking Program, http://www.navajocourts.org/index5.htm (both accessed December 11, 2008). The operation of these courts is illustrated in the video *Winds of Change: A Matter of Promises,* a PBS documentary (1990).

30. The Navajo Nation has recently authorized establishing a gaming operation on trust land just off its main reservation land base, seeming to be an experimental or transitional activity (2006).

31. The Miami Indians in Indiana have had experiences similar to the Mashpee in struggling for, and so far failing to gain, recognition. Their saga is recounted in Rafert 1996.

RECOMMENDED READINGS

Blackhawk, Ned. 2006. *Violence over the Land: Indians and Empires in the Early American West.* Cambridge, MA: Harvard University Press.
    An account of the northern Southwest with special focus on the relations of Ute and Paiute peoples with European intruders.
Carmean, Kelli. 2002. *Spider Woman Walks This Land: Traditional Cultural Properties and the Navajo Nation.* Walnut Creek, CA: AltaMira Press.
    Examines the meanings of various areas and formations to Navajo culture and shows how they are still an essential part of Navajo culture today.
Deloria, Vine Jr., and David E. Wilkins. 1999. *Tribes, Treaties, and Constitutional Tribulations.* Austin: University of Texas Press.
    Comprehensive, masterful review of the legal underpinnings of tribal sovereignty.
Fenelon, James V. 1998. *Culturicide, Resistance, and Survival of the Lakota ("Sioux Nation").* New York: Garland.
    Comprehensive historiography of the Lakota and development of the Sioux Nation, reservations, and contemporary politics, utilizing some world-systems analysis.
Mario Gonzalez, Mario, and Elizabeth Cook-Lynn. 1998. *The Politics of Hallowed Ground: Wounded Knee and the Struggle for Indian Sovereignty.* Urbana: University of Illinois Press.
    Lakota history with a focus on the 1868 treaty and twentieth-century movements.
Hall, Thomas D. 1989. *Social Change in the Southwest, 1350–1880.* Lawrence: University Press of Kansas.

An account from a world-systems perspective of how various indigenous nations were affected by and resisted assorted European invaders.

Iverson, Peter. 2002. *Diné: A History of the Navajos.* Albuquerque: University of New Mexico Press.

An excellent history of the Navajo.

Kehoe, Alice Beck. 2002. *America Before the European Invasions.* London: Longman.

An account of the land that became the United States before the arrival of Europeans.

Mandell, Daniel R. 1996. *Behind the Frontier: Indians in Eighteenth-Century Eastern Massachusetts.* Lincoln: University of Nebraska Press.

———. 2008. *Tribe, Race, History: Native Americans in Southern New England, 1780–1880.* Baltimore, MD: Johns Hopkins University Press.

Two excellent histories of interactions between indigenous peoples and settlers in New England.

Web Resources

On the Wampanoag and Plimoth Plantation, see http://plimoth.org/features/homesite.php (accessed December 11, 2008).

Sites on Lakota "Sioux" culture and history, http://www.native-languages.org/dakota_culture. htm (accessed December 11, 2008).

California Indians, http://ceres.ca.gov/nahc/califindian.html (accessed December 11, 2008).

Links to all tribes and sites: http://www.kstrom.net/isk/maps/ca/california.html.

You can also look up any reservation by name, such as Standing Rock: http://www. standingrock.org/ (accessed December 11, 2008).

CHAPTER 6

Indigenous Peoples

Global Perspectives and Movements

I N THIS CHAPTER WE MOVE TO A GLOBAL, long-term change perspective of indigenous peoples, with particular focus on social movements arising from resistance and revitalization. We build on both the previous chapters and other work (Hall and Fenelon 2005a, 2005b, 2007, 2008; Fenelon and Hall 2005, 2008). We also build on the arguments and insights of Terry Boswell and Christopher Chase-Dunn (2000) that globalization, especially capitalist globalization, engenders resistance movements, and that both move in reaction to each other in a spiral path. Often what first appears as revolution in a next turn of the spiral appears as reform, and in the following turn becomes "normal" processes. This gloss is far too simplistic, yet there is a general pattern that follows this form. Another key insight of world-systems analysis is the cyclical nature of many of its processes, especially those involving changes in hegemonic control of the system itself (Chase-Dunn and Babones 2006; Hall and Chase-Dunn 2006; Friedman and Chase-Dunn 2005a, 2005b; Chase-Dunn and Anderson 2005; Wallerstein 2004; Boswell and Chase-Dunn 2000; Grimes 2000; Thompson 2000; Chase-Dunn and Hall 1997; Goldstein 1988). These cycles form a larger context within which all sorts of social processes occur, especially those of resistance, reform, and revolution. There are two broad categories of resistance, reform, and revolution: (1) those that occur along the expanding edges of the world-system; and (2) those that occur within the states and territories that make up the world-system. Indigenous peoples have always been involved in the first type, and once incorporated into a world-system they also become involved in the second type. We return to an opening theme that indigenous movements are special in this regard even while sharing some characteristics with other movements.

Specifically, we argue that there is a continuum or range of antisystemic movements. Counterhegemonic movements may, or may not, be counter-systemic, or antisystemic. If the goal of a movement is to eliminate hegemony, it would be antisystemic. If, however, its goal is either to replace a specific hegemon or speed up the hegemonic cycle, then it is not antisystemic, but "reformist." We further argue that the timing, the relative density of such movements, and especially their potential for success or failure are limited by hegemonic cycles that are products of changing international political systems, which are themselves part of globalization processes (Smith and Johnston 2002; Smith and Weist 2006; Smith 2008). We illustrate our argument with eleven cases of indigenous peoples. We suggest that periods of hegemonic transition are particularly dangerous times (Boswell 2004; Kentor 2004), especially for indigenous movements and peoples. Key factors are their levels of sovereignty, autonomy, or minority status, issues we have already discussed.

We begin with four caveats or cautions. The first concerns the issue of cycles. By *cycles* we do not necessarily mean smooth, sinusoidal patterns, but rather repeating patterns of rise and fall, or instability around some equilibrium point. The existence of cycles is evidence that there is a system, no matter how incoherent and/or unstable (see Boswell 1995; Boswell and Chase-Dunn 2000; Grimes 2000; Boswell and Sweat 1991; Goldstein 1988; Thompson 2000). The second caveat revolves around the issue of agency. Structural explanations often seem, but are not necessarily, deterministic. Rather, they sketch the limits of agency and—where sufficiently detailed—the probabilities of effectiveness of human agency. Our third caveat recognizes that all cultures change continually, typically sporadically and unevenly (e.g., Bodley 1988, 1990; Burger 1987; Hill 1996; Sanderson and Alderson 2005; Smith et al. 1988; Sponsel 1995b, 2000b). As we have indicated in previous chapters, many contemporary indigenous movements are part of continuing processes of adaptation to changing environments—ecological and social—and are *not* nostalgic efforts to recapture a golden past. This chapter is more suggestive than definitive. The empirical cases are illustrations, not conclusive evidence. Finally, most of these cases are drawn from the United States, where the rule of law has had, at least recently, more force than many other regions of the world, especially in peripheral or semiperipheral areas such as Central America, parts of Latin America, and Southeast Asia. In those areas, conflicts may be much more violent and vicious. While to some degree suggestive, we present our analysis in terms that render it susceptible to future empirical investigations.

We begin with a brief recap of earlier arguments and discussions.

HOW INDIGENOUS MOVEMENTS ARE DIFFERENT FROM OTHER MOVEMENTS

Our fundamental claim is that survival of indigenous groups, and hence movements intended to promote their survival, are inherently antisystemic because they promote the legitimate right of groups of humans to organize and live their lives in ways other than those permitted or favored by neoliberal capitalism (see McMichael 2003; Sklair 2002; and Robinson 2004 for more elaborate definitions of neoliberalism). As we have seen, they challenge privatization, commodification, conventional gender roles, conventional family organizations, and conventional views and practices of the fundamental relations between human beings and their environment. Nearly all seek to preserve some aspects of ancient ways of living while adapting to contemporary social conditions.

For most indigenous movements—even those that are highly self-conscious and theoretically driven, such as the EZLN—the immediate goal is not to destroy or replace the system but to carve out social space where they can continue to exist. This is what many have called a "war of position" in Gramscian terms (Gills 2000; Morton 2000). Still, such movements constitute fundamental challenges to neoliberal capitalism, even if they are not serious threats to it, because there is no conceptual, political, or social "space" within neoliberalism to allow the continued existence of indigenous groups and their continued autonomy (Fenelon and Hall 2005, 2008; Hall and Fenelon 2008). Yet, that is precisely what is happening on a limited scale, both in terms of resistance movements (especially within core countries that have been forced to accept at least limited sovereignty) and in terms of pure cultural survival (especially within peripheral countries that maintain indigenous peoples in tightly controlled minority status). Hence, these struggles entail political, cultural, and economic struggles over sovereignty, limited autonomy, and a minority status and rights. Furthermore, indigenous struggles are for group rights, including continued existence as groups and at least partial or limited autonomy from all other polities. This is significantly different from human rights struggles that focus almost exclusively on individual rights.

Nearly all other antisystemic, antiglobalization, or antineoliberal movements are directed against the continued growth of the neoliberal project, or seek a better position within the contemporary system, or seek to invert it—though to be sure, some do seek to subvert or overthrow the neoliberal project. To revert to a common metaphor, they seek either a larger slice of the pie or to tinker with the recipe for the pie. Most indigenous movements, in contrast, reject pies in all forms, or try to live outside them. This is why indigenous movements are inherently more fundamental, if not as threatening, than other antiglobalization movements (Fenelon and Hall 2005, 2008; Hall and Fenelon 2008).

Actual movements, of course, demonstrate more nuanced and a much wider range of goals and intentions. This, however, is not new, but has been occurring since states were first invented some 5,000 years ago. Here we recognize that most indigenous groups have disappeared either directly through genocide, or indirectly via absorption into state societies leading to ethnocide and/or culturicide—that is, destruction of their distinct identities, or of their distinctive cultures (Fenelon 1995, 1997, 1998; Hall 1998a). To reiterate our third caveat, those groups that have survived are not static relics of an ancient past but products of complex and frequently intense adaptations that have allowed them to preserve some aspects of their distinctive ways even while adopting and adapting others.

By rethinking movement goals and strategies, we seek to place indigenous movements within a context of movements that are antisystemic, antiglobalization, or seek reform. We hope that such theorizing will facilitate comparisons among different types of movements and ultimately build bridges among movements with shared goals.

CONTINUUM OF MOVEMENT GOALS

Briefly, we describe the contemporary world-system as a globalizing version of late industrial capitalism, intensely pursuing the neoliberal project of a system run entirely by market principles, tempered only by parallel efforts to keep current elites in powerful positions (Bodley 2003; Boswell and Chase-Dunn 2000; Chase-Dunn 1999; Chase-Dunn et al. 2000; Manning 1999; McMichael 2003; Sklair 2002; Robinson 2004).

Many movements are directed against globalization or seek to minimize its effects. Bruce Podobnik (2005) labels these types of globalization movements, since many are not so much oppositional as reformist. Such movements represent a continuum from those that explicitly seek to stop or reverse globalization processes, to those that seek to reform globalization into a "kinder, gentler" global capitalism that gives due consideration to the quality of life of some segment or all of the planet's residents, to movements that pursue other goals, but which either as an indirect consequence or a secondary goal reject some part of contemporary neoliberal globalization. Examples of the first include overt global social democratic movements like those described by Boswell and Chase-Dunn (2000). In the middle range are movements that seek to reform globalization processes, such as those pursued by Ralph Nader, and a number of other "Green" movements. The indirect globalization movements include those directed at preserving this or that piece of land in a "natural" condition, those advocating larger shares of worker control of working conditions, and, of course, most indigenous movements that seek rights to continued group existence and as least partial autonomy from all other polities.

No doubt, this range of movements could be arrayed in other ways (see Gills 2000; Bennholdt-Thomsen et al. 2001; Smith and Johnston 2002; Smith and Weist 2006; and Smith 2008). We posit this continuum as a heuristic device for sorting a wide range of movements.[1] We also note that movements may shift rapidly, or even be placed at two points on the continuum simultaneously. This is especially the case for the often shaky alliances, sometimes sympathetic and occasionally hostile, between indigenous movements and green movements (e.g., Gedicks 1993, 2001; Sponsel 1995a, 1995b, 2000a, 2000b). Clearly, too, many movements transform themselves in the course of their activities, exemplified in the Zapatistas.

CYCLES, HEGEMONY, AND MOVEMENTS

One of the more frustrating experiences in examining indigenous movements is that there is no ready correspondence among various world-systemic cycles, especially hegemony and K-waves, and vagaries of policy toward indigenous peoples in the United States. Table 6.1 summarizes various approaches to these cycles by several researchers (Boswell 1995; Boswell and Chase-Dunn 2000; Cornell 1988). Because many factors impinge on policy toward indigenous populations, any underlying regularities are masked. However, there appears to be a counterpoint between pressures for assimilation and policies toward indigenous peoples. Albert Bergesen's work on hegemonic decline (2000) suggests that a general decline of an authoritative approach to cultural norms opens space for a variety of identities to emerge. This opens social space for movements that reassert formerly submerged or suppressed identities and for assorted new identities.

Shortly after the United States closed immigration after World War I, the Indian Citizenship Act (1924) granted citizenship to all American Indians. By then many Native Americans had already gained citizenship through allotment or other avenues. The Merriam Report (1928) was one of many factors behind the Indian Reorganization Act (1934) that moved the government toward increased self-determination for indigenous populations. The aftermath of World War II gave rise to both the Indian Claims Commission (1946), which sought to finalize all land claims, and the move for termination in the 1950s, which sought to eliminate the special status of American Indians (Valandra 2006). In the late 1960s and early 1970s there was a strong move back to Indian self-determination (Cornell 1988; Wilkins 2006). These changes are shown in the penultimate column in Table 6.1. Comparison of these policy changes with the hegemonic cycle, or with the U.S. world-system position (last column of Table 6.1), yields no neat correspondence between these policy shifts and either K-wave phase or hegemonic phase. Why this is so remains an open question, though we suspect that it is due to the counteracting effects of a changing U.S. world-system position, its hegemonic phase (once in the core), and the vagaries of internal ethnic politics in the United States.

However, the last move toward self-determination was fueled by what might be called *contagion effects* from other civil rights movements, the rise of activism generally, and the legacies of the boarding school movements and relocation programs that accompanied termination. The allotment era (ca. 1887 through 1934) was marked by extensive use of boarding schools that forced American Indians to learn English and to adopt or at least partially adapt to American mainstream culture—itself a changing entity. Because boarding schools mixed children from various Indian nations and taught them English, they created several cohorts of Indians who were able to see and act upon similarities in their relations with the U.S. government. Similarly, the relocation programs in the 1950s brought many Indian individuals and families from reservations to large cities. They shared urban experiences and were able to observe various civil rights struggles closely.

Table 6.1 K-Waves, Hegemony, Leading Sectors, and Indigenous Relations

K-Wave Phase	Hegemonic Phase[1]	Leading Sector/ Innovation	Geographic Concentration	World Leaders/ Hegemonies	Cornell Phase[2]	U.S. World-Systems Position
1496 B	1492 A	Direct Spice Trade	Portugal			Peripheral
1509 A	1519 V	Explorers	Portugal			Peripheral
1529 B	1526 M	American Silver	Spain/Portugal	Portugal 1517–1541		Peripheral
1539A		Colonial Conquest	Spain/Portugal	Hapsburgs 1526–1556		Peripheral
1559 B	1556 D	Baltic Trade	Low Countries	(Spain 1594–1597)	Market	Peripheral
1575 A	1575 A	Fluyt Ships	Low Countries	(Spain 1594–1597)	Market	Peripheral
1595 B	1609 V	Asian Trade	Netherlands	United Netherlands 1609–1635	Market	Peripheral
1621 A	1621 M	East India Company	Netherlands	United Netherlands 1648–1667	Market	Peripheral
1650 B	1655 D	Atlantic Trade	American Colonies		Market	Peripheral
1689 A	1667 C	Slave Plantations	American Colonies		Market	Peripheral
1720 B		Colonial Trades	English Colonies	United Kingdom 1715–1739	Market	Peripheral
1747 A		Colonial Expansion	English Colonies	United Kingdom 1715–1739	Market	Peripheral
1762 B		Cotton Textiles	United Kingdom		Market	Peripheral
1790 A	1789 A	Industrialization	France		Conflict	Peripheral
1814 B	1815 V	Railroads	United Kingdom	United Kingdom 1816–1849	Conflict	Semiperipheral

table continues on next page

Table 6.1 (continued)

K-Wave Phase	Hegemonic Phase[1]	Leading Sector/ Innovation	Geographic Concentration	World Leaders/ Hegemonies	Cornell Phase[2]	U.S. World-Systems Position
1848 A	1850 M	Wage/Factory System	United Kingdom	United Kingdom 1850–1873	Conflict	Semiperipheral
1872 B	1873 D	Steel, Chemicals	United States (Germany)		Reservation	Semiperipheral
1893 A	1897 A	Mass Production	United States (Germany)		Reservation	Semiperipheral
1917 B	1918 V	Autos, Air, Electric	United States	United States 1945–1974	Reservation	Core
1940 A	1945 M	Multicorporation	United States	United States 1945–1974	IRA	Core
1968 B	1974 D	Information, Flexible Specialization	Japan/United States		Termination	Core
1990s A?		Information, Flexible Specialization	Japan/United States		Self-Determiniation	Core
			United States			

Source: Based on table 1, p. 39, in Boswell and Chase-Dunn 2000.
K-wave phase: B = stagnation period; A = expansion period

A = ascent
V = victory
M = maturity
D = decline
C = competitive

Notes: 1. From Boswell 1995, Table 2. 2. From Cornell 1988, 14.

Joane Nagel (1996) analyzes how these conditions helped foment several different movements and to some extent reshaped American Indian identities. One interesting effect was that many people who were either Native American or had some Native American ancestry and who has "passed" as white reasserted their native heritage. This led to what at first was a puzzling jump in U.S. Census figures for the Native American population that exceeded biological growth (see Nagel 1996; Liebler 2004).

In both Canada and the United States, native peoples have been able to use the legal systems to support movements, but often at the price of accepting the principles of those systems (Biolsi 1995, 2001; Wilkins 2006). Movements have often been accompanied or supported by extralegal actions, including the occupation of Alcatraz (1969), the trail of broken treaties march and the occupation of the BIA in the early 1970s, and the takeover of Wounded Knee in 1973. More recently there have been the various legal battles surrounding Indian gaming in the United States (Fenelon 2000, 2002) and the founding of Nunavut in Canada (2000). But in peripheral areas and the global south, movements have not met with the same degree of success. Al Gedicks (2001) argues that these legal avenues have helped core indigenous populations resist encroachment somewhat more successfully than peripheral indigenous peoples. Yet, both sets of indigenous peoples have cooperated with each other, and indigenous activists from peripheral areas have come to the United States to work with American sympathizers in various stockholder and legal moves against U.S.-based corporations (Gedicks 2001).

Indeed, it is these latter alliances and actions that suggest the nature of the "game" is changing, due in no small part to increased global communications. The role of the Internet in mobilizing defense for the Zapatistas and the EZLN is well known, but as Gedicks (2001) documents, this is truly a global phenomenon that is making links with other globalization movements. This raises the question of whether this new situation is an opportunity for new forms of resistance or a dangerous time where past gains might be endangered.

To answer this question it is necessary to review some of the indigenous movements that have succeeded, and some that have failed, with an eye to the world-systemic, contextual circumstances that contributed to their success or failure. Furthermore, it is necessary to critique Stephen Cornell's (1988) analysis in two important ways. First, different Indian nations or indigenous groups within the United States (or its colonial predecessors) actually experienced incorporation, conquest, domination, and policy periods at different times in different regions and in ways that varied with the processes of colonial and U.S. expansion. Second, indigenous peoples (who rarely receive recognition as "nations") in semiperipheral or peripheral regions of the Americas (Central and South America) have experienced quite different relations within their developing states and in relation to their hegemonic cycles.[2]

Immanuel Wallerstein (2004) has pointed to a strong reliance by global capitalism on the interstate system and its multitude of connections to military-political networks (Chase-Dunn et al. 2005) that prop up and enforce economic systems and domination. Indigenous peoples represent an alternative to capitalist accumulation (we pointedly do not mean Marx's primitive communism, but a literal and real distributive political economy) that by its very nature poses a perplexing problem if not a fundamental challenge to formal state sovereignty.

The United States has the most well-developed and codified relationship with its indigenous peoples, with Canada following closely. Some analysts argue that Canada has surpassed the United States by recognizing the oral tradition of its "First Nations" (Perry 1996). Although nearly all colonial systems conducted forms of genocide well into the nineteenth century, most did not develop treaty-based legal systems. Central and South America incorporated native peoples into systems of racial subordination, segregation, and partial assimilation as minority groups.

States have used two key concepts to justify expansion over the Western Hemisphere: the Doctrine of Discovery and the Prince's Rights to Conquest (Deloria and Lytle 1984; Wilkins 1997, 2002; Fenelon 1997; Deloria and Wilkins 1999). The first colonial relationships were with strong native nations. They were predicated on treaties and various "nonintercourse" acts, meant to contain and control indigenous peoples within one state in the expanding world-system. In the United States such relationships became known as "tribal sovereignty" for surviving indigenous peoples.

This relationship evolved into a complex set of "dual sovereignty" relationships (Fenelon 2002): federal sovereignty was supreme, followed by the sovereignty of the original thirteen and later fifty individual states making up the United States, and the contested tribal sovereignties. The new states in the Western Hemisphere assumed they could extinguish claims to tribal sovereignty at a later date (Champagne et al. 2005; Champagne 2007). Generally, that did not happen. Over time, indigenous resistance to domination has taken on many forms, shaped in part by hegemonic cycles in the world-system.

We illustrate this in Box 6.1. A few key concerns arise in the relationships among the legacy of systemic domination, individual sociopolitical statuses (tribe/nation), and contemporary sociopolitical position in the world-system:

- Presence or absence of sovereignty claims by indigenous peoples and recognition by states within existing hegemonic systems;
- Nature of any autonomous relations over political, economic, and cultural realms of social life, again with states and hegemonic systems; and
- Status as "minority" peoples relative to cultural domination and claims to differential treatment, again within states and hegemonic systems.

The effects of hegemonic cycles in core areas are different from those in peripheral areas. They are mediated through processes of nationalism and nation-building and are also part of a larger shift from tributary world-systems to an increasingly global capitalist world-system. Survival is also highly problematic, especially in the contemporary world-system (Hall 1987; Carlson 2001).

**Box 6.1 Levels and Types of Indigenous Survival
Within Hegemonic Nation-State Systems**

Sovereignty Recognized Level 1—SR

Political—systems recognized by nation-state and even by hegemonic regimes

Economic—limited or in some cases full control over internal institutions

Cultural—intact or assimilated, no longer under strict cultural domination

Sovereignty Contested Level 2—SC

Political—quasi- or no recognition by nation-state or by hegemonic regimes

Economic—trade and land tenure contested externally, internally controlled

Cultural—assimilated or hidden, under legalized cultural domination (policies)

Autonomy Bounded Level 3—AB

Political—boundaries noted internally by nation-state or by hegemonic regimes

Economic—all trade and land tenure under external controls, contested internally

Cultural—segregated, assimilated, or secreted, legalized cultural domination

Autonomy Contested Level 4—AC

Political—boundaries shaped and penetrated by nation-state/hegemonic regimes

Economic—trade, land tenure, and property under external and internal controls

Cultural—segregated, assimilated, suppressed, or secreted, cultural domination

Minority Status Defined Level 5—MD

Political—no boundaries, relations defined by nation-state/hegemonic regimes

Economic—trade, land tenure, and property under total dominant group policies

Cultural—dominated, suppressed, or secreted (language policy, group property)

Minority Status Subsumed Level 6—MS

Political—no separate legal status, as defined by nation-state/hegemonic regimes

Economic—trade, land tenure, property dominated by elites and nation-state law

Cultural—distorted, suppressed, or secreted (discriminatory systems encouraged)

In Table 6.2 we identify eleven indigenous peoples from the Western Hemisphere and suggest levels of domination, current status, and world-system position. We argue that these cases represent the legacy of systematic domination and resulting sociopolitical status of colonized and conquered societies. These historical and contemporary sociopolitical positions in the world-system are connected to hegemonic decline, as will be discussed.

The Mohawk in Canada, referred to now as a "First Nation," were relegated to a subsumed and segregated reserve status following the U.S. policy treatment, until the 1980s, when the Canadian courts and political processes gave more credence to both historical treaty rights and contemporary laws concerning a separate sovereignty. During their 300–400 years of cultural domination, they have experienced the full range of relationships, including exchange of gunfire with the military as late as the 1990s at Oka. The Mohawk exist under different laws but similar status on both sides of the U.S.-Canada border, and thus make a fascinating case of transnational historical ethnicity divided by artificial political borders imposed on them by the dominant groups.

The Lakota (Sioux nations) represent about 200 years of conflicts ranging from war, regionally until 1890 and on a smaller scale well into the 1970s, and formal treaty-making with the United States in spectacular negotiations clearly and primarily revolving around claims to sovereignty and control over land (Valandra 2006). The Lakota were forcefully broken up into six different reservation groups only roughly conforming to tribal relationships, without recognition of the 1868 treaty lands or rights until recent antihegemonic social movements brought these agreements, broken only by the United States on multiple occasions, back to the table and to the courts.

The Cherokee were militarily removed under genocidal conditions by the U.S. military, orchestrated by President Andrew Jackson in direct opposition to Supreme Court rulings and all legal and moral constraints of the time in respect to the Five Civilized Tribes, forcing what many analysts believe is the single best example of a constitutional crisis, in that all three sovereigns were in play—federal, tribal, state—and all three divisions of the U.S. government were at odds, with raw power to remove Indian peoples winning out. The primary result was the United States ignored its manufactured crisis over sovereignty, mainly for the purposes of expanding its realm of control and limiting Indian country.

The Puyallup make another good example of what started out as another treaty-tribe, essentially over the environs of what is now Tacoma, Washington. Although they were believed to have been driven out of existence, the Puyallup made a stunning comeback in the late twentieth century to reclaim portions, albeit small, of their earlier claims. The Pequot make an even more compelling story: thought to have been eliminated for over 300 years, before the creation of the United States, they now receive formal recognition partially by congressional fiat and have built a legal anomaly into a stunning economic success through Indian gaming, based entirely on sovereignty. Wampanoag peoples represent the flip side of that

Table 6.2 Eleven Indigenous Societies in Comparative World-Systems Analysis

Society, People, or "Nation"	Legacy of Systematic Domination	Sociopolitical Statuses (i.e., tribe/nation)	Historical and Contemporary Sociopolitical Position in the World System (connected to hegemonic system decline)
Mohawk [U.S.] (Canada)	Treaty—U.S. British Colonial Reserve – FN	Segregated Canada (U.S.) reserves	First Nations sovereignty claim in Canada, internal semiperipheral status, mixed self-determination controlled by state structure
Lakota [regional] (Dakotas)	Treaty—U.S. Int.-Colony Reservation	Reservations (separated) 6 tribe/nation	Indian tribal sovereignty in the U.S., treaty-based claims with self-determination, state-controlled internal semiperiphery
Cherokee [removal] (U.S.-SE)	Treaty—U.S. Relocation Reservations	Spatial tribe segregation 2 tribe/nation	Indian tribal sovereignty in the U.S., self-determination, state-controlled internal colonial, assimilated semi-periphery
Puyallup [urban] (U.S.-NW)	Int.-Colony Treaty with U.S.	Reservations (separated) tribe/nation	U.S. tribal sovereignty, with some treaties, current self-determination, state-controlled, internal assimilation as "minority"
Pequot Wampanoag (U.S.-NE)	Genocide, dependence after U.S.	Reservations (separated) tribe/nation	U.S. tribal sovereignty, lost and recognized, current self-determination, state-controlled, assimilated as "minority" special legal claim

table continues on next page

Table 6.2 (continued)

Yaqui Tarahumara (U.S.-SW)	Colonizing Int.-Colony Mexico/U.S.	Yaqui-U.S. "tribe" status unclear in Mexico	U.S. tribal sovereignty, some later treaties, Mexico *ejido* system, all state-controlled, nonassimilation and "minority" status
Mayan [Guatemala] (in Chiapas)	Colonial, I.C. genocidal, conquests	Suppressed rural groups w/o legality	Subordinated status with little recognition, revolutionary struggle in Chiapas gaining limited autonomy
Miskito [Honduras] (Nicaragua)	Int.-Colonial conquest by colonizing	Recently won autonomous status—legal	Subordinated "minority" recently winning limited autonomy under armed struggle, socioeconomic inclusion as internal colony
Yanomami [Brazil] (Venezuela)	"Genocidal" Int.-Colony current	Separated territory, few protections	Recent conflicts mediated by state controls, Brazil genocidal, Venezuela limited "tribal" protections, isolated territories
Quechuan Ecuador (Peruvian)	Colonial long-term, Int.-colonial	Suppressed minority populations	Dispersed broadly based general population, recent separatist movements increasingly mediated by state structures
Hawaiian Native	Conquered neo-state, Int.-colonial	Suppressed minority, factionalized	Submerged "minority" assimilation, recently reinvigorated indigenous sovereignty, treaty-like claims, U.S. constitutional law

story, from once-great nations first supporting and then warring with English colonists, who obtained only a limited, partial recognition through the court system, with nominal sovereignty, until the most recent court decisions granted them recognition (see Mandell 1996, 2008 for further details).

The Yaqui complete the U.S. examples. Straddling the border with Mexico, and sometimes warring with both countries, the Yaqui ultimately received recognition, having grown substantially in the past two decades in terms of their territorial claim. Mexico, although historically an assimilative nation toward indigenous peoples, treated most of its "Indians" with segregated and discriminatory repression, existent today. Tarahumara peoples, with difficult relationships with the *ejido* system of land tenure, represent state control over these autonomously bounded peoples.

Mayan-descent peoples in Chiapas exhibit both armed and sociopolitical resistance to globalization. They argue that their struggle has been for "500 years" and is against transnational capitalism, hemispheric hegemony, and the repression of the peasant Indian for economic profits. Revolutionary struggle has linked with indigenous resistance that has percolated over hundreds of years under various regimes and economic domination, again primarily with sovereignty and claims to the land as its basis. Legal, socioeconomic, and cultural factors driving indigenous mountain peoples to take up arms are perfectly representative of how world-systems affect microeconomic relations, especially when hegemonic decline changes their positions and the activities of dominating elites.

The Miskito in Nicaragua perversely prove these contentions in reverse. There, a socialist-armed revolutionary government tried to impose modernized conditions, boundaries, and forced removal, albeit not truly capitalist (for instance, see Harff and Gurr 2004). The Sandinistas were, no doubt, responding to hegemonic forces that attempted to employ Miskito people in Honduras to support the Contras. However, the central concerns were against incursions over a limited but existing sovereignty, or in the Miskito case, "autonomy" over their lands and sociopolitical life. Whereas the capitalist system tends to be more invasive to both cultural and political forms of autonomy, socialist systems also seek exclusive sovereignty—including over indigenous peoples, prompting resistance to domination. These patterns become more apparent when hegemonic systems are in decline.

Yanomami people are found in both Venezuela and Brazil, facing an artificially imposed state political border. They were subject to genocidal internal colonialism in Brazil. Venezuela, in contrast, has developed reserve areas, similar to North American patterns, with limited protections but a still invasive market economy with trading posts and timber companies. Gold mines and mineral companies operate freely in Brazilian economic expansion, peripheralizing Yanomami land where they cannot even be a minority group. Hegemonic decline seems to hasten these activities and puts reserved lands and laws in Venezuela into contention, again over forms of sovereignty or limited autonomy.

Quechuan people in Ecuador, and in a more complicated set of relationships in Peru, maintain a sizable demographic presence that at times must be taken into consideration—for example, in the recent elections followed by a near military coup, indigenous groups were key to swinging political parties behind one side or another. However, once the immediate objective, always associated with political machinations connected in some manner or form with natural resource extraction, has been achieved, defeated, or no longer matters, the Quechuan peoples are subsumed into the general population again. Separatist movements, as in Peru, Venezuela, and Colombia, attempt to make short-lived coalitions similar to the dominant groups.

Last, we consider Native Hawaiians, who have achieved limited sovereignty through the practice of legal and political recognition. In this case, we also observe states ensconced in the international system of trade believing they are forced to recognize minority separatist groups with documented claims, such as a treaty or formal agreement. Ironically, core countries such as the United States find themselves no longer able to forcefully eliminate or assimilate indigenous peoples undergoing incorporation processes; instead they enter into negotiations that abide by previous contractual or treaty-like rules, similar to the contracts of international trade and economic development.

What remains to be sorted out is how these patterns are shaped and affected by changes in the hegemonic cycle. A key component to this survival is degree of autonomy or sovereignty. As we noted earlier and in Box 6.1, sovereignty is a complex legal-political relationship.

When systems are in hegemonic decline, there are opportunities to take the aforementioned relationships and change them—either through force or political maneuvering—into new political relationships more advantageous to indigenous peoples. However, states may also contract and respond with greater oppression toward indigenous peoples if they threaten the existing status quo, or simply in an attempt to consolidate those parts of their society under their total control. When indigenous peoples straddle borders, these issues become more acute, depending on the particular states involved and the relative strength of the region. Thus, hegemonic decline provides *both* potential opportunities and sometimes grave threats for indigenous groups.

In Box 6.1 we identify six levels of indigenous survival with respect to sovereignty, autonomy, and a minority status. Box 6.1 further analyzes three distinct social spheres of domination—political, economic, and cultural. Levels 1 and 2, sovereignty formally recognized or at least legally contested, seem to offer the greatest opportunity during times of hegemonic decline, with some caveats. The primary caution is that core states or their close affiliates benefit from the international system of trade and economic dominance. Another caution seems to be that existing treaties or legal documents can be put into play. The Mohawk, Lakota, Cherokee, Puyallup, Pequot, perhaps Yaqui, and Native Hawaiian cases appear to be operating in all three spheres on these levels.

Levels 3 and 4, with autonomy in two or more of the social spheres bounded, or at least undergoing formal contestation, are both fraught with peril and loaded with opportunity. These peoples are much more likely to be involved in an armed struggle, with assets such as land and mineral rights, or labor and trade rights, being determined by a struggle characterized by extreme domination often contradicting the mores of the society itself. Levels of development and position in the global economy of the particular state also seem to have an effect. Poorer countries are much more likely to employ military forces against their indigenous peoples. The Mayan and the Miskito cases are examples.

Because a "minority status" is dependent on the dominant policies of the state, levels 5 and 6 hold the most dangerous possibilities for indigenous groups, unless they can engineer movement to the higher levels by gaining some form of autonomy or even limited sovereignty. Being forced into an oppressive minority status was a common feature in the European expansion throughout the Western Hemisphere, but currently less developed or poorer countries are most likely to oppress their indigenous peoples through such definition or complete subordination of political, economic, and cultural rights. The Yanomami and Quechuan are examples in such highly vulnerable positions.

This brief discussion suggests that the consequences of degree of sovereignty can differ in political, economic, and cultural spheres. These three areas overlap and interact. We further question whether and to what degree various effects are different in core, peripheral, or semiperipheral regions. Though it will take further research to confirm this, we suggest that core states have developed highly codified laws relative to the interstate system that they must acknowledge on some level or another.[3] They are thus more likely to offer recognition of some form of autonomy or of sovereignty. In peripheral states the reverse appears to be the case. Indeed, extralegal and state violence (direct or indirect) are much more common in peripheral states.

Although the evidence is far from clear, it suggests that a global historical survey will be necessary to tease out the nuances of the relations among indigenous survival, indigenous movements, hegemony, and world-system position. We suspect that these relations are quite sensitive to world-system time. That is, location in a declining hegemon in the late eighteenth century is very different from location in a declining hegemon in the late twentieth or early twenty-first century. Some First Nations, such as the Mohawk of the Haudenosaunee as represented in the flag shown in Plate 6.1, have survived, resisted, and revitalized in both these hegemonic systems.

With all these suggestive findings, we draw some provisional conclusions.

DISCUSSION AND CONCLUSIONS

A key issue is the maintenance, or not, of sovereignty. Once a group has become a minority group with no special legal status, it is well on its way to full absorption into the dominant state. Movements among such groups are almost always of the "bigger piece of the pie" type. Where any degree of sovereignty is maintained, there is room, or social space, for stronger movements that reject some or all of

Plate 6.1. Flag representing the traditional Mohawk and Haudenosaunee (Iroquoian) Confederacy, thus modern cultural sovereignty, outside Oka, Quebec, Canada. (Photo courtesy of James V. Fenelon)

the larger system. These movements are more typically of "change the recipe for the pie" or "reject the pie outright" type.

Furthermore, we argue there is an important distinction between movements that are overtly and clearly antisystemic (as are many leftist movements) versus others, like indigenous movements, and many fundamentalisms, which have some other primary goal but carry an important "secondary" agenda of being antisystemic. Finally, we argue that the potential for success of such movements, and conversely the potential for being crushed, varies with the hegemonic cycle, but in complex ways. As we suggested earlier, location in a core, as opposed to peripheral, region shapes these processes in important ways. These results are a matter of motivation and interpretations, with all sides "spinning" what all others are saying or trying to do.

These kinds of differences make for the very messy politics of movements that sometimes form alliances and sometimes are at each other's throats, such as the uneasy alliances and occasional hostilities between indigenist movements and green movements (see Gedicks 2001). Yet, indigenist movements are fundamentally antisystemic, and probably more so than many—but far from all—green movements because they advocate a right to maintain a different form of social life that is inherently antisystemic. It also appears that as some indigenous peoples become more fully incorporated in core countries, with or without autonomy, they become less antisystemic and more reformative or transformative.

When hegemony is either weak or strong, such movements have a better chance of success, but for different reasons. When hegemony is weak, states cannot afford the resources, the political capital, or the moral standing needed to crush them. When hegemony is strong, the state often has "bigger fish to fry" and finds it not worth the effort to crush the movements; it can occasionally gain moral standing by "tolerating" them or using "kinder, gentler" ways to deter them. The termination movement in the 1950s and 1960s in the United States might be such an instance—"getting rid of Indians by converting them into minorities." But it did not work. Furthermore, by the time the U.S. state figured out that it was not working, the government had moved into hegemonic decline and it became too expensive to crush the movements, as Indians gained favor with the U.S. public through the publicity surrounding the occupation of Alcatraz, the Trail of Broken Treaties, and the siege at Wounded Knee (Nagel 1996). Furthermore, more oppression was less of an option precisely because of involvement in, if not leadership of, a still somewhat hegemonic state in a globalized system.

Times of changing hegemony, whether rapid or slow, however, are indeed dangerous times. Even while the various activities of the late 1960s and early 1970s were gaining press coverage and popular support, the U.S. government did mount serious efforts against rebellious minorities, like the Black Panthers, and the American Indian Movement via COINTELPRO efforts (Churchill and Vander Wall 1988). The most notorious example was on the Pine Ridge (Oglala) Lakota Reservation in South Dakota, which became a veritable zone of low-intensity conflict, with over sixty unsolved murders, including the ones that led to the incarceration of Leonard Peltier (Churchill 1996, 231–270). Similar, if less intense, repression occurred elsewhere in the United States, but as we have noted, much more violence occurs elsewhere, especially in peripheral and semiperipheral states. Indeed, another goal for future research is to verify this empirically and develop some measures of the differences in degree of violence.

Clearly, these results are still preliminary. However, we argue that even this evidence is compelling in terms of showing a need for further research on indigenous movements and their roles in changes in the world-system, specifically in terms of survival and revitalization. It is not a matter of "political correctness" nor of legitimate concern for wrongs done to others, though these are vital concerns, but it is also a matter of a full understanding of antiglobalization movements and the impacts of changes in hegemony.

We now turn to some general conclusions, suggest directions for future empirical research, speculate on what that research might show, note recent struggles that illustrate our discussion, and try to tease out some of the implications of these possibilities for future struggles for indigenous survival.

NOTES

1. In the conceptionalization presented here both Transnational Social Movements (TSMs) and the New Social Movements (NSMs) would fit in portions of this continuum toward the "seek to stop or reverse globalization processes" region. Thus, our conceptionalization of the range of types of movements is broader than those reviewed in Chapter 4.

2. Weber 2005 provides an overview of Spanish dealings with nonsedentary indigenous populations. His account reveals broad similarities embedded within myriad local particulars.

3. See the UN's Permanent Forum on Indigenous Issues, http://www.un.org/issues/m-indig.html, accessed December 11, 2008. See also Biolsi 1995, 2001. China poses an intriguing

and relevant case with this analysis, not only in the numerous examples in southern regions, but also in its clear attempt to force Tibetan peoples out of autonomous relationships and into minority status.

RECOMMENDED READINGS

Gedicks, Al. 2001. *Resource Rebels: Native Challenges to Mining and Oil Corporations.* Cambridge, MA: South End Press.

A global survey of indigenous movements with much information of their complicated relationships with green movements.

Nabokov, Peter. 2002. *A Forest of Time: American Indian Ways of History.,* Cambridge, UK: Cambridge University Press.

A comprehensive historical perspective with an indigenous point of view of history.

Nagel, Joane. 1996. *American Indian Ethnic Renewal: Red Power and the Resurgence of Identity and Culture.* Oxford, UK: Oxford University Press.

An empirical study of movements in the United States, with a comprehensive discussion of changing concepts of identity in the social sciences and among U.S. native peoples.

Weber, David J. 2005. *Bárbaros: Spaniards and Their Savages in the Age of Enlightenment.* New Haven, CT: Yale University Press.

A thorough overview of how Spanish rulers treated natives they saw as uncivilized.

Web Resources

Contemporary issues from activist perspectives: http://indianz.com/ (accessed December 11, 2008).

H-Amindian list serve of and by historians who study Native peoples in the United States, http://www.asu.edu/clas/asuhistory/h-amindian/index.html?q=h-amindian/index.html.

Indian Country Today (leading national newspaper on American Indians), http://indiancountry.com.

United Nations Permanent Forum on Indigenous Issues, http://www.un.org/issues/m-indig.html (accessed December 11, 2008).

CHAPTER 7

Conclusions

Indigenous Peoples, Globalization, and Future Prospects

O N SEPTEMBER 13, 2007, the United Nations General Assembly voted to adopt the Declaration on the Rights of Indigenous Peoples.[1] This landmark legislation, in active turmoil for three decades, acknowledges self-determination and autonomous relationships of indigenous peoples as separate communities with the right to organize their own governance, relationship to the land, economic practices, and sense of identity and membership, as we have written about here. Only four countries voted against it: the United States, Canada, New Zealand, and Australia. Interestingly, each of these countries has at least somewhat of a treaty-basis with indigenous peoples, has a strong and violent history of colonization by the English during the expansion out of Europe into the modern world-system that we describe here, and is deeply ensconced in the hegemonic forces of globalization that have proven to be the enemy of indigenous peoples. In addition, each country claims to be under laws that respect its citizenry and their cultural origins. We argue that understanding how these states resist a recognition of indigenous nations and peoples is perfectly exemplary of the issues we have discussed in this book.[2]

John C. Mohawk (1955–2006) captured the essence of these struggles when observing, during that initial presentation to the United Nations in 1977, that

[the] Haudenosaunee position is derived from a philosophy which sees The People with historical roots which extend back tens of thousands of years. It is a geological kind of perspective, which sees modern man as an infant, occupying a very short

139

space of time in an incredibly long spectrum. It is the perspective of the oldest elder looking into the affairs of a young child and seeing that he is committing incredibly destructive folly. It is, in short, the statement of a people who are ageless but who trace their history as a people to the very beginning of time. And they are speaking, in this instance, to a world which dates its existence from a little over 500 years ago, and perhaps, in many cases, much more recently than that. (Mohawk 2007)[3]

These Haudenosaunee (Iroquois) representatives, in our parlance people's spokespersons, captured both an indigenous perspective of resistance and revitalization and aspects of a world-system focus over long periods of time. Oren Lyons, Onondaga faithkeeper and Haudenosaunee delegate in 1977, asked, "After all, we are peoples, are we not?" He wrote that they were indeed peoples "in the full international sense of the word," and that held significance for "the millions of indigenous for whom this declaration begins a new era of recognition," in that "we are and have always been peoples 'in the eyes of the Creator'" (Lyons 2007).[4]

The Onondaga had been crushed by General George Washington's forces in the Revolutionary War and again by U.S. forces years later, as the Mohawk found themselves on both sides during wars that established the border drawn between Canada and the United States of America. However, it is not merely a denial of these histories that has led both of these countries to negate the Declaration on the Rights of Indigenous Peoples, but very real contemporary struggles to retain and practice sovereignty, and over the natural resources and territorial integrity of the land base that was once the Haudenosaunee (Iroquois) confederated lands. Roadblocks have been set up in New York State when the government tried to illegally tax the reservation businesses there, along with periodic violence around gaming casinos, when land tenure was questioned. More ominously, there have been direct military fights between various Mohawk nations in Canada over Kanehsata:ke lands and sovereignty, especially at a shooting standoff at Oka in 1990. Linkage of the Mohawk (Kanehsata:ke) and Iroquois conflicts with other indigenous nations is represented in Plate 7.1 shows a sign just outside Oka, Canada. These struggles are linked to oil leases in the north, timber operations, and treaty rights of First Nations. As in the struggles we have discussed in this book, this revitalization and resistance has taken many forms that are connected to the broader global issues documented in the Declaration on the Rights of Indigenous Peoples.

We have argued that the struggles of indigenous peoples fall into three broad analytical categories—over sovereignty, as with First Nations in Canada or native nations in the United States; over autonomy, as with the Mayan-descent Zapatistas in Mexico, Miskito in Nicaragua, Kurds in Iraq, or recent Aymara developments in Bolivia; and minority group status, as with the Adevasi peoples in India, most *pueblos indigenas* in Latin America, the Zulu "tribals" in South Africa, and Indigenous Australians. There are many exceptions and variations to this list, including recently declared tribal areas or even new states in India; the Māori, who have both sovereignty and racial minority struggles; recognition

Watkwanonhwerá:ton ne ne tsi
weriáhsaien ne Kanehsatà:ke
Kanien'kéhá:ka rontathá:wi tsi
ronnatonhwentsiá:te.

Welcome to the heart of Kanehsatà:ke,
Kanien'kéha sovereign territory.

S I X   N A T I O N S
Y O U   A R E
N O T   A L O N E

Plate 7.1. Sign proclaiming support for the "Six Nations" by Kanehsata:ke sovereign authority, outside Oka, Quebec, Canada. (Photo courtesy of James V. Fenelon)

fights in the United States and Canada by previously subsumed native peoples such as Native Hawaiians; and so on, seemingly endlessly.

As we have noted in several places, often citing the work of Duane Champagne (2005, 2007), the natural world is not separate from the human world, and when animal or plant life is taken for and by humans, something is returned, and respect is shown for this "sacrifice." In this worldview the cosmos is not disturbed by the overly greedy takings of so much life that it cannot reproduce. For some indigenous people, like the Nahua (central Mexico indigenous peoples descendant of the Aztecs) or in the community of Yora in the Peruvian Amazon, living in isolation from the outside world, holistically, has been preferable to the vagaries of modernity.[5] Timber and oil resources are attracting invasions by corporate interests, as demonstrated with the Achuar in Ecuador's Amazon region. They note a "legacy of deforestation and environmental damage" and have brought suit with the United Nations.[6] We observe a continual unfolding of these age-old conflicts with the modern world-system.

A RECAP OF EARLIER CHAPTERS

We have argued that indigenous peoples are organizing and comparing their sociopolitical relations with dominant elites in terms of their habitation as survivors. These alliances have not only proven to be more effective in terms of resistance and cultural survival but are producing new forms of indigeneity that influence existing relations, including claims to sovereignty, the land, and social justice issues. These efforts for rights and autonomy differ in key ways from efforts of many other societies, in their historical depth, their community bases, their decision-making processes, their direct and spiritual ties to the land and sea, their traditional economic distribution networks (which are generally oriented toward egalitarian sharing), and their group characteristics.

Our case studies illustrate regional differences that are reflected in our two models (see Figures 2.2 and 2.3), one indigenous revitalization, another resistance to state and globalization forces, that facilitate analyses of diverse situations and peoples. Struggles over sovereignty and autonomy are important conflict points for indigenous peoples in continuing to develop relationships with dominant states. Resistance, ranging from sociocultural maintenance to violent revolution, is a vital part of cultural and political survival and the community empowerment supporting long-term social change rooted in a collective memory.

Lakota, Navajo, Wampanoag, and California Indian peoples in the United States; the Warli and Gond Adevasi in India; the Māori peoples in New Zealand; and the Zapotec and Zapatista-led Tzotzil peoples in Mexico all have diverse backgrounds and social systems that are represented in the models. Networks have given rise to new sites of resistance, new forms of cultural survival, new types of indigeneity, and continued social change, within larger globalizing processes. These changes need to be studied in world-system time, attending to historical context, phases of world-systemic cycles, and position within the world-system.

We have noted that Māoris, a treaty-based indigenous people living in lands dominated by the Pakeha, share many characteristics with First Nations and American Indians from North America. As a treaty people (Waitangi), they struggle over the meaning of sovereignty and face social discrimination. The Adevasi of India have a history of thousands of years, from being a true periphery to the British colonial rule, to the stratification and suppression by government and corporate forces, involving struggles over land, forests, dams, relocation, and urban issues. Indigenous Australians experienced genocide and social suppression via racial and ethnic discrimination as victims of both imperial, internal colonial, and globalizing conquest. Native Hawaiians are involved in struggles over sovereignty claims, cultural autonomy, and recognition in their homelands. These indigenous peoples illustrate a wide diversity of indigeneity in their struggles to revitalize their communities in a world increasingly hostile to collective societies, where globalization is synonymous with neoliberal individualism and the sociopolitical submersion of them.

We have also discussed how Mexico seldom used treaties or agreements during periods of conquest and domination. The San Andreas Accords, arising from violent struggle with the Zapatistas, used *normas y costumbres* to establish rights to collective land ownership. The accords are a form of "self-determination" and "autonomy" meant to maintain separate communities, even while participating in the larger state system. With this, Mexico is becoming explicitly multiethnic.

This is a fundamental assault on the concept of nation-state and nation-building, with emphasis on collective ownership of land and maintenance of traditions, in reaction to the cultural aspects of globalization. Examples from Mexico and Latin America show an emergence of an immense variety of forms of indigenous activism and resistance to colonization and assimilation. Underlying unity maintains some level of autonomy, and where possible, legal sovereignty, although this is problematic in states dealing with globalized and transnational capitalism.

For the Zapatistas, armed rebellion became nonviolent in an effort to implement local control by providing culturally sensitive mediating services. Those indigenous peoples who have survived these conflicts have adapted to changing systems of domination and have nearly always included cultural constructs around land tenure, collective distribution, traditional group leadership, and a strong focus on the community. Increasingly this has also meant claims for autonomy of one sort or another, especially in the area of resisting many neoliberal economic forces attempting to penetrate their region.

Communidades Indigenas have formed social movements with local leaders in alliances within their states, as identified with Bolivia and Ecuador. The Miskito in Nicaragua indicate that it is not solely capitalism that is at issue, but also modernity per se. We also find that theories of racialization and indigeneity are severely distorted when they rely solely on the study of processes in the United States, or conversely solely on Latin American cases. Complex interactions among states, historical processes, and aboriginal indigenous social organizations are socially constructed and transformed over time and give rise to a large variety of forms of resistance and revitalization. The underlying unity is a continuing struggle for survival and some degree of autonomy on the part of indigenous peoples. The election of individuals such as Evo Morales indicates how these movements adapt to political realities and how they are alienated by neoliberalism with its notions of private property and corporatization.

We also noted how many American Indian groups have been proactive in defending themselves from outside encroachments and genocide, using myriad strategies and tactics that varied widely in effectiveness (see Plate 7.2 for an example of how U.S. museums struggle to present these histories). Most accounts come from survivors who have faced problems that originated in geopolitics, or "reasons of state," such as national politics of the American Civil War, or the discovery of gold. States attempt to use indigenous peoples as pawns, but this usually leads to further resistance.

Indigenous survival and resistance are shaped by local, regional, national, and especially global forces and factors. To omit any level of these interactions is to distort and fundamentally misunderstand indigenous survival and resistance. Simple accounts or explanations of indigenous survival and resistance are flawed. Survival and resistance *are* complex and have deep historical roots. These circumstances often are remembered better in and by indigenous communities.

Key among the issues in North America is sovereignty. Native Americans have been recognized as separate nations, even if interpreted as "domestic,

Plate 7.2. North Dakota Heritage Center (Historical Society) installation noting "Indian resistance" with regalia, Lakota leaders, and history markers. (Photo courtesy of James V. Fenelon)

dependent nations" that became the reservation system. Connections to the land are more vital to identity and spiritual well-being, shown by the Mashpee Wampanoags and some California "Mission Bands" who have survived despite recognition issues. The long history of indigenous survival and resistance may equip Native Americans to face the winds of change emanating from forces of globalization better than their fellow citizens, who have seldom had to resist such forces.

In the United States, Indian "racial" identity was constructed with the concept of blood quantum, tying racial with ethnic forms of domination, with small benefits sometimes accruing from this status, usually accompanied by discrimination and social injustice. Navajo experiences show ways that indigenous people have adjusted while maintaining traditions. Struggles over sovereignty and autonomy still render it difficult to adapt foreign institutions to traditional cultures, as when Pueblo peoples wove theocracy into governance and justice, or some Northwest Coast peoples used systems of partial and/or temporary banishment to isolated areas. Navajo "Peacemaker Courts" are an example of indigenizing an institution.

Lakota peoples were undercut by the division into six different reservations, each now considered a "nation" with separate governments, and deep racism. The fight over regaining their sacred land, the Black Hills, though not yet successful, provided the basis for continued struggle with the United States, as seen in legal battles that have continued into the twenty-first century. Resistance by elder councils, as seen in renewals of the SunDance, gives hope and sustenance to many other Indian nations and First Nations to persevere. The smaller base of Wampanoag and many California Natives may have aided survival. As genocide survivors, these native nations have powerful stories to tell about the expansion of the modern world-system and its contemporary struggles with globalization.

We have argued in several places that an issue for indigenous peoples is the maintenance of sovereignty and autonomy over their own affairs and social organizations. Once a group has become a minority group with no special legal status, it is on a path to full absorption into the dominant state. We argue that there is an important distinction between movements that are overtly and clearly antisystemic and others, like indigenous movements and many fundamentalisms, which have some other primary goal but carry an important "secondary" agenda of being antisystemic. And we argue that the potential for success of such movements, and the potential for being crushed, varies with the hegemonic cycle in complex ways. Location in a core, as opposed to peripheral, region also shapes these processes in important ways.

Indigenist movements are fundamentally antisystemic, probably more so than many—but far from all—green movements because they advocate a right to maintain a different form of social life that is inherently antisystemic.[7] It also appears that some indigenous peoples become more fully incorporated in core countries, with or without autonomy, as they become less antisystemic and more reformative or transformative.

When hegemony is weak, states cannot afford the resources, the political capital, or the moral standing needed to crush them. When hegemony is strong the state often has "bigger fish to fry" and finds it not worth the effort to crush the movements; occasionally the state can gain moral standing by "tolerating" them, or using "kinder, gentler" ways to deter them. Times of changing hegemony, whether rapid or slow, however, are dangerous times. Intense repression has been used by the United States against internal movements. Similar, if less intense, repression occurred elsewhere in the United States, and much more violence occurs elsewhere, especially in peripheral and in semiperipheral states. Plate 7.3 is a Chilean visual description of centuries of struggles by their indigenous peoples. One goal for future research is to verify this empirically and develop some measures of the differences in degree of violence. It is also a matter of a full understanding of antiglobalization movements and the impacts of changes in hegemony.

GLOBALIZATION, WORLD-SYSTEMS, AND INDIGENOUS PEOPLES

Throughout this book we have tried to connect indigenous peoples, movements, resistance, and survival to world-systemic processes. Our most important point

Plate 7.3. "Presencia de America Latina" mural at the University de Concepcion, Chile, representing struggle and survival of indigenous peoples. (Photo courtesy of James V. Fenelon)

for social sciences and for world-system analysts in particular is that these movements are *not* new. They are as old as states, some five millennia. Following closely on the heels of this point are a few others. First, indigenous peoples have more enemies than either capitalism or neoliberal globalization. States are, *qua* states, a problem. As Immanuel Wallerstein noted over three decades ago (1974), capitalism is not a twentieth- or even nineteenth-century invention. It goes back at least 500 years. To be sure, the rise and spread of European mercantilism, capitalism, and colonialism brought a new level of contact and conflict between states and indigenous peoples. But that was a transformation of by then already millennia-old conflicts. These conflicts occurred with a new intensity and with a new viciousness, but they were not entirely new. Nor can they be blamed solely on capitalism or neoliberal globalization.

Second, indigenous movements are not a "new flavor" or a "new color" in various rainbow coalitions of globalization-spawned movements (see Hall and Fenelon 2008, and above). Rather, they are old movements, predating the "new social movements" of the late twentieth and early twenty-first centuries. In forming alliances with Greens and globalization-spawned movements, indigenous peoples are doing what they have been doing for millennia: adapting, adjusting, and adopting to changing circumstances to maintain their autonomy. Since the Peace of Westphalia (1648) they have also been seeking to maintain their sovereignty. That they are trying to do this is not surprising. What is surprising, noted over a decade ago by Franke Wilmer (1993), is that there have been many successes in these efforts—especially when we see the small amount of political, military, economic, or demographic power indigenous peoples possess.

This suggests a third point deriving from the antiquity of indigenous resistance, namely that the timing and often techniques of indigenous resistance, like much else, are tied to world-systemic processes and forces. Whenever *any* set of social movements occurs, world-systems analysis asks Why now? Why not some other time? and Which world-systemic cycles and processes have contributed to the timing? We have suggested that indigenous movements are in some sense countercyclical, that is, they occur when world-system hegemony is relatively weak and when states are otherwise occupied with jockeying for world-system position. Furthermore, we have suggested that internal to any one state, but especially in core states like late-nineteenth and twentieth-century United States, such indigenous movements are again countercyclical as the state becomes preoccupied with both internal strength and presenting a suitable "face" to the rest of the world. These remain suggestions, because there is nothing like a global or even United States catalog of indigenous movements.

This discussion points to a fourth aspect of the antiquity of indigenous survival. Despite volumes of histories on or about indigenous peoples, there is no compendium of acts of resistance. As we have noted often in the preceding chapters, such movements are often overlooked, not only because indigenous peoples have quite often been "the people without history" (Wolf 1982) but also because many forms of resistance are far from obvious and they have changed form over millennia, centuries, or even decades. Too often historians and others have thought of such movements by their presenting form, missing the underlying goals. An attempt to compile such a master list may well be a fool's errand. Still, many gaps could be filled. Our case studies have indicated some of the range of types of movements that should be considered, compared, and contrasted. But with such a relative paucity of data, all conclusions must remain provisional. They may well be artifacts of biased data or information. Still, by advancing hypotheses and provisional conclusions, we hope to suggest new avenues of research that will eventually lead to more complete information and allow the drawing of more refined conclusions. Thus do science and knowledge always advance.

These points all grow from the antiquity of indigenous survival and resistance seen in the light of long-term world-systems analysis. They all point to a much larger conclusion. Indigenous peoples are not "quaint," nor are they the (sole?) province of anthropology, or the odd specialist in social history. Understanding them is vital to understanding long-term social change and the transformations of human societies. In short, including indigenous peoples in social analyses is not a matter of inclusiveness, or multiculturalism, or "political correctness." It is a matter of good science and accurate history. Including indigenous peoples in all social analyses is hard work. Doing so requires reexamining foundational assumptions, greatly complicates comparisons, and requires rethinking many concepts. The "trick" here is to generalize sufficiently to allow broad comparisons, but to do so without turning everything into meaningless abstractions.

To ignore groups like the Adevasi would make it much harder to understand that it is not solely capitalism or neoliberal globalization that is problematic for indigenous peoples, but that it is states in general. Once that point is accepted, analysts can then turn to questions about just exactly what is peculiar to capitalism and neoliberal globalization. This also shows that as harmful as European expansion has been to indigenous peoples everywhere, it is far from a European monopoly. *All* states cause problems for indigenous peoples. We should note here that this must include states indigenous to the Americas, such as the Maya and their forerunners, the Aztecs or Triple Alliance and their forerunners, or the Inka and their forerunners. Recent work shows that these states, too, conquered, reorganized, and attempted to absorb neighboring indigenous groups. Hence, oppression of indigenous groups is not solely a matter of race, no matter how that concept is conceptualized. It is a matter of human beings.[8]

SOME FINAL THOUGHTS

As much as we have tried to draw defensible generalizations, there are exceptions. For instance, Native Hawaiians had elite leaders who resembled monarchs more than appointed spokespersons for councils. And as just noted, some indigenous states conquered nonstate indigenous peoples.

Another observation is that indigenous social movements are not always revolutionary, nor for that matter do they all require major regime reform. Various authors (noted in earlier chapters) make the case that even, or especially, in Mexico, indigenous groups sometimes accept a middle road. They compromise by accepting the hegemony of a particular state rather than facing a more conservative, repressive, and potentially more destructive political atmosphere.[9]

We also observe the manipulation of ideologies flowing in the opposite direction, as in the *terra nullis* (empty or uninhabited earth) concept used by some negotiators in relation to the Māori "first occupier" arguments, employed by the Australian government against its indigenous peoples, literally stating they are not there or do not matter. We also note that others have falsely—at times knowingly, at other times unwittingly—applied the doctrine of *terra nullis* to territories that while technically partially "empty" were in fact emptied often by disease and other deleterious consequences of contact at a distance.

As we noted, the UN Declaration of September 13, 2007, was something of a victory for indigenous peoples and their allies. Yet it is a victory that comes with a cost. The United States, Canada, New Zealand, and Australia are still opposing what appears to be a relatively simple declaration of rights and limited self-determination and social survival. So, we can ask, why the stiff and unyielding opposition? These four states all inherited treaty rights that they have been attempting to suppress or deny for hundreds of years, although with Australia it may be more a denial of racism than treaty rights per se.

The very large and complex numbers of indigenous peoples on the continent of Africa are not discussed much in our analysis, though they present similar yet also different sets of problems. For one thing, there is a much longer history of interactions among peoples in Africa (Kopytoff 1987). Then, too, there are the very complex effects of centuries of the slave trades. Also the concept of *indigenous* is more complex in Africa, compounded by the colonial and postcolonial use of *tribal* to demean various peoples.[10] South Africa is instructive in this respect, as systems of stratification and the sublimation of "tribal" peoples throughout the state are being reproduced in spite of its independence from the brutal, racist apartheid system from the preceding decades (Alexander 2002). Nearby, the San people in Botswana have won a rough court recognition of their lands and property undergoing "dispossession." Perhaps this will lead to the restoration of their indigenous rights and protection of their traditional living areas. If so, this would be very significant for the surrounding region in that it includes an acknowledgment of their historical oppression.[11]

Perhaps the most difficult to understand, and likewise having the most powerful potential to inform and transform our future collective efforts, are indigenous people such as the Moken of Thailand, and native inhabitants of India's Andaman and Nicobar islands, who managed to anticipate the great tsunami in December 2004 and its dangerous waves of destruction both by withdrawing from the coastline (inland, out to sea) and by traditional housing that "moves with the earth" on reinforced stilts.[12]

Without stereotyping or pigeonholing their particular experiences, we can ask very difficult but important questions: Is it possible to learn how they have knowledge like this, and where it comes from? Is it possible to learn from these people the foundations of how to relate to the earth, the climate, and indeed the cosmos in order to produce a better prediction of human societies for the next few hundred years? Besides the obvious environmental and cultural survival aspects to these questions, we should begin to pay attention to the broader issues that arise in the social sciences, none more important than the social and climatic results of the Industrial Revolution and modernity, and globalization that destroys these forms of traditional knowledge. Surely, world-systems analysis is in a good place to conduct such studies, since it has developed the analysis of large-scale systems arising from capitalist societal controls and yet can identify micro processes of social change on the level of community.

The Inuit from the circumpolar areas of the Arctic make another compelling example of the centrality of indigenous peoples struggles over the environment in respect to global warming, industrial policies and modernity, and traditional knowledge. As the Arctic areas undergo a "horrific global reality" of melting permafrost, changes in animal species, decreasing glaciers, and thinning ice floes, the Inuit have often predicted and dealt with the climactic changes to their lifestyles. Their treatment, usually a kind of rejection as being primitive, has led them to be called the "Miner's Canary" of indigenous peoples and the world.[13]

Duane Champagne has studied social change and the cultural continuity of native nations, finding that their covenant with the natural world—animals, plants, even stones and the mountains—and connections with environmental issues and concerns have survived the many onslaughts of "civilization" and the cultural distance "far removed from Western emphasis on self-interest and individualism" as "radical separation" from nature (2007, 334ff). He has called for us to consider interdisciplinary indigenous studies that are more multinational in their scope and intent. In this respect, as indigenous scholars and traditional leaders have been telling us for some time, or perhaps warning us, we can say that there are indeed alternatives to the neoliberal cry, "TINA" (There Is No Alternative [to neoliberal capitalism]). These include a focus on the following:

- Communities with a convergence of collectivity and stressing social harmony;
- Economic relations as public goods, as value systems, where the local is first, not markets;
- Decision making or governance responsive to local councils, not or less so than individual leaders; and
- Land as collective, symbiotic relationships, with spirituality and tenure for public good.

We cannot state with certainty what any indigenous group or nation would do if free of the penetrating and invasive forces of globalization. But we can and do argue that many indigenous peoples have had, and many still do have, alternative forms of constructing society that would mean less interstate violence, less inequality and injustice in social institutions, more citizen participation along the lines of a respected caucus or councils, and much healthier relationships to the nonhuman world, including forests and plant life, animals of all makings, and the earth itself.

Our arguments suggest that if the rest of the world will listen and observe, indigenous groups *may* point to other ways of existing, even thriving, within a global industrial system. In this they are simultaneously a hope, a promise, a puzzle, and a threat. They, too, by their very continued existence, say to those blinded by the TINA assumption: TATA (There Are Thousands of Alternatives), and these alternative views of the world often share philosophical underpinnings, as shown in the Mayan traditional cross in Plate 7.4. These are far from our last

Plate 7.4. Mayan traditional cross, using four directions and medicine wheel representation, made entirely with natural ingredients. San Cristóbal de las Casas, Chiapas, Mexico. (Photo courtesy of James V. Fenelon)

words about indigenous peoples, and most assuredly not from indigenous peoples themselves, but for now TATA is a strong metaphor for the work ahead of us.[14]

In acknowledging four directions, each of which must be understood, and an accompanying centrality of one's own social circles of relatives and friendships, relating outward to ultimately encompass the earth and the cosmos itself, indigenous peoples have developed ways of knowing and societies that can adapt to new directions while retaining traditions. It is this philosophy and worldview with which we end this book, in what the Lakota mean when they invoke powerful speeches or ceremonial language:

"Oh-mitakuye-Oyasin" (We are all related, as relatives let us show respect).

NOTES

1. This can be found on many websites; an official one is http://www.iwgia.org/sw248.asp, accessed December 11, 2008.

2. "Sept. 13, 2007, will stand as a day of victory for indigenous peoples worldwide. On that day, the U.N. General Assembly voted overwhelmingly to finally adopt the Declaration on the Rights of Indigenous Peoples. The landmark declaration, adopted by a vote of 143 in favor to 4 against, was the culmination of many decades of negotiation and conflict over recognition of Native individual and collective rights. The declaration provides for the strengthening of cultural identities, protection of Native lands and resources, and emphasizes the indigenous right of self-determination." From "Septembers to Remember for Indigenous Peoples," *Indian Country Today,* http://www.indiancountry.com, December 11, 2008.

3. John C. Mohawk in *Indian Country Today,* http://www. indiancountry.com, December 11, 2008, original "From the Natural People to the Western World," in *A Basic Call to Consciousness: The Hau de no sau nee Address to the Western World,* edited by Six Nations (Mohawk Nation, Rooseveltown, NY: Akwesasne Notes).

4. Ibid., "Preamble."

5. "Peru's Hidden People at Risk," *Indian Country Today,* http://www.indiancountry.com, October 16, 2006.

6. Michale Voss, "Ecuador Tribes Vow to Fight Oil Threat," *BBC News,* March 3, 2005.

7. Some newer green movements are advocating that the entire biosphere and its constituent members have, or should have, rights comparable to those of humans. These movements are probably even more antisystemic.

8. For excellent summaries, see Mann 2005. Note, though, that even his accounts of South America are becoming rapidly dated as new archaeological evidence radically challenges the heretofore accepted accounts of social change there. See, too, La Lone 2000 for a detailed example.

9. Some scholars argue that contemporary Indian gaming tribes with high-stakes casinos are just such a compromise. See Fenelon 2006a.

10. See Hodgson 2002 for a detailed account of indigenous movements and organizations she calls INGOs, that is, Indigenous Non-Governmental Organizations. Macharia 2003 discusses many of the complexities of indigenous identities in Africa.

11. Jerry Reyonolds, "Africa's Indigenous San Win in Court, Now Face Regulations," *Indian Country Today,* http://www.indiancountry.com, December 29, 2006.

12. Moken indigenous people (or "sea gypsies") of Thailand and native inhabitants of India's Andaman and Nicobar islands anticipated the tsunami; http://academic.evergreen.edu/g/grossmaz/LEEPERFY/, accessed July 17, 2008.

13. "Inuit, as 'Miners' Canary,' Lead Fight for the World," editor's report, *Indian Country Today*, http://www.indiancountry.com, December 30, 2005; also "Getting a Bead on Felix Cohen's 'Miner's Canary,'" ibid., August 31, 2006.

14. The expression *TATA* is taken from John Foran (2005, 277 and 348n63), who borrowed it from Robert Ware, who heard it someplace else.

RECOMMENDED READINGS

Champagne, Duane. 2007. *Social Change and Cultural Continuity Among Native Nations.* Lanham, MD: AltaMira Press.

  A collection of Champagne's essays, many on the possible futures for indigenous peoples. Some of these essays were originally published in hard-to-find publications.

Champagne, Duane, and Ismael Abu-Saad, eds. 2003. *The Future of Indigenous Peoples: Strategies for Survival and Development.* Los Angeles: UCLA American Indian Studies Center.

  A recent collection with multiple examinations of possible futures for indigenous peoples.

Fenelon, James V., ed. 2008. "Indigenous Peoples: Globalization, Resistance, and Revitalization." *American Behavioral Scientist* 52, 12 (August): 1656–1918.

  This special issue of this journal contains several comprehensive articles, many by indigenous scholars, from Latin and North America, India, New Zealand, the Middle East, and other areas, covering a wide range of topical issues revolving around their struggles and movements.

Epilogue

AS WE NOTED IN THE PREFACE, many events and processes have occurred while we were writing this book. Some of those events strengthened our arguments, a few may weaken them, but most suggest further ways to think about the issues we have raised. Struggles of indigenous peoples have continued over thousands of years, markedly so for 500 years of the Western expansion over the Americas and the colonization of much of the world—all of which subsumed indigenous peoples in the lower layers of domination. Resistance movements and revitalization have arisen and have been suppressed throughout these centuries. We expect that these cycles will not end any time soon. As noted in Chapters 5 and 6, it is likely that they will follow hegemonic cycles of rise and decline mitigated by the reactions of individual states.

We present a few events and give a brief assessment of how they would (re-) shape our discussions. We address the following in stories from both South and Central America, various American Indian peoples, Māori, and far Eastern Asian indigenous peoples.

The evolving situation in Bolivia with the election and presidency of an indigenous leader, Evo Morales, is both encouraging and problematic for resistance struggles. Indigenous rights, as we have noted elsewhere, are thrust into international review (Romero 2008) even as internal struggles for dominance have splintered the mestizo elite, and perhaps the electorate as well. The Bolivian elite are resisting land reform vigorously. Meanwhile, poor farmers and working rural classes have joined with indigenous organizations supporting and pursuing the promises that Morales has made about land reform (Kearns 2008).

Coalitions between indigenous and nonindigenous peoples hold great prospect throughout Latin America but are hardly the only arena for action that is constantly changing. As noted in our chapter on Mexico, the Zapatistas reached out to American Indian resistance groups, notably the Lakota and Mohawk, in their international *Encuentros*. Besides aligning with the Bolivian leader Evo Morales, Venezuelan president Hugo Chavez has promised the support of Citgo

Petroleum Corporation and other organizations for indigenous peoples in the United States, including the Lakota on the Cheyenne River Reservation in South Dakota. Receiving that support, Joseph Brings Plenty, chairman of the Cheyenne River Sioux Tribe, was invited to and attended an international indigenous summit in Caracas where networks were established and the commonality of struggles were identified:

> I landed in the sprawling Venezuelan capital of Caracas Aug. 8 and, upon arrival, took full advantage of a busy schedule of meetings and events with the leaders of indigenous tribes from across the Americas, including Colombia, Cuba, Bolivia, Ecuador, Chile, Peru and Argentina.... I visited with the indigenous brother from Argentina.... [He told] me the story of an Incan prophecy about a condor and an eagle. He said the Condor and the Eagle will meet in the air and join together, at which time will begin 1,000 years of peace on Earth. This Indian man believes that the Eagle represents the North American nations of indigenous people and the Condor represents the South American tribes. (Brings Plenty 2008)

Brings Plenty tells of how another indigenous leader had received a *pipa* (pipe) long ago. The tradition is that it had come from the Northern peoples, which he believes were certainly the Lakota. In discussing the oppression by the Spanish, he noted how it was similar to Lakota struggles. Brings Plenty discussed how the family (community), land, shared resources, and leadership by responsibility to councils and the people have shaped these indigenous movements from both American continents.

In contemporary times, we can find both the rise from oppression to recognition and new conflicts arising throughout the Americas. This includes a powerful story from Paraguay, where quasi-slavery, mass killings, and kidnapping of children were all too common until the 1990s. The Ache Guayaki chief Margarita Mbywangi personally experienced these events. She later rose to become Minister of Indigenous Affairs of Paraguay on August 19, 2008, the first indigenous minister in a country with a high percentage of "Indians" living in poverty (Kearns 2008). Concurrent with this progress, mixed indigenous and rural activists in Oaxaca have been suppressed, including some "death squads" who targeted Indian leaders, especially women who had made radio broadcasts (Gibler 2008).

One book author recently observed a similarity of struggles by the Mapuche and Pehuenche people in Chile with Lakota and other native nations from North America. Since the Pinochet regime brutally repressed civil and indigenous rights in their region, indigenous peoples have been rebuilding. However, now there are greater divisions over privatized land, community leadership, and economic growth in the agricultural sector. Some resistance groups have burned international corporations' timber holdings and buildings of absentee landowners. The Mapuche note how their leader, Toqui Lautaro, operating on horseback, defeated Spanish invaders long ago. He made treaties and agreements with invading Spaniards. Spanish officials later broke these treaties and even destroyed local knowledge of their very existence.[1]

As we have noted elsewhere, the United Nations Declaration of the Rights of Indigenous Peoples has given recognition of how dominant societal descriptions of indigenous peoples have contributed to their suppression. Canada joined many states in making apologies (again) to "aboriginals." The United States considered such a move but, as always before, shelved this important acknowledgement (Associated Press 2008).

We can see how powerful these relations are in recent and continuing actions by the Māori. They have reached the largest land settlement in New Zealand to date (Faucette 2008), even while the Foreshore and Seabed Debates rage. All of these actions are touted in a long historical view that begins with the Waitangi Treaty. Events with their relatives, the Native Hawaiians, have escalated, forcing court decisions on who qualifies and what actions are to be taken on these long-contested islands.

Japan has finally moved to recognize the Ainu on the island of Hokkaido. These indigenous peoples experienced oppression and identity suppression remarkably similar to those of indigenous peoples throughout the world (Ito 2008; Batten 2003). Despite hostility, Ainu peoples have kept deep philosophies about the land and sea.

These events, which are only the tip of the iceberg of indigenous actions, lead us to predict discussions like this for China, Russia, and other states with large and diverse indigenous populations. We foresee both great progress and great duress for indigenous peoples in the coming decades. The rise and demise of hegemonic forces and the recognition of and continuing suppression of specific indigenous peoples by individual states will continue to shape, but not entirely determine, the actions. We are encouraged by the movements and many international meetings of indigenous peoples, which is to say they are "international" in two senses: across state boundaries, but more significantly, among indigenous nations. The movements continue to react to and to use the forces and processes of globalization like communications, travel, "international" meetings, and growing global civil society to aid their efforts. Indigenous peoples will maintain a strong focus on the land of their grandmothers, the communities formed by their grandmothers and grandfathers, economies that support all the people, and creation of new forms and institutions of leadership. All of this not only will aid their continued survival and success, but, if states and scholars try to learn rather than control, it will offer vital lessons for the future to nonindigenous peoples.

NOTE

1. Interviews and discussions of James V. Fenelon with Mapuche and Pehuenche scholars and leaders in September 2008, in and around Concepcion, Chile.

Bibliography

Aberle, David F. 1982. *The Peyote Religion Among the Navaho.* Chicago: University of Chicago Press.

Acuña, Rodolfo. 1988. *Occupied America: A History of Chicanos,* 3rd ed. New York: Harper and Row.

Adams, David Wallace. 1995. *Education for Extinction: American Indians and the Boarding School Experience, 1875–1928.* Lawrence: University Press of Kansas.

Alexander, Neville. 2002. *Ordinary Country: Issues in the Transition from Apartheid to Democracy in South Africa.* Pietermaritzburg, South Africa: University of Natal Press.

Allard, Francis. 2006. "Frontiers and Boundaries: The Han Empire from Its Southern Periphery." Pp. 233–254 in *Archaeology of Asia,* edited by Miriam T. Stark. Malden, MA: Blackwell.

Álvarez Fabela, Martin. 2000. *Acteal de los mártires: Infamia para no olvidar.* Mexico City, Mexico: Plaza y Valdés.

Amarante, Leonor. 1986. "Indians Bring Video to the Amazon." *World Paper* 16 (February), 6.

American Indian Higher Education Consortium. 2000. *Tribal College Contributions to Local Economic Development.* Alexandria, VA: AIHEC. Available online at http://www.aihec.org/resources/documents/TC_contributionsLocalEconDevmt.pdf (accessed July 13, 2008).

———. 2000. "Tribal Colleges and Universities (TCUs) Roster." http://www.aihec.org/colleges/TCUroster.cfm.

América Profunda. 2003. América Profunda colloquium, December, Mexico City, Mexico.

Anderson, Benedict. 1991. *Imagined Communities: Reflections on the Origin and Spread of Nationalism.* London: Verso.

Anderson, Gary Clayton. 1984. *Kinsmen of Another Kind: Dakota–White Relations in the Upper Mississippi Valley, 1650–1862.* Lincoln: University of Nebraska Press.

Arquilla, John, and David Ronfeldt. 2000. *Swarming and the Future of Conflict.* Santa Monica, CA: Rand Corporation.

Associated Press. 2008. "Congress May Apologize to American Indians." Diverse: Issues in Higher Education, February 22, http://www.diverseeducation.com (accessed October 9, 2008).

Baird-Olson, Karen, and Carol Ward. 2000. "Recovery and Resistance: The Renewal of Traditional Spirituality Among American Indian Women." *American Indian Culture and Research Journal* 24, 4: 1–35.

156

Barber, Benjamin R. 1995. *Jihad vs. McWorld.* New York: Times Books.

Barlow, Maude, and Heather-Jane Robertson. 1996. "Homogenization of Education." Pp. 60–70 in *The Case Against the Global Economy and for a Turn Toward the Local,* edited by Jerry Mander and Edward Goldsmith. San Francisco, CA: Sierra Club Books.

Barrera, Mario. 1979. *Race and Class in the Southwest: A Theory of Racial Inequality.* Notre Dame, IN: University of Notre Dame Press.

Barta, Tony. 1987. "Relations of Genocide: Land and Lives in the Colonization of Australia." Pp. 237–251 in *Genocide and the Modern Age: Etiology and Case Studies of Mass Death,* edited by Isador Wallimann and Michael N. Dobkowski. New York: Greenwood Press.

Bartlett, Robert. 1993. *The Making of Europe: Conquest, Colonization, and Cultural Change, 950–1350.* Princeton, NJ: Princeton University Press.

Bates, Crispin. 1995. "'Lost Innocents and the Loss of Innocence': Interpreting *Adivasi* Movements in South Asia." Pp. 103–120 in *Indigenous Peoples of Asia,* edited by R. H. Barnes, Andrew Gray, and Benedict Kingsbury. Monograph and Occasional Papers Series, No. 48. Ann Arbor, MI: Association for Asian Studies.

Batten, Bruce L. 2003. *To the Ends of Japan: Premodern Frontiers, Boundaries, and Interactions.* Honolulu: University of Hawaii Press.

Belich, James. 1996. *Making Peoples: A History of the New Zealanders, from Polynesian Settlement to the End of the Nineteenth Century.* Honolulu: University of Hawaii Press.

Bennholdt-Thomsen, Veronika, Nicholas Fraclas, and Claudia Von Werlhof. 2001. *There Is an Alternative: Subsistence and Worldwide Resistance to Corporate Globalization.* London: Zed Books.

Berger, Peter L. 1997. "Four Faces of Global Culture." *National Interest* 49 (Fall): 23–29.

Berger, Peter L., and Samuel P. Huntington, eds. 2002. *Many Globalizations: Cultural Diversity in the Contemporary World.* New York: Oxford University Press.

Bergesen, Albert J. 2000. "Postmodernism Explained." Pp. 181–192 in *A World-Systems Reader: New Perspectives on Gender, Urbanism, Cultures, Indigenous Peoples, and Ecology,* edited by Thomas D. Hall. Lanham, MD: Rowman and Littlefield.

Berkhofer, Robert. 1978. *The White Man's Indian.* New York: Random House.

Bijoy, C. R. 2001. "The Adivasis of India: A History of Discrimination, Conflict, and Resistance." *Indigenous Affairs* 1/01 (March) : 54–61.

———. 2008. "Forest Rights Struggle: The Adivasis Now Awaits a Settlement." *American Behavioral Scientist* 51, 12 (August): 1755–1773.

Biolsi, Thomas. 1995. "Bringing the Law Back In: Legal Rights and the Regulation of Indian-White Relations on the Rosebud Reservation." *Current Anthropology* 36, 4 (August–October): 543–571.

———. 2001. *Deadliest Enemies: Law and the Making of Race Relations on and off Rosebud Reservation.* Berkeley: University of California Press.

Blanton, Richard, Stephen A. Kowalewski, Gary Feinman, and Laura M. Finsten. 1993. *Ancient Mesoamerica: A Comparison of Change in Three Regions,* 2nd ed. New York: Cambridge University Press.

Bodley, John H., ed. 1988. *Tribal Peoples and Development Issues: A Global Overview.* Mountain View, CA: Mayfield Publishing.

———. 1990. *Victims of Progress,* 3rd ed. Mountain View, CA: Mayfield Publishing.

———. 2003. *Power of Scale: A Global History Approach.* Armonk, NY: M. E. Sharpe.

Bond, Patrick. 2006. *An Ordinary Country: Issues in the Transition from Apartheid to Democracy in South Africa.* London and Pietermaritzburg: Zed Books and University of KwaZulu-Natal Press.

Bonfil Batalla, Guillermo. 1996. *Mexico Profundo: Reclaiming a Civilization.* Translated by Phillip A. Dennis. Austin: University of Texas Press.

Boswell, Terry. 1995. "Hegemony and Bifurcation Points in World History." *Journal of World-Systems Research* 1, 15. Available online at http://jwsr.ucr.edu/index.php.
———. 2004. "Hegemonic Decline and Revolution: When the World Is Up for Grabs." Pp. 149–161 in *Globalization, Hegemony, and Power: Antisystemic Movements and the Global System,* edited by Thomas E. Reifer. Boulder, CO: Paradigm Publishers.
Boswell, Terry, and Christopher Chase-Dunn. 2000. *The Spiral of Capitalism and Socialism: The Decline of State Socialism and the Future of the World-System.* Boulder, CO: Lynne-Rienner.
Boswell, Terry, and Mike Sweat. 1991. "Hegemony, Long Waves, and Major Wars: A Time Series Analysis of Systemic Dynamics, 1496–1967." *International Studies Quarterly* 35, 2 (June): 123–149.
Boyer, Paul. 1997. *Native American Colleges: Progress and Prospects.* An Ernest L. Boyer Project of the Carnegie Foundation for the Advancement of Teaching. Princeton, NJ: Carnegie Foundation for the Advancement of Teaching.
Brings Plenty, Joseph. 2008. "North, South: We're in It Together." *Indian Country Today,* October 3, http://wwwindiancountry.com (accessed October 9, 2008).
Brooks, James F. 2002. *Captives and Cousins: Slavery, Kinship, and Community in the Southwest Borderlands.* Chapel Hill: University of North Carolina Press.
Brown, Dee. 1970. *Bury My Heart at Wounded Knee: An Indian History of the American West.* New York: Holt, Rinehart, and Winston.
Brown, Kaye. 1976. "Quantitative Testing and Revitalization Behavior: On Carroll's Explanation of the Ghost Dance." *American Sociological Review* 41 (August): 740–744.
Bruhn, Kathleen. 1999. "Antonio Gramsci and the Palabra Verdadera: The Political Discourse of Mexico's Guerrilla Forces." *Journal of Interamerican Studies and World Affairs* 41, 2: 29–55.
Buchan, Bruce. 2002. "Withstanding the Tide of History: The Yorta Yorta Case and Indigenous Sovereignty." *Borderlands* 1, 2. Special Indigenous Sovereignty Edition (e-journal, http://www.borderlands.net.au/ (accessed December 11, 2008).
Buck, Sir Peter (Te Rangi Hiroa). 1949. "The Coming of the Maori." Christchurch, New Zealand: Whitcombe and Tombes.
Burger, Julian. 1987. *Report from the Frontier: The State of the World's Indigenous Peoples.* London: Zed Books.
Cabazon. 1987. *Californian v. Cabazon Band of Mission Indians,* 480 U.S. 202, 1987.
Cadwalader, Sandra D., and Vine Deloria, Jr., eds. 1984. *The Aggressions of Civilization: Federal Indian Policy Since the 1880s.* Philadelphia: Temple University Press.
Calliou, Brian. 2005. "The Culture of Leadership: North American Indigenous Leadership in a Changing Economy." Pp. 47–68 in *Indigenous People and the Modern State,* edited by Duane Champagne, Karen Torjesen, and Susan Steiner. Walnut Creek, CA: AltaMira Press.
Campbell, Howard. 1994. *Zapotec Renaissance: Ethnic Politics and Cultural Revivalism in Southern Mexico.* Albuquerque: University of New Mexico Press.
Cancian, Frank. 1965. *Economic and Prestige in a Maya Community: The Religious Cargo System in Zinacantán.* Stanford, CA: Stanford University Press.
Carlson, Jon D. 2001. "Broadening and Deepening: Systemic Expansion, Incorporation, and the Zone of Ignorance." *Journal of World-Systems Research* 7, 2 (Fall): 225–263. Available online at http://jwsr.ucr.edu/index.php.
———. 2002. "The 'Otter-Man' Empires: The Pacific Fur Trade, Incorporation, and the Zone of Ignorance." *Journal of World-Systems Research* 8, 3 (Fall): 389–442. Available online at http://jwsr.ucr.edu/index.php.
Carmack, Robert M., Janine Gasco, and Gary H. Gossen. 1996. *The Legacy of Mesoamerica:*

History and Culture of a Native American Civilization. Upper Saddle River, NJ: Prentice Hall.

Cavalli-Sforza, Luigi Luca, and Francesco Cavalli-Sforza. 1995. *The Great Human Diasporas: The History of Diversity and Evolution*. Translated by Sarah Thorne. New York: Addison-Wesley.

Center for Sami Studies, University of Tromso, http://www.sami.uit.no/indexen.html.

Centro de Derechos Humanos Fray Bartolomé de Las Casas A. C. 2005. *La política genocida en el conflicto armado en Chiapas*. http://www.laneta.apc.org/cdhbcasas/genocidio/genocidio.htm.

Champagne, Duane. 1983. "Social Structure, Revitalization Movements, and State Building: Social Change in Four Native American Societies." *American Sociological Review* 48 (December): 754–763.

———. 1989. *American Indian Societies: Strategies and Conditions of Political and Cultural Survival*. Cambridge, MA: Cultural Survival.

———. 1992. *Social Order and Political Change: Constitutional Governments Among the Cherokee, the Choctaw, the Chickasaw, and the Creek*. Stanford, CA: Stanford University Press.

———. 1999a. "Introduction." Pp. 7–10 in *Contemporary Native American Cultural Issues, edited by Duane Champagne*. Walnut Creek, CA: AltaMira Press.

———, ed. 1999b. *Contemporary Native American Cultural Issues*. Walnut Creek, CA: AltaMira Press.

———. 2003a. "Indigenous Strategies for Engaging Globalism." Pp. xix–xxxii in *The Future of Indigenous Peoples: Strategies for Survival and Development*, edited by Duane Champagne and Ismael Abu-Saad. Los Angeles: UCLA American Indian Studies Center.

———. 2003b. "Renewing American Indian Nations: Cosmic Communities and Spiritual Autonomy." Pp. 167–181 in *Diversity and Community: A Critical Reader*, edited by Philip Anderson. Oxford, UK: Blackwell. Republished as pp. 9–24 in *Social Change and Cultural Continuity Among Native Nations*, edited by Duane Champagne. Lanham, MD: AltaMira Press, 2007.

———. 2005. "Rethinking Native Relations with Contemporary Nation-States." Pp. 1–33 in *Indigenous People and the Modern State*, edited by Duane Champagne, Karen Torjesen, and Susan Steiner. Walnut Creek, CA: AltaMira Press.

———. 2007. *Social Change and Cultural Continuity Among Native Nations*. Lanham, MD: AltaMira Press.

Champagne, Duane, and Ismael Abu-Saad, eds. 2003. *The Future of Indigenous Peoples: Strategies for Survival and Development*. Los Angeles: UCLA American Indian Studies Center.

Champagne, Duane, Karen Torjesen, and Susan Steiner, eds. 2005. *Indigenous People and the Modern State*. Walnut Creek, CA: AltaMira Press.

Chance, John K., and William B. Taylor. 1985. "Cofradías and Cargos: An Historical Perspective on the Mesoamerican Civil-Religious Hierarchy." *American Ethnologist* 12, 1 (February): 1–26.

Chase-Dunn, Christopher. 1999. "Globalization: A World-Systems Perspective." *Journal of World-Systems Research* 5, 2 (Summer): 156–185. Available online at http://jwsr.ucr.edu/index.php.

Chase-Dunn, Christopher, Alexis Alvarez, and Daniel Pasciuti. 2005. "Power and Size: Urbanization and Empire Formation in World-Systems." Pp. 92–112 in *The Historical Evolution of World-Systems*, edited by Christopher Chase-Dunn and Eugene Anderson. New York: Palgrave.

Chase-Dunn, Christopher, and E. N. Anderson, eds. 2005. *The Historical Evolution of World-Systems*. New York and London: Palgrave.

Chase-Dunn, Christopher, and Salvatore Babones. 2006. *Global Social Change: Comparative and Historical Perspectives*. Baltimore, MD: Johns Hopkins University Press.

Chase-Dunn, Christopher, and Thomas D. Hall. 1997. *Rise and Demise: Comparing World-Systems*. Boulder, CO: Westview Press.

———. 1998. "World-Systems in North America: Networks, Rise and Fall, and Pulsations of Trade in Stateless Systems." *American Indian Culture and Research Journal* 22, 1: 23–72.

Chase-Dunn, Christopher, Yukio Kawano, and Benjamin D. Brewer. 2000. "Trade Globalization Since 1795: Waves of Integration in the World-System." *American Sociological Review* 65, 1 (February): 77–95.

Chase-Dunn, Christopher, and Kelly M. Mann. 1998. *The Wintu and Their Neighbors: A Very Small World-System in Northern California*. Tucson: University of Arizona Press.

Childs, Matt. 1995. "An Historical Critique of the Emergence and Evolution of Ernesto Che Guevara's Foco Theory." *Journal of Latin American Studies* 27, 3 (October): 593–624.

Chirot, Daniel. 1977. *Social Change in the Twentieth Century*. New York: Harcourt, Brace, Jovanovich.

Chiste, Katherine Beaty. 1994. "Aboriginal Women and Self-Government: Challenging Leviathan." *American Indian Culture and Research Journal* 18, 3: 19–43. Reprinted as pp. 71–90 in *Contemporary Native American Cultural Issues*, edited by Duane Champagne. Walnut Creek, CA: AltaMira Press, 1999.

———. 1986. *Social Change in the Modern Era*. New York: Harcourt, Brace, Jovanovich.

Churchill, Ward. 1994. *Indians Are Us: Culture and Genocide in Native North America*. Monroe, ME: Common Courage Press.

———. 1996. From *A Native Son: Selected Essays on Indigenism, 1985–1995*. Boston: South End Press.

Churchill, Ward, and Jim Vander Wall. 1988. *Agents of Repression: The FBI's Secret Wars Against the Black Panther Party and American Indian Movement*. Boston: South End Press.

Cleaver, Harry. 1998. "The Zapatista Effect: The Internet and the Rise of an Alternative Political Fabric." *Journal of International Affairs* 51, 2 (Spring): 621–640.

Coates, Ken S. 2004. *A Global History of Indigenous Peoples: Struggle and Survival*. New York: Palgrave.

Cobo, Jose R. Martinez. 1986. "Problem of Discrimination Against Indigenous Populations." U.N. Doc. E/CN:4/Sub.2/1986/7 & Adds.4, PARAS. 380. Available online at http://www.un.org/esa/socdev/unpfii/documents/PFII%202004%20WS.1%203% 20Definition.doc.

———. 1987. *Estudio del problema de la discriminacion contra las oblaciones indigenas (vol. V, Conclusiones, propuestas y recomendaciones)*. New York: United Nations.

Collier, George A., with Elizabeth Lowery Quaratiello. 1999. *Basta! Land and the Zapatista Rebellion in Chiapas*. Oakland, CA: Food First Books.

Cook, Sherburne F. 1976. *The Population of the California Indians, 1769–1970*. Berkeley: University of California Press.

Cornell, Stephen. 1988. *The Return of the Native: American Indian Political Resurgence*. New York: Oxford University Press.

Corntassel, Jeff F. 2003. "Who Is Indigenous? 'Peoplehood' and Ethnonationalist Approaches to Rearticulating Indigenous Identity." *Nationalism and Ethnic Politics* 9, 1 (Spring): 75–100.

Couch, Jen. 2001. "Imagining Zapatismo: The Anti-Globalization Movement and the Zapatistas." *Communal/Plural* 9, 2: 243–260.

Crosby, Alfred W., Jr. 1972. *The Columbian Exchange: Biological and Cultural Consequences of 1492.* Westport, CT: Greenwood Press.

Cutter, Charles R. 1995a. "Judicial Punishment in Colonial New Mexico." *Western Legal History* 8, 1 (Winter/Spring): 115–129.

———. 1995b. *The Legal Culture of Northern New Spain, 1700–1810.* Albuquerque: University of New Mexico Press.

Daniel, John, Adam Habib, and Roger Southall, eds. 2004. *State of the Nation: South Africa 2003–2004.* Cape Town, South Africa: Human Sciences Research Council Press.

De Janvry, Alain, Gustavo Gordillo, and Elisabeth Sadoulet. 1997. *Mexico's Second Agrarian Reform: Household and Community Responses.* La Jolla, CA: Center for U.S.-Mexican Studies, University of California, San Diego.

Dello Buono, Richard A., and Joseì Bell Lara, eds. 2007. *Imperialism, Neoliberalism, and Social Struggles in Latin America.* Boston: Brill.

Deloria, Ella C. 1979 [1933]. *Speaking of Indians.* Vermillion, SD: Dakota Press.

Deloria, Vine, Jr. 1969. *Custer Died for Your Sins: An Indian Manifesto.* New York: Avon. Reprinted 1988, Norman: University of Oklahoma Press.

———. 1994. *God Is Red: A Native View of Religion.* Golden, CO: North American Press.

———. 1997. *Red Earth, White Lies: Native Americans and the Myth of Scientific Fact.* New York: Scribner.

Deloria, Vine, Jr., and Clifford Lytle. 1984. *The Nations Within: The Past and Future of American Indian Sovereignty.* New York: Pantheon Books.

Deloria, Vine, Jr., and David E. Wilkins. 1999. *Tribes, Treaties, and Constitutional Tribulations.* Austin: University of Texas Press.

DeMallie, Raymond J. 1982. "The Lakota Ghost Dance: An Ethnohistorical Account." *Pacific Historical Review* 51 (October): 385–405.

———. 1984. *The Sixth Grandfather : Black Elk's Teachings Given to John G. Neihardt.* Lincoln: University of Nebraska Press.

DeMallie, Raymond J., and Douglas R. Parks, eds. 1987. *Sioux Indian Religion: Tradition and Innovation.* Norman: University of Oklahoma Press.

Díaz-Polanco, Héctor. 1997. *La rebelión Zapatista y la autonomía.* Mexico City, Mexico: Siglo Veintiuno Editores.

Downs, James. 1971. *The Navajo.* New York: Holt, Rinehart, and Winston.

Dunaway, Wilma A. 1994. "The Southern Fur Trade and the Incorporation of Southern Appalachia into the World-Economy, 1690–1763." *Review* 18, 2 (Spring): 215–242.

———. 1996a. *The First American Frontier: Transition to Capitalism in Southern Appalachia, 1700–1860.* Chapel Hill: University of North Carolina Press.

———. 1996b. "Incorporation as an Interactive Process: Cherokee Resistance to Expansion of the Capitalist World-System, 1560–1763." *Sociological Inquiry* 66, 4 (Fall): 455–470.

———. 1996c. "The Incorporation of Mountain Ecosystems into the Capitalist World-System." *Review* 19, 4 (Fall): 355–381.

———. 1997. "Rethinking Cherokee Acculturation: Women's Resistance to Agrarian Capitalism and Cultural Change, 1800–1838." *American Indian Culture and Research Journal* 21, 1: 231–268.

———. 2000. "The International Fur Trade and Disempowerment of Cherokee Women, 1680–1775." Pp. 195–210 in *A World-Systems Reader: New Perspectives on Gender, Urbanism, Cultures, Indigenous Peoples, and Ecology,* edited by Thomas D. Hall. Lanham, MD: Rowman and Littlefield.

———. 2001. "The Double Register of History: Situating the Forgotten Woman and Her Household in Capitalist Commodity Chains." *Journal of World-System Research* 7, 1 (Spring): 2–31. Available online at http://jwsr.ucr.edu/index.php.

————. 2003. "Ethnic Conflict in the Modern World-System: The Dialectics of Counter-hegemonic Resistance in an Age of Transition." *Journal of World-Systems Research* 9, 1 (Winter): 3–34. Available online at http://jwsr.ucr.edu/index.php.

Eidheim, Harald. 1969. "When Ethnic Identity Is a Social Stigma." Pp. 39–57 in *Ethnic Groups and Boundaries,* edited by Frederik Barth. Boston: Little, Brown. Reprinted 1998, Prospect Heights, IL: Waveland Press.

El Comité Clandestino Revolucionario Indígena-Comandancia General del EZLN. 1994. "Pliego de demandas." In *EZLN: Documentos y comunicados, 1 de enero/8 de agosto de 1994.* Mexico City, Mexico: Ediciones Era.

Eldredge, Nancy, and Linda Coombs. http://www.plimoth.org/learn/history/wampanoag/wampanoag.asp.

Esteva, Gustavo. 1999. "The Zapatistas and People's Power." *Capital and Class* 68: 153–182.

————. 2001. "The Meaning and Scope of the Struggle for Autonomy." *Latin American Perspectives* 28, 2 (March): 120–148.

————. 2003. *Sin Maiz No Hay Pais.* Mexico: Consejo Nacional Para la Cultura y Las Artes (Museo Nacional de Culturas Populares).

Faiman-Silva, Sandra L. 1997. *Choctaws at the Crossroads: The Political Economy of Class and Culture in the Oklahoma Timber Region.* Lincoln: University of Nebraska Press.

Farris, Nancy M. 1984. *Maya Society Under Colonial Rule: The Collective Enterprise of Survival.* Princeton, NJ: Princeton University Press.

Faucette, Judith. 2008. "Historic Maori Land Compensation Agreement." *Australian Indigenous Peoples,* June 28, http://australian-indigenous-peoples.suite101.com (accessed October 9, 2008).

Featherstone, Mike, ed. 1990. *Global Culture: Nationalism, Globalization, and Modernity.* Newbury Park, CA: Sage Publications.

Featherstone, Mike, Scott Lash, and Roland Robertson, eds. 1995. *Global Modernities.* Newbury Park, CA: Sage Publications.

Feinman, Gary M., and Linda M. Nicholas. 1991a. "The Monte Albán State: A Diachronic Perspective on an Ancient Core and Its Periphery." Pp. 240–276 in *Core/Periphery Relations in Precapitalist Worlds,* edited by Christopher Chase-Dunn and Thomas D. Hall. Boulder, CO: Westview Press.

————. 1991b. "New Perspectives on Prehispanic Highland Mesoamerica: A Macroregional Approach." *Comparative Civilizations Review* 24 (Spring): 13–33.

Fenelon, James V. 1995. "Culturicide, Resistance, Survival: The Cultural Domination of Lakota Oyate." Doctoral diss., Northwestern University. Ann Arbor: University of Michigan.

————. 1997. "From Peripheral Domination to Internal Colonialism: Socio-Political Change of the Lakota on Standing Rock." *Journal of World-Systems Research* 3, 2 (Spring): 259–320. Available online at http://jwsr.ucr.edu/index.php.

————. 1998. *Culturicide, Resistance, and Survival of the Lakota (Sioux Nation).* New York: Garland Publishing.

————. 1999. "Indian Icons in the World Series of Racism: Institutionalization of the Racial Symbols Wahoos and Indians." Pp. 25–45 in *The Global Color Line: Racial and Ethnic Inequality and Struggle from a Global Perspective,* edited by Pinar Batur-Vanderlippe and Joe Feagin. *Research in Politics and Society* 6. Stamford, CT: JAI Press.

————. 2002. "Dual Sovereignty of Native Nations, the United States, and Traditionalists." *Humboldt Journal of Social Relations* 27, 1: 106–145.

————. 2006. "Indian Gaming: Traditional Perspectives and Cultural Sovereignty." *American Behavioral Scientist* 50, 3 (November): 381–409.

Fenelon, James V., and Mary Louise Defender-Wilson. 2004. "Voyage of Domination,

'Purchase' as Conquest, Skakawea for Savagery: Distorted Icons from Misrepresentation of the Lewis and Clark Expedition." *Wicazo Sa Review* 19, 1 (Spring): 85–104.

Fenelon, James V., and Thomas D. Hall. 2005. "Indigenous Struggles over Autonomy, Land, and Community: Anti-Globalization and Resistance in World-Systems Analysis." Pp. 107–122 in *Latin@s in the World-System: Decolonization Struggles in the 21st-Century U.S. Empire,* edited by Ramón Grosfoguel, Nelson Maldonado-Torres, and Jose David Saldivar. Boulder, CO: Paradigm Publishers.

———. 2008. "Revitalization and Indigenous Resistance to Globalization and Neoliberalism." *American Behavioral Scientist* 51, 12 (August): 1867–1901.

Fenelon, James V., and D. LeBeau. 2006. "Four Directions for Indian Education: Curriculum Models for Lakota/Dakota Teaching and Learning." Pp. 21–68 in *Indigenous and Minority Education,* edited by Duane Champagne and Ibraham Abu-Saad. Beer Sheba, Israel: Negev Center for Regional Development.

Fools Crow, Frank. 1976. "To My People from Eagle Bear, Better Known as Chief Frank Fools Crow." *Fools Crow.* Denver: Tatanka Records.

———. 1979. *Fools Crow.* Recorded, edited by Thomas Mails and Dallas Chief Eagle. Garden City, NY: Doubleday.

Foran, John. 2005. *Taking Power: On the Origins of Third World Revolutions.* Cambridge, UK: Cambridge University Press.

Forbes, Jack. 1998. "The Urban Tradition Among Native Americans." *American Indian Culture and Research Journal* 22, 4: 15–41.

Forero, Juan, and Larry Rohter. 2006. "Bolivia's Leader Solidifies Region's Leftward Tilt." *New York Times,* January 22.

Foster, Michael S., and Shirley Gorenstein, eds. 2000. *Greater Mesoamerica: The Archaeology of West and Northwest Mexico.* Salt Lake City: University of Utah Press.

Frank, Andre Gunder. 1966. "The Development of Underdevelopment." *Monthly Review* (September): 17–31.

———. 1978. *World Accumulation, 1492–1789.* New York: Monthly Review Press.

———. 1992. *A World Economic Interpretation of East-West European Politics.* Maarssen: Department of International Relations and Public International Law, University of Amsterdam.

Frank, Andre Gunder, and Barry K. Gills, eds. 1993. *The World System: Five Hundred Years or Five Thousand?* London: Routledge.

Fried, Stephanie. 2003. "Writing for Their Lives: Bentian Dayak Authors and Indonesian Development Discourse." Pp. 142–183 in *Culture and the Question of Rights: Forests, Coasts, and Seas in Southeast Asia,* edited by Charles Zerner. Durham, NC: Duke University Press.

Friedman, Jonathan. 1994. *Cultural Identity and Global Process.* Thousand Oaks, CA: Sage Publications.

———. 1998. "Transnationalization, Socio-political Disorder, and Ethnification as Expressions of Declining Global Hegemony." *International Political Science Review* 19, 3 (July): 233–250.

———. 1999. "Indigenous Struggles and the Discreet Charm of the Bourgeoisie." *Journal of World-Systems Research* 5, 2 (Summer): 391–411. Available online at http://jwsr.ucr.edu/index.php.

Friedman, Jonathan, and Christopher Chase-Dunn, eds. 2005a. *Hegemonic Declines: Present and Past.* Boulder, CO: Paradigm Publishers.

———. 2005b. "Introduction: Hegemonic Declines." Pp. 1–4 in *Hegemonic Decline: Present and Past,* edited by Jonathan Friedman and Christopher Chase-Dunn. Boulder, CO: Paradigm Publishers.

Froehling, Oliver. 1997. "The Cyberspace of 'War of Ink and Internet' in Chiapas." *Geographical Review* 87, 2 (April) 291–307.

Fuentes, Carlos. 1997 [1994]. *A New Time for Mexico*. Translated by Marina Gutman Castañeda. Berkeley: University of California Press.

Gedicks, Al. 1993. *The New Resource Wars: Native and Environmental Struggles Against Multinational Corporations*. Boston: South End Press.

———. 2001. *Resource Rebels: Native Challenges to Mining and Oil Corporations*. Cambridge, MA: South End Press.

Gell, Simeran Man Singh. 1992. *The Ghotul in Muria Society*. Philadelphia: Harwood Academic Publishers.

Gibler, John. 2008. "Death Squads in Oaxaca: The Mexican Government Ignores the Assassination of Two Community Radio Activists." *These Times,* June 10, http://www.inthesetimes.com (accessed October 9, 2008).

Gills, Barry K. 2000. *Globalization and the Politics of Resistance*. London: Routledge.

Global Exchange. 2000. *Always Near, Always Far: The Armed Forces in Mexico*. San Francisco: Global Exchange.

Goddard, Ives. 2004. "Endangered Knowledge: What We Can Learn from Native American Languages." *Anthronotes* 25, 2 (Fall): 1–8.

Goldberg, Carol. 1999. "Public Law 280 and the Problem of 'Lawlessness' in California Indian Country." Pp. 197–225 in *Contemporary Native American Political Issues,* edited by Troy Johnson. Walnut Creek, CA: AltaMira Press.

Goldstein, Joshua. 1988. *Long Cycles: Prosperity and War in the Modern Age*. New Haven, CT: Yale University Press.

Gonzalez, Mario, and Elizabeth Cook-Lynn. 1999. *The Politics of Hallowed Ground: Wounded Knee and the Struggle for Indian Sovereignty*. Urbana: University of Illinois Press.

Goodman, Ronald. 1992. *Lakota Star Knowledge: Studies in Lakota Stellar Theology*. Rosebud, ND: Sinje Gleska University.

Green, Michael. 1995. "Cultural Identities: Challenges for the Twenty-First Century." In *Issues in Native American Cultural Identity,* edited by Michael K. Green. New York: Peter Lang.

Grimes, Peter. 2000. "Recent Research on World-Systems." Pp. 29–55 in *A World-Systems Reader: New Perspectives on Gender, Urbanism, Cultures, Indigenous Peoples, and Ecology,* edited by Thomas D. Hall. Lanham, MD: Rowman and Littlefield.

Guidry, John A., Michael D. Kennedy, and Mayer N. Zald, eds. 2000. *Globalizations and Social Movements: Culture, Power, and the Transnational Public Sphere*. Ann Arbor: University of Michigan Press.

Guillermoprieto, Alma. 2002. *Looking for History: Dispatches from Latin America*. New York: Pantheon Books.

Gurr, Ted Robert. 1993. *Minorities at Risk: A Global View of Ethnopolitical Conflicts*. Washington, DC: United States Institute of Peace Press.

———, ed. 2000. *Peoples Versus States: Minorities at Risk in the New Century*. Washington, DC: United States Institute of Peace Press.

Gutiérrez, Ramón A. 1991.*When Jesus Came, the Corn Mothers Went Away: Marriage, Sexuality, and Power in New Mexico, 1500–1846*. Stanford, CA: Stanford University Press.

Guy, Donna J., and Thomas E. Sheridan, eds. 1998. *Contested Ground: Comparative Frontiers on the Northern and Southern Edges of the Spanish Empire*. Tucson: University of Arizona Press.

Hale, Charles. 1994. *Resistance and Contradiction: Miskitu Indians and the Nicaraguan State, 1894-1987*. Stanford, CA: Stanford University Press.

Hall, Thomas D. 1983. "Peripheries, Regions of Refuge, and Nonstate Societies: Toward a Theory of Reactive Social Change." *Social Science Quarterly* 64: 582–597.

———. 1986. "Incorporation in the World-System: Toward a Critique." *American Sociological Review* 51 (June): 390–402.

———. 1987. "Native Americans and Incorporation: Patterns and Problems." *American Indian Culture and Research Journal* 11, 2: 1–30.

———. 1989a. "Is Historical Sociology of Peripheral Regions Peripheral?" Pp. 349–372 in *Studies of Development and Change in the Modern World*, edited by Michael T. Martin and Terry R. Kandal. New York: Oxford University Press.

———. 1989b. *Social Change in the Southwest, 1350–1880*. Lawrence: University Press of Kansas.

———. 1989c. "Historical Sociology and Native Americans: Methodological Problems." *American Indian Quarterly* 13, 3: 223–238.

———. 1998a. "The Effects of Incorporation into World-Systems on Ethnic Processes: Lessons from the Ancient World for the Contemporary World." *International Political Science Review* 19, 3 (July): 251–267.

———. 1998b. "The Rio de La Plata and the Greater Southwest: A View from World-System Theory." Pp. 150–166 in *Contested Ground: Comparative Frontiers on the Northern and Southern Edges of the Spanish Empire*, edited by Donna Guy and Thomas Sheridan. Tucson: University of Arizona Press.

———, ed. 2000a. *A World-Systems Reader: New Perspectives on Gender, Urbanism, Cultures, Indigenous Peoples, and Ecology*. Lanham, MD: Rowman and Littlefield.

———. 2000b. "World-Systems Analysis: A Small Sample from a Large Universe." Pp. 3–27 in *A World-Systems Reader: New Perspectives on Gender, Urbanism, Cultures, Indigenous Peoples, and Ecology*, edited by Thomas D. Hall. Lanham, MD: Rowman and Littlefield.

———. 2000c. "Frontiers, Ethnogenesis, and World-Systems: Rethinking the Theories." Pp. 237–270 in *A World-Systems Reader: New Perspectives on Gender, Urbanism, Cultures, Indigenous Peoples, and Ecology*, edited by Thomas D. Hall. Lanham, MD: Rowman and Littlefield.

———. 2002. "World-Systems Analysis and Globalization: Directions for the Twenty-First Century." Pp. 81–122 in *Theoretical Directions in Political Sociology for the 21st Century, Research in Political Sociology*, vol. 11, edited by Betty A. Dobratz, Timothy Buzzell, and Lisa K. Waldner. Oxford, UK: Elsevier Science Ltd.

———. 2004. "Ethnic Conflict as a Global Social Problem." Pp.139–155 in *Handbook of Social Problems: A Comparative International Perspective*, edited by George Ritzer. Thousand Oaks, CA: Sage Publications.

Hall, Thomas D., and Christopher Chase-Dunn. 2006. "Global Social Change in the Long Run." Pp.33–58 in *Global Social Change: Comparative and Historical Perspectives*, edited by Christopher Chase-Dunn and Salvatore Babones. Baltimore, MD: Johns Hopkins University Press.

Hall, Thomas D., and James V. Fenelon. 2003. "Indigenous Resistance to Globalization: What Does the Future Hold?" Pp. 173–188 in *Emerging Issues in the 21st-Century World-System: Vol. I: Crises and Resistance in the 21st-Century World-System*, edited by Wilma A. Dunaway. Westport, CT: Praeger.

———. 2004. "The Futures of Indigenous Peoples: 9-11 and the Trajectory of Indigenous Survival and Resistance." *Journal of World-Systems Research* 10, 1 (Winter): 153–197.

———. 2005a. "Indigenous Peoples and Hegemonic Change: Threats to Sovereignty or Opportunities for Resistance?" Pp. 205–225 in *Hegemonic Decline: Present and Past*, edited by Jonathan Friedman and Christopher Chase-Dunn. Boulder, CO: Paradigm Publishers.

————. 2005b. "Trajectories of Indigenous Resistance Before and After 9/11." Pp. 95–110 in *Transforming Globalization: Challenges and Opportunities in the Post 9/11 Era,* edited by Bruce Podobnik and Thomas Reifer. Leiden, the Netherlands: Brill.

————. 2008. "Indigenous Movements and Globalization: What Is Different? What Is the Same?" *Globalizations* 4, 3 (September): 1–11.

Hall, Thomas D., and Joane Nagel. 2000. "Indigenous Peoples." Pp. 1295–1301 in *The Encyclopedia of Sociology,* vol. 2, rev. ed. , edited by Edgar F. Borgatta and Rhonda J. V. Montgomery. New York: Macmillan Reference.

————. 2006. "Indigenous Peoples." Pp. 2278–2283 in *The Encyclopedia of Sociology,* vol. 5, edited by George Ritzer. Oxford, UK: Blackwell.

Harff, Barbara, and Ted Robert Gurr. 2004. *Ethnic Conflict in World Politics,* 2nd ed. Boulder, CO: Westview Press.

Harris, Betty J. 1990. "Ethnicity and Gender in the Global Periphery: A Comparison of Basotho and Navajo Women." *American Indian Culture and Research Journal* 14, 4: 15–38.

Harvard Project on American Indian Economic Development (HPAIED: Eric C. Henson, Jonathan B. Taylor, Catherine E. A. Curtis, Stephen Cornell, Kenneth W. Grant, Miriam R. Jorgensen, Joseph P. Kalt, Andrew J. Lee). 2008. *The Sate of the Native Nations: Conditions under U.S. Policies of Self-Determination.* New York: Oxford University Press.

Harvey, Neil. 1998. *The Chiapas Rebellion: The Struggle for Land and Democracy.* Durham, NC: Duke University Press.

Hayden, Tom, ed. 2002. *The Zapatista Reader.* New York: Thunder's Mouth Press/Nation Books.

Healy, Kevin. 2004. "An Andean Food Revolution: Bringing Ancient Nutrition to the Modern Marketplace." *Native Americas* 21, 2: 46–51.

Heizer, Robert, F., ed. 1978. *Handbook of North American Indians, Volume 8: California.* Washington, DC: Smithsonian Institution.

Hellman, Judith Adler. 1999. "Real and Virtual Chiapas: Magic Realism and the Left." Pp. 161–186 in *Necessary and Unnecessary Utopias: Socialist Register 2000,* edited by Leo Panitch, and Colin Leys. New York: Merlin Press/Fernwood Press/Monthly Review Press.

Henare, Manuka. 2001. *"Tapu, Mana, Mauri, Hau, Wairua:* A Maori Philosophy of Vitalism and Cosmos." In *Indigenous Traditions and Ecology: The Interbeing of Cosmology and Community,* edited by John Grim. Cambridge, MA: Harvard University Press.

Henck, Nick. 2007. *Subcommander Marcos: The Man and the Mask.* Durham: Duke University Press.

Hill, Jonathan D., ed. 1996. *History, Power, and Identity: Ethnogenesis in the Americas, 1492–1992.* Iowa City: University of Iowa Press.

Himmel, Kelly D. 1999. *The Conquest of the Karankawas and the Tonkawas: A Study in Social Change, 1821–1859.* College Station: Texas A&M University Press.

Hodgson, Dorothy L. 2002. "Precarious Alliances: The Cultural Politics and Structural Predicaments of the Indigenous Rights Movement in Tanzania." *American Anthropologist* 104, 4 (December): 1086–1097.

Hollis, Shirley. 2004. "Crafting Europe's 'Clean Slate' Advantage: World-System Expansion and the Indigenous Mississippians of North America." *American Indian Culture and Research Journal* 28, 3: 77–101.

————. 2005. "Contact, Incorporation, and the North American Southeast." *Journal of World-Systems Research* 11, 1 (July): 95–130. Available online at http://jwsr.ucr.edu/index.php.

Holton, Robert J. 2005. *Making Globalization.* New York: Palgrave Macmillan.

Honeychurch, William, and Chunag Amartuvshin. 2006. "States on Horseback: The Rise of Inner Asian Confederations and Empires." Pp. 255–278 in *Archaeology of Asia,* edited by Miriam T. Stark. Malden, MA: Blackwell.

Horsley, Peter. 2008. "The Foreshore and Seabed Debate in Aotearoa: Maori Resistance, Judicial Innovation, and State Control." *American Behavioral Scientist* 51, 12 (August): 1656–1671.

Hsiao, H. H. Michael. 2002. "Coexistence and Synthesis: Cultural Globalization and Localization in Contemporary Taiwan." Pp. 48–67 in *Many Globalizations: Cultural Diversity in the Contemporary World,* edited by Peter L. Berger and Samuel P. Huntington. New York: Oxford University Press.

Hughes, Lotte. 2003. *The No-Nonsense Guide to Indigenous Peoples.* London: Verso.

Huntington, Samuel P. 1996. *The Clash of Civilizations and the Remaking of World Order.* New York: Simon and Schuster.

Hurtado, Albert L. 1988. *Indian Survival on the California Frontier.* New Haven, CT: Yale University Press.

International Work Group for Indigenous Affairs, http://www.iwgia.org/ (last accessed July 13, 2008).

Ito, Shingo. 2008. "Japan Recognises Indigenous People." Agence France Presse, English, June 6, http://asia.news.yahoo.com (accessed October 9, 2008).

Iverson, Peter. 1981. *The Navajo Nation.* Albuquerque: University of New Mexico Press.

———. 1994. *When Indians Became Cowboys: Native Peoples and Cattle Ranching in the American West.* Norman: University of Oklahoma Press.

———. 1999. *"We Are Still Here": American Indians in the Twentieth Century.* Wheeling, IL: Harlan Davidson.

Iverson, Peter, and Linda MacCannell. 1999. *Riders of the West: Portraits from Indian Rodeo.* Seattle: University of Washington Press.

Jaimes, M. Annette, with Halsey, Theresa. 1992. "American Indian Women: At the Center of Indigenous North America." Pp. 311–344 in *The State of Native America: Genocide, Colonization, and Resistance,* edited by M. Annette Jaimes. Boston: South End Press.

Jennings, Francis. 1975. *The Invasion of America: Indians, Colonialism, and the Cant of Conquest.* Chapel Hill: Institute of Early American History and Culture, University of North Carolina Press.

Johnston, José. 2000. "Pedagogical Guerrillas, Armed Democrats, and Revolutionary Counterpublics: Examining Paradox in the Zapatista Uprising in Chiapas, Mexico." *Theory and Society* 29, 4 (August): 463–505.

Johnston-Dodds, Kimberly. 2002. "Early California Laws and Policies Related to California Indians." California Research Bureau, California State Library, http://www.library .ca.gov/crb/02/14/02-014.pdf (accessed July 14, 2008).

Jorgensen, Joseph J. 1972. *The Sun Dance Religion: Power for the Powerless.* Chicago: University of Chicago Press.

Kardulias, P. Nick. 1990. "Fur Production as a Specialized Activity in a World System: Indians in the North American Fur Trade." *American Indian Culture and Research Journal* 14, 1: 25–60.

Katzenberger, Elaine, ed. 1995. *First World, Ha Ha Ha! The Zapatista Challenge.* San Francisco: City Lights Books.

Kavanaugh, Thomas K. 1996. *Comanche Political History: An Ethnohistorical Perspective, 1706–1875.* Lincoln: University of Nebraska Press.

Kearns, Rick. 2008. "From Slavery to Government: The Rise of Ache Guayaki Chief Margarita Mbywangi of Paraguay." *Indian Country Today,* October 3, http://www.indiancountry .com (accessed October 9, 2008).

Keenan, Danny. 2002. "Bound to the Land: Maori Retention and Assertion of Land and

Identity." In *Environmental Histories of New Zealand,* edited by Eric Pawson and Tom Brooking. Melbourne: Oxford University Press.

Kentor, Jeffery. 2004. "Quantifying Hegemony in the World Economy." Pp. 74–87 in *Globalization, Hegemony, and Power: Antisystemic Movements and the Global System,* edited by Thomas E. Reifer. Boulder, CO: Paradigm Publishers.

Kçpa, Mere, and Linitâ Manu'atu. 2008. "Pedagogical Decolonization: Impacts of the European/Pâkehâ Society on the Education of Tongan People in Aotearoa-New Zealand." *American Behavioral Scientist* 51, 12 (August): 1801–1816.

Kessell, John H. 2002. *Spain in the Southwest: A Narrative History of Colonial New Mexico, Arizona, Texas, and California.* Norman: University of Oklahoma Press.

King, Anthony D., ed. 1997. *Culture, Globalization, and the World-System: Contemporary Conditions for the Representation of Identity.* Minneapolis: University of Minnesota Press.

Kopytoff, Igor. 1987. *The African Frontier: The Reproduction of Traditional African Societies.* Bloomington: Indiana University Press.

Krauze, Enrique. 2002. "Chiapas: The Indians' Prophet." Pp. 395–417 in *The Zapatista Reader,* edited by Tom Hayden. New York: Thunder's Mouth Press/Nation Books.

Kuecker, Glen. 2004. "Latin American Resistance Movements in the Time of the Posts." *History Compass* 2: 1–126.

La Barre, Weston. 1964. *The Peyote Cult.* Hamden, CT: Shoe String Press.

Laczko, Leslie S. 2000. "Canada's Linguistic and Ethnic Dynamics in an Evolving World-System." Pp. 131–142 in *A World-Systems Reader: New Perspectives on Gender, Urbanism, Cultures, Indigenous Peoples, and Ecology,* edited by Thomas D. Hall. Lanham, MD: Rowman and Littlefield.

La Lone, Darrell. 2000. "Rise, Fall, and Semiperipheral Development in the Andean World-System." *Journal of World-Systems Research* 6, 1 (Spring): 68–99. Available online at http://jwsr.ucr.edu/index.php.

Landsman, Gail. 1979. "The Ghost Dance and the Policy of Land Allotment." *American Sociological Review* 44 (February): 162–166.

Langer, Eric, ed. 2003. *Contemporary Indigenous Movements in Latin America.* Wilmington, DE: Scholarly Resources.

Langman, Lauren, D. Morris, and J. Zalewski. 2003. "Cyberactivism and Alternative Globalization Movements." Pp. 218–235 in *Emerging Issues in the 21st-Century World-System: Vol. 1: Crises and Resistance in the 21st-Century World-System,* edited by Wilma A. Dunaway. Westport, CT: Praeger.

Lassiter, Luke E. 1997. "Southwestern Oklahoma, the Gourd Dance, and 'Charlie Brown.'" *American Indian Culture and Research Journal* 21, 4: 75–103. Reprinted as pp. 145–166 in *Contemporary Native American Cultural Issues,* edited by Duane Champagne. Walnut Creek, CA: AltaMira Press, 1999.

Latané, Bibb, and John M. Darley. 1970. *The Unresponsive Bystander: Why Doesn't He Help?* New York: Appleton-Century Crofts.

Lazarus, Edward. 1991. *Black Hills, White Justice: The Sioux Nation Versus the United States, 1775 to the Present.* New York: Harper Collins.

Liebler, Carolyn A. 2004. "American Indian Ethnic Identity: Tribal Nonresponse in the 1990 Census." *Social Science Quarterly* 85, 2 (June): 310–323.

Lyons, Oren. 2007. "Septembers to Remember for Indigenous Peoples." *Indian Country Today,* September 20, http://www.indiancountry.com (accessed October 9, 2008).

Macharia, Kinuthia. 2003. "Resistant Indigenous Identities in the 21st-Century World-System: Selected African Cases." Pp. 189–200 in *Emerging Issues in the 21st-Century World-System: Vol. 1: Crises and Resistance in the 21st-Century World-System,* edited by Wilma A. Dunaway. Westport, CT: Praeger.

MacLachlan, Colin M., and Jaime E. Rodriguez. 1980. *Forging the Cosmic Race: A Reinterpretation of Colonial Mexico.* Berkeley: University of California Press.

Maldonado Alvarado, Benjamin. 2002. *Autonomia y Communalidad India, enfoques y propuestas desde Oaxaca. INAH, Secretaria de Asuntos Indigenas,* Oaxaca, Mexico: CEDI.

Mallon, Florencia. 1997. *Peasant and Nation: The Making of Postcolonial Mexico and Peru.* Berkeley: University of California Press.

Mandell, Daniel R. 1996. *Behind the Frontier: Indians in Eighteenth-Century Eastern Massachusetts.* Lincoln: University of Nebraska Books.

———. 2008. *Tribe, Race, History: Native Americans in Southern New England, 1780–1880.* Baltimore, MD: Johns Hopkins University Press.

Mander, Jerry, and Edward Goldsmith, eds. 1996. *The Case Against the Global Economy and for a Turn Toward the Local.* San Francisco: Sierra Club Books.

Mann, Charles C. 2005. *1491: New Revelations of the Americas Before Columbus.* New York: Alfred A. Knopf.

Manning, Susan, ed. 1999. "Introduction [to special issue on Globalization]." *Journal of World-Systems Research* 5, 2 (Summer): 137–141. Available online at http://jwsr.ucr.edu/index.php (issue 137-461).

Marcos, Sylvia. 2005. "We Come to Ask for Justice, Not Crumbs." Pp. 97–108 in *Indigenous People and the Modern State,* edited by Duane Champagne, Karen Torjesen, and Susan Steiner. Walnut Creek, CA: AltaMira Press.

Marin, C. 1998. "Plan del ejercito en Chiapas desde 1994." *Proceso* (January 4): 6–11.

Marsden, Maori. 2003. *The Woven Universe: Selected Writings of Rev. Maori Marsden, Te Ahukaramu* (editor) Charles Royal, Estate of Rev. Marsden, Te Wananga-o-Raukawa, Otaki.

Mathien, Frances Joan, and Randall McGuire, eds. 1986. *Ripples in the Chichimec Sea: Consideration of Southwestern-Mesoamerican Interactions.* Carbondale: Southern Illinois University Press.

Mattern, Mark. 1996. "The Powwow as a Public Arena for Negotiating Unity and Diversity in American Life." *American Indian Culture and Research Journal* 21, 4: 75–103. Reprinted as pp. 129–143 in *Contemporary Native American Cultural Issues,* edited by Duane Champagne. Walnut Creek, CA: AltaMira Press, 1999.

Matthiessen, Peter. 1983. *In the Spirit of Crazy Horse.* New York: Viking.

Mattiace, Shannan L. 2003. *To See with Two Eyes: Peasant Activism and Indian Autonomy in Chiapas, Mexico.* Albuquerque: University of New Mexico Press.

Maybury-Lewis, David. 2002. "Genocide Against Indigenous Peoples." Pp. 43–53 in *Annihilating Difference: The Anthropology of Genocide,* edited by Alexander Hinton. Berkeley: University of California Press.

McAdam, Doug, Sidney Tarrow, and Charles Tilly. 2001. *Dynamics of Contention.* Cambridge: Cambridge University Press.

McCarty, Teresa L. 2003. "Revitalising Indigenous Languages in Homogenising Times." *Comparative Education* 39, 2: 147–163.

McLeod, Leonard (producer). 2001. *In the Light of Reverence: Protecting America's Sacred Lands.* Oley, PA: Bullfrog Films. http://www.sacredland.org/.

McMichael, Philip. 2003. *Development and Social Change: A Global Perspective,* 3rd ed. Thousand Oaks, CA: Pine Forge Press.

McNamara, Patrick J. 2007. *Sons of the Sierra: Juárez, Díaz, and the People of Ixtlán, Oaxaca, 1855–1920.* Chapel Hill: University of North Carolina Press.

McNeill, William H. 1986. *Polyethnicity and National Unity in World History.* Toronto: University of Toronto Press.

Menchu, Rigoberta. 1984. *I, Rigoberta Menchuì : An Indian Woman in Guatemala.* Edited by Elisabeth Burgos-Debray; translated by Ann Wright. New York: Verso.

Meyer, Jean. 2000. *Samuel Ruiz en San Cristóbal.* Mexico: Tusquets.

Meyer, Melissa L. 1990. "Signatures and Thumbprints: Ethnicity Among the White Earth Anishinaabeg, 1889–1920." *Social Science History* 14, 3 (Fall): 305–345.

————. 1991. "'We Cannot Get a Living as We Used To': Dispossession and the White Earth Anishinaabeg, 1889–1920." *American Historical Review* 96, 2: 368–394.

————. 1994. *The White Earth Tragedy: Ethnicity and Dispossession at a Minnesota Anishinaabe Reservation, 1889–1920.* Lincoln: University of Nebraska Press.

Mignolo, Walter D. 2002. "The Zapatista's Theoretical Revolution: Its Historical, Ethical, and Political Consequences." *Review* 25, 3: 245–275.

Miller, Bruce G. 1994. "Contemporary Tribal Codes and Gender Issues." *American Indian Culture and Research Journal* 18, 2: 43–74. Reprinted as pp. 103–126 in *Contemporary Native American Cultural Issues,* edited by Duane Champagne. Walnut Creek, CA: AltaMira Press, 1999.

Mohawk, John C. 2000. *Utopian Legacies: A History of Conquest and Oppression in the Western World.* Santa Fe, NM: Clear Light Publishers.

————. 2007. *Indian Country Today,* September 20, http://www.indiancountry.com. Originally published as "From the Natural People to the Western World." In *A Basic Call to Consciousness: The Hau de no sau nee Address to the Western World,* edited by Six Nations. Mohawk Nation, Rooseveltown, NY: Akwesasne Notes.

Montejano, David. 1981. "Is Texas Bigger Than the World-System? A Critique for a Provincial Point of View." *Review* 4, 3 (Winter): 597–628.

————. 1987. *Anglos and Mexicans in the Making of Texas, 1836–1986.* Austin: University of Texas Press.

Moon, Paul. 2002. *Te Ara Ki Te Tiriti: The Path to the Treaty of Waitangi.* Auckland, New Zealand: David Ling Publishing.

Mooney, James. 1973 [1896]. *The Ghost Dance Religion and Wounded Knee.* New York: Dover Publications.

Mörner, Magnus. 1967. *Race Mixture in the History of Latin America.* New York: Little, Brown.

————. 1973. "The Spanish American Hacienda: A Survey of Recent Research and Debate." *Hispanic American Historical Review* 53, 2 (May): 183–216.

————. 1983. "Economic Factors and Stratification in Colonial Spanish America with Special Regard to Elites." *Hispanic American Historical Review* 63, 2 (May): 335–369.

Morton, Adam David. 2000. "Mexico, Neoliberal Restructuring, and the EZLN: A Neo-Gramscian Analayis." Pp. 255–279 in *Globalization and the Politics of Resistance,* edited by Barry K. Gills. New York: St. Martin's Press.

Moses, A. Dirk. 2000. "An Antipodean Genocide? The Origins of the Genocidal Moment in the Colonization of Australia." *Journal of Genocide Research* 2, 1: 89–106.

————. 2004. "Genocide and Settler Society in Australian History." In *Genocide and Settler Society: Frontier Violence and Stolen Indigenous Children in Australian History,* edited by A. Dirk Moses. New York: Berghan Books.

Mullis, Angela, and David Kamper. 2000. *Indian Gaming: Who Wins?* Los Angeles: Native American Studies.

Muñoz Ramírez, Gloria. 2003. *EZLN: 20 y 10, el fuego y la palabra.* Mexico, DF: La Jornada Ediciones [rev. ed.: Muñoz Ramírez, Gloria. 2008. *The Fire and the Word: A History of the Zapatista Movement.* San Francisco: City Lights].

Nagel, Joane. 1996. *American Indian Ethnic Renewal: Red Power and the Resurgence of Identity and Culture.* New York: Oxford University Press.

Nash, June. 2001. *Mayan Visions: The Quest for Autonomy in an Age of Globalization.* New York: Routledge.

National Tribal Justice Resource Center, http://www.tribalresourcecenter.org/personnel/ (last accessed July 13, 2008).

Navajo Nation Peacemaking Program, http://www.navajocourts.org/index5.htm (last accessed July 13, 2008).

Navarro, Luis Hernández, and Ramón Vera Herrera, eds. 1998. *Acuerdos de San Andrés.* Mexico: Ediciones Era.

Nee-Benham, Maenette, and Ronald H. Heck. 1998. *Culture and Educational Policy in Hawaii: The Silencing of Native Voices.* Mahwah, NJ: Lawrence Erlbaum Associates.

Nesper, Larry. 2002. *The Walleye War: The Struggle for Ojibwe Spearfishing and Treaty Rights.* Lincoln: University of Nebraska Press.

Nettle, Daniel, and Suzanne Romaine. 2000. *Vanishing Voices: The Extinction of the World's Languages.* New York: Oxford University Press.

Niezen, Ronald. 2003. *The Origins of Indigenism: Human Rights and the Politics of Identity.* Berkeley: University of California Press.

Nostrand, Richard L. 1980. "The Hispano Homeland in 1900." *Annals of the Association of American Geographers* 70, 3 (September): 382–396.

———. 1984. "Hispano Cultural Distinctiveness: A Reply." *Annals of the Association of American Geographers* 74, 1 (April): 164–169.

———. 1992. *The Hispano Homeland.* Norman: University of Oklahoma Press.

———. 2003. *El Cerrito, New Mexico: Eight Generations in a Spanish Village.* Norman: University of Oklahoma Press.

Noyce, Phillip. (director) 2002. *Rabbit-Proof Fence.* Australia: Miramax.

O'Brien, Patricia. 1992. "The 'World-System' of Cahokia Within the Middle Mississippi Tradition." *Review* 15, 3 (Summer): 389–417.

Omi, Michael, and Howard Winant. 1994. *Racial Formation in the United States: From the 1960s to the 1990s,* 2nd ed. New York: Routledge.

Ortiz, Roxanne Dunbar. 1984. *Indians of the Americas: Human Rights and Self-determination.* New York: Praeger.

———. 1985. "The Fourth World and Indigenism: Politics of Isolation and Alternatives." *Journal of Ethnic Studies* 12 (Spring): 79–105, 2: 113–120.

Parezo, Nancy J. 1983. *Navajo Sandpainting: From Religious Act to Commercial Art.* Albuquerque: University of New Mexico Press.

Peregrine, Peter N. 1992. *Mississippian Evolution: A World-System Perspective.* Monographs in World Archaeology No. 9. Madison, WI: Prehistory Press.

———. 1995. "Networks of Power: The Mississippian World-System." Pp. 132–143 in *Native American Interactions,* edited by M. Nassaney and K. Sassaman. Knoxville: University of Tennessee Press.

Peregrine, Peter N., and Gary M. Feinman, eds. 1996. *Pre-Columbian World-Systems.* Monographs in World Archaeology No. 26. Madison, WI: Prehistory Press.

Perry, Richard J. 1996. *From Time Immemorial: Indigenous Peoples and State Systems.* Austin: University of Texas Press.

Peters, Russell. M. 1987. *The Wampanoags of Mashpee: An Indian Perspective on American History.* Washington, DC: Smithsonian Institute Indian Spiritual and Cultural Training Council.

Pickering, Kathleen. 2000. *Lakota Culture, World Economy.* Lincoln: University of Nebraska Press.

Pilkington Garimara, Doris. 2001. *Follow the Rabbit-Proof Fence.* St Lucia, Australia: University of Queensland Press.

Pineda, F. 1996. "*La guerra de baja intensidad.*" Pp. 173–196 in *Chiapas 2,* edited by Andres Barreda et al. Mexico: Instituto de Investigaciones Economicas.

Pitt, Leonard. 1966. *The Decline of the Californios.* Berkeley: University of California Press.

Podobnik, Bruce. 2005. "Resistance to Globalization: Cycles and Trends in the Globalization Protest Movement." Pp. 51–68 in *Transforming Globalization: Challenges and Opportunities in the Post 9/11 Era,* edited by Bruce Podobnik and Thomas Reifer. Leiden, the Netherlands: Brill.

Poniatowska, Elena. 1998. *La noche de Tlatelolco: Testimonios de historia oral.* Mexico: Ediciones Era.

Postero, Nancy. 2005. "Indigenous Responses to Neoliberalism: A Look at the Bolivian Uprising of 2003." *PoLAR: Political and Legal Anthropology Review* 28, 1: 73–92.

Powers, William. 1986. *Sacred Language: The Nature of Supernatural Discourse in Lakota.* Norman: University of Oklahoma Press.

Prabhu, Pradip. 2001. "In the Eye of the Storm: Tribal Peoples of India." Pp. 47–69 in *Indigenous Traditions and Ecology: The Interbeing of Cosmology and Community,* edited by John Grim. Cambridge, MA: Harvard University Press.

———. 2004. "Nature, Culture, and Diversity—The Indigenous Way of Life." Pp. 39–82 in *The Value of Nature: Ecological Politics in India,* edited by Imtiaz Smitu Kothari and Helmut Reifeld. New Delhi: Rainbow Publishers.

"Preamble," in *A Basic Call to Consciousness: The Hau de no sau nee Address to the Western World,* edited by Six Nations. Mohawk Nation, Rooseveltown, NY: Akwesasne Notes.

Preston, Julia, and Sam Dillon. 2004. *Opening Mexico: The Making of a Democracy.* New York: Farrar, Straus, and Giroux.

Prucha, Francis Paul. 1975. *Documents of United States Indian Policy.* Lincoln: University of Nebraska Press.

———. 1984. *The Great Father, the United States Government, and the American Indians.* Lincoln: University of Nebraska Press.

———. 1990. *Documents of United States Indian Policy.* Lincoln: University of Nebraska Press.

Public Broadcasting System. 1990. *Winds of Change: A Matter of Promises.*

Rafert, Stewart. 1996. *The Miami Indians of Indiana: A Persistent People, 1654–1994.* Indianapolis: Indiana Historical Society.

Ragin, Charles. 1994. *Constructing Social Research: The Unity and Diversity of Method.* Thousand Oaks, CA: Pine Forge Press.

Rainforestweb, http://www.rainforestweb.org/Rainforest_Information/Indigenous_Peoples/?state=more (accessed July 13, 2008).

Reichard, Gladys A. 1950. *Navajo Religion: A Study of Symbolism.* Princeton, NJ: Princeton University Press.

Reséndez, Andrés. 2005. *Changing National Identities at the Frontier: Texas and New Mexico, 1800–1850.* Cambridge, MA: Cambridge University Press.

Reyes, Reynaldo, and F. J. K. Wilson. 1992. *Rafaga: The Life Story of a Nicaraguan Miskito Comandante.* Norman: University of Oklahoma Press.

Reynolds, Jerry. 2006. "Africa's Indigenous San Win in Court, Now Face Regulations." *Indian Country Today,* December 20, http://www.indiancountry.com (accessed October 9, 2008).

Riggs, Fred W. 1994. "Ethnonationalism, Industrialism, and the Modern State." *Third World Quarterly* 15, 4: 583–611.

———, ed. 1998a. "Ethnic Nationalism and the World Systemic Crisis." Special issue of *International Political Science Review* 19, 3 (July): 227–332.

———. 1998b. "Ethnic Nationalism and the World Systemic Crisis: A Preface." *International Political Science Review* 19, 3 (July): 227–229.

————. 1998c. "The Modernity of Ethnic Identity and Conflict." *International Political Science Review* 19, 3 (July): 269–288.

Robertson, Roland. 1992. *Globalization: Social Theory and Global Culture.* London: Sage Publications.

————. 1995. "Glocalization: Time-Space and Homogeneity-Heterogeneity." Pp. 25–24 in *Global Modernities,* edited by Mike Featherstone, Scott Lash, and Roland Robertson. Newbury Park, CA: Sage Publications.

Robinson, William I. 2004. *A Theory of Global Capitalism: Production, Class, and State in a Transnational World.* Baltimore, MD: Johns Hopkins University Press.

Roessel, Ruth. 1973. *Navajo Stories of the Long Walk.* Tsaile, AZ: Navajo Community College Press.

Romero, Simon. 2008. "A Vote That May Strengthen Bolivian Leader." *New York Times,* August 9.

Rose, Wendy. 1992. "The Great Pretenders: Further Reflections on Whiteshamism." Pp. 403–421 in *The State of Native America: Genocide, Colonization, and Resistance,* edited by M. Annette Jaimes. Boston: South End Press.

Ross, John. 1995. *Rebellion from the Roots: Indian Uprising in Chiapas.* Monroe, ME: Common Courage Press.

Rubin, Jeffrey W. 1997. *Decentering the Regime: Ethnicity, Radicalism, and Democracy in Juchitán, Mexico.* Durham, NC: Duke University Press.

Russ, William Adam. 1992. *The Hawaiian Revolution (1893–94).* Monmouth Junction, NJ: Associated University Presses.

Russell, James. W. 1994. *After the Fifth Sun: Class and Race in North America.* Englewood Cliffs, NJ: Prentice-Hall.

Sanderson, Stephen K., and Arthur S. Alderson. 2005. *World Societies: The Evolution of Human Social Life.* Boston: Pearson, Allyn, and Bacon.

Scheduled Tribes (Recognition of Forest Rights) Bill. 2005. New Dehli: Ministry of Environment and Forest, Government of India.

Scott, James C. 1985. *Weapons of the Weak: Everyday Forms of Peasant Resistance.* New Haven, CT: Yale University Press.

Selverston, Melinda H. 1998. "Pachacutik: Indigenous People and Democracy in Ecuador." *Native Americas* 15, 2: 12–21.

Shannon, Thomas R. 1996. *An Introduction to the World-System Perspective,* 2nd ed. Boulder, CO: Westview Press.

Shoemaker, Nancy, ed. 1995. *Negotiators of Change: Historical Perspectives on Native American Women.* New York: Routledge.

Sinopoli. Carla M. 2006. "Imperial Landscapes in South Asia." Pp. 324–349 in *Archaeology of Asia,* edited by Miriam T. Stark. Malden, MA: Blackwell.

Six Nations. 1978. *A Basic Call to Consciousness: The Hau de no sau nee Address to the Western World.* Mohawk Nation, Rooseveltown, NY: Akwesasne Notes.

Sklair, Lelsie. 2002. *Globalization: Capitalism, and Its Alternatives,* 3rd ed. Oxford, UK: Oxford University Press.

————. 2006. "Competing Conceptions of Globalization." Pp. 59–78 in *Global Social Change: Comparative and Historical Perspectives,* edited by Christopher Chase-Dunn and Salvatore Babones. Baltimore, MD: Johns Hopkins University Press.

Smedley, Audrey. 1999. *Race in North America: Origin and Evolution of a Worldview,* 2nd ed. Boulder, CO: Westview Press.

Smith, Claire Heather Burke, and Graeme K. Ward. 2000. "Globalisation and Indigenous Peoples: Threat or Empowerment?" Pp. 1–24 in *Indigenous Cultures in an Interconnected*

World, edited by Claire Smith and Graeme K. Ward. St. Leonards, NWS Australia: Allen and Unwin.

Smith, Jackie. 2008. *Social Movements for Global Democracy.* Baltimore, MD: Johns Hopkins University Press.

Smith, Jackie, and Hank Johnston, eds. 2002. *Globalization and Resistance: Transnational Dimensions of Social Movements.* Lanham, MD: Rowman and Littlefield.

Smith, Jackie, and Dawn Wiest. 2006. "National and Global Foundations of Global Civil Society." Pp. 289–313 in *Global Social Change: Comparative and Historical Perspectives,* edited by Christopher Chase-Dunn and Salvatore Babones. Baltimore, MD: Johns Hopkins University Press.

Smith, Joan, Jane Collins, Terence K. Hopkins, and Akhbar Muhammed, eds. 1988. *Racism, Sexism, and the World-System.* New York: Greenwood Press.

Smith, Keri E. Iyall. 2008. "Comparing State and International Protections of Indigenous Peoples' Human Rights." *American Behavioral Scientist* 51, 12 (August): 1817–1883.

Smith, Linda Tuwahi. 1999. *Decolonizing Methodologies Research and Indigenous Peoples.* Dunedin, New Zealand, and London: University of Otago Press and Zed Books.

Snipp, C. Matthew. 1986. "Who Are American Indians? Some Observations About the Perils and Pitfalls of Data for Race and Ethnicity." *Population Research and Policy Review* 5: 237–252.

———, ed. 1988a. *Public Policy Impacts on American Indian Economic Development.* Albuquerque, NM: Native American Studies (Development Series No 4).

———. 1988b. "Public Policy Impacts and American Indian Economic Development." Pp. 1–22 in *Public Policy Impacts on American Indian Economic Development.* Albuquerque, NM: Native American Studies (Development Series No 4).

———. 1989. *American Indians: The First of This Land.* New York: Russell Sage Foundation.

———. 1992. "Sociological Perspectives on American Indians." *Annual Review of Sociology* 18: 351–370.

Snow, Dean R. 1994. *The Iroquois.* New York: Blackwell.

Spicer, Edward E. 1962. *Cycles of Conquest: The Impact of Spain, Mexico, and the United States on the Indians of the Southwest, 1533–1960.* Tucson: University of Arizona Press.

Spolsky, Bernard. 1970. "Navajo Language Maintenance: Six-Year-Olds in 1969." *Language Sciences* 13 (December): 63–73.

———. 2002. "Prospects for the Survival of the Navajo Language: A Reconsideration." *Anthropology and Education Quarterly* 33, 2: 139–162.

Sponsel, Leslie E. 1995a. "Relationships Among the World System, Indigenous Peoples, and Ecological Anthropology in the Endangered Amazon." Pp. 263–283 in *Indigenous Peoples and the Future of Amazonia: An Ecological Anthropology of an Endangered World,* edited by Leslie E. Sponsel. Tucson: University of Arizona Press.

———. 1995b. *Indigenous Peoples and the Future of Amazonia: An Ecological Anthropology of an Endangered World.* Tucson: University of Arizona Press.

———. 2000a. "Identities, Ecologies, Rights, and Futures: All Endangered." Pp. 1–22 in *Endangered Peoples of Southeast and East Asia: Struggles to Survive,* edited by Leslie E. Sponsel. Westport, CT: Greenwood Press.

———. 2000b. *Endangered Peoples of Southeast and East Asia: Struggles to Survive.* Westport, CT: Greenwood Press.

Stahler-Sholk, Richard. 2005. "Time of the Snails: Autonomy and Resistance in Chiapas." *NACLA: Report on the Americas* 38, 5 (March–April): 34–40.

Stahler-Sholk, Richard, Harv E. Vanden, and Glen David Kuecker, eds. 2008. *Latin American*

Social Movements in the Twenty-First Century: Resistance, Power, and Democracy. Lanham, MD: Rowman and Littlefield.

Standing Bear, Luther. 1933. *Land of the Spotted Eagle, by Chief Standing Bear.* Boston: Houghton Mifflin Company.

Stannard, David E. 1992. *American Holocaust: Columbus and the Conquest of the New World.* New York: Oxford University Press.

Stark, Miriam T. 2006a. *Archaeology of Asia.* Malden, MA: Blackwell.

———. 2006. "Contextualizing an Archaeology of Asia." Pp. 3–13 in *Archaeology of Asia,* edited by Miriam T. Stark. Malden, MA: Blackwell.

Stavenhagen, Rodolfo. 1990. *The Ethnic Question: Conflicts, Development, and Human Rights.* Tokyo: United Nations Press.

Steinmetz, George, ed. 2005. *The Politics of Method in the Human Sciences: Positivism and Its Epistemological Others.* Durham, NC: Duke University Press.

Stephen, Lynn. 2002. *Zapata Lives! Histories and Cultural Politics in Southern Mexico.* Berkeley: University of California Press.

———. 2005. *Zapotec Women: Gender, Class, and Ethnicity in Globalized Oaxaca.* Durham, NC, and London: Duke University Press.

Stern, Steve J. 1988a. "Feudalism, Capitalism, and the World-System in the Perspective of Latin America and the Caribbean." *American Historical Review* 93, 4 (October): 829–872.

———. 1988b. "Reply: 'Ever More Solitary.'" *American Historical Review* 93, 4 (October): 886–897.

Stewart, Omer C. 1987. *Peyote Religion: A History.* Norman: University of Oklahoma Press.

Stonich, Susan C. 2001. *Endangered Peoples of Latin America: Struggles to Survive and Thrive.* Westport, CT: Greenwood Press.

Stucki, Larry R. 1971. "The Case Against Population Control: The Probable Creation of the First American Indian State." *Human Organization* 30, 4 (Winter): 393–426.

Swett, Charles. 1995. *Strategic Assessment: The Internet.* Office of the Assistant Secretary of Defense for Special Operations and Low-Intensity Conflict (Policy Planning), http://www.fas.org/cp/swett.html (accessed July 14, 2008).

Tatz, Colin. 1999. *Genocide in Australia.* Canberra: Aboriginal Studies Press.

———. 2003. *With Intent to Destroy: Reflecting on Genocide.* New York: Verso.

Thompson, William R. 2000. "K-Waves, Leadership Cycles, and Global War: A Nonhyphenated Approach to World Systems Analysis." Pp. 83–104 in *A World-Systems Reader: New Perspectives on Gender, Urbanism, Cultures, Indigenous Peoples, and Ecology,* edited by Thomas D. Hall. Lanham, MD: Rowman and Littlefield.

Thornton, Russell. 1986. *We Shall Live Again: The 1870 and 1890 Ghost Dance Movements as Demographic Revitalization.* New York: Cambridge University Press.

———. 1987. *American Indian Holocaust and Survival.* Norman: University of Oklahoma Press.

United Nations Development Program, http://www.undp.org/ (accessed July 13, 2008).

United Nations High Commission on Refugees, http://www.unhcr.org/cgi-bin/texis/vtx/home, (accessed July 13, 2008).

United Nations Permanent Forum on Indigenous Issues, http://www.un.org/esa/socdev/unpfii/ (accessed July 13, 2008).

Utley, Robert M. 1984. *The Indian Frontier of the American West, 1846–1890.* Albuquerque: University of New Mexico Press.

———. 1993. *The Lance and the Shield: The Life and Times of Sitting Bull.* New York: Henry Holt.

Valandra, Edward Charles. 2006. *Not Without Our Consent: Lakota Resistance to Termination, 1950–59.* Champaign-Urbana: University of Illinois Press.

Vestal, Stanley. 1932. *Sitting Bull: Champion of the Sioux*. New York: Houghton Mifflin.

Walker, James R. 1980. *Lakota Belief and Ritual*. Edited by Raymond J. DeMallie and Elaine A. Jahner. Lincoln: University of Nebraska Press.

———. 1982 [1917]. *Lakota Society*. Edited by Raymond J. DeMallie. Lincoln: University of Nebraska Press.

———. 1983. *Lakota Myth*. Edited by Elaine A. Jahner. Lincoln: University of Nebraska Press.

Wallace, Anthony. 1956. "Revitalization Movements." *American Anthropologist* 58, 2 (April): 264–281.

———. 1969. *The Death and Rebirth of the Seneca Movement*. New York: Knopf.

Wallerstein, Immanuel. 1974. *The Modern World-System: Capitalist Agriculture and the Origins of European World-Economy in the Sixteenth Century*. New York: Academic Press.

———. 1988. "Comments on Stern's Critical Tests." *American Historical Review* 93, 4 (October): 873–885.

———. 2004. *World-Systems Analysis: An Introduction*. Durham, NC: Duke University Press.

Ward, Carol, Elon Stander, and Yodit Solom. 2000. "Resistance Through Healing Among American Indian Women." Pp. 211–236 in *A World-Systems Reader: New Perspectives on Gender, Urbanism, Cultures, Indigenous Peoples, and Ecology*, edited by Thomas D. Hall. Lanham, MD: Rowman and Littlefield.

Ward, Kathryn B. 1993. "Reconceptualizing World-system Theory to Include Women." Pp. 43–68 in *Theory on Gender/Feminism on Theory*, edited by Paula England. New York: Aldine.

Weber, David J. 1982. *The Mexican Frontier, 1821–1846*. Albuquerque: University of New Mexico Press.

———. 1992. *The Spanish Frontier in North America*. New Haven, CT: Yale University Press.

———, ed. 1999. *What Caused the Pueblo Revolt?* Boston: Bedford/St. Martin's Press.

———. 2005. *Bárbaros: Spaniards and Their Savages in the Age of Enlightenment*. New Haven, CT: Yale University Press.

Weinberg, Bill. 2000. *Homage to Chiapas: The New Indigenous Struggles in Mexico*. New York: Verso.

White, Richard. 1983. *The Roots of Dependency: Subsistence, Environment, and Social Change Among the Choctaws, Pawnees, and Navajos*. Lincoln: University of Nebraska Press.

———. 1991. *"It's Your Misfortune and None of My Own": A New History of the West*. Norman: University of Oklahoma Press.

———. 1994. "Winning of the West: The Expansion of the Western Sioux in the Eighteenth and Nineteenth Centuries." In *Major Problems in American Indian History*, edited by Albert L. Hurtado and Peter Iverson. Lexington, MA: D. C. Heath.

Whitt, Laurie Anne. 1995. "Indigenous Peoples and the Cultural Politics of Knowledge." Pp. 223–272 in *Issues in Native American Cultural Identity*, edited by Michael K. Green. New York: Peter Lang.

Wilkins, David E. 1997. *American Indian Sovereignty and the U.S. Supreme Court: The Masking of Justice*. Austin: University of Texas Press.

———. 2006. *American Indian Politics and the American Political System*, 2nd ed. Lanham, MD: Rowman and Littlefield.

Wilmer, Franke. 1993. *The Indigenous Voice in World Politics: Since Time Immemorial*. Newbury Park, CA: Sage Publications.

———. 2002. *The Social Construction of Man, the State and War: Identity, Conflict, and Violence in Former Yugoslavia*. New York: Routledge.

Wissler, Clark. 1912. *Societies and Ceremonial Associations in the Oglala Division of the Teton-Dakota.* New York: The Trustees.

Wolf, Eric R. 1982. *Europe and the People Without History.* Berkeley: University of California Press.

———. 1999. *Envisioning Power: Ideologies of Dominance and Crisis.* Berkeley: University of California Press.

Womack, John. 1999. "Chiapas, the Bishop of San Cristóbal, and the Zapatista Revolt." Pp. 3–59 in *Rebellion in Chiapas: An Historical Reader,* edited by John Womack. New York: New Press.

Wood, Houston. 1999. *Displacing Natives: The Rhetorical Production of Hawaii.* Lanham, MD: Rowman and Littlefield.

Zamosc, Leon. 1994. "Agrarian Protest and the Indian Movement in the Ecuadorian Highlands. *Latin American Research Review* 29, 3: 37–68.

Zolbrod, Paul. G. 1984. *Diné bahané: The Navajo Creation Story.* Albuquerque: University of New Mexico Press.

Credits

In writing this book we have borrowed heavily from our many published papers. We thank all these journals and presses for permission to reuse material that first appeared in them, albeit in significantly different form. (Where applicable we note the chapters where we most used this material.)

Fenelon, James V. 2007. "The Struggle of Indigenous Americans: A Socio-Historical View." Pp. 15–38 in *Handbook of the Sociology of Racial and Ethnic Relations,* edited by Hernan Vera and Joseph Feagin. New York: Springer Press. Background material.

Fenelon, James V., and Mary L. Defender-Wilson. 2004. "Voyage of Domination, 'Purchase' as Conquest, Sakakawea for Savagery: Distorted Icons from Misrepresentations of the Lewis and Clark Expedition." *Wicazo Sa Review* 19, 1 (Spring): 85–104. Background material.

Fenelon, James V., and Thomas D. Hall. 2005. "Indigenous Struggles over Autonomy, Land, and Community: Anti-Globalization and Resistance in World Systems Analysis." Pp. 107–122 in *Latin@s in the World-System: Decolonization Struggles in the 21st Century U.S. Empire,* edited by Ramón Grosfoguel, Nelson Maldonado-Torres, and Jose David Saldivar. Boulder, CO: Paradigm Publishers. Chapter 4 and others.

———. 2008. "Revitalization and Indigenous Resistance to Globalization and Neo-liberalism." *American Behavioral Scientist* 51, 12 (August): 1867–1901. Chapter 2.

Hall, Thomas D., and James V. Fenelon. 2003. "Indigenous Resistance to Globalization: What Does the Future Hold?" Pp. 173–188 in *Emerging Issues in the 21st-Century World-System: Vol.1: Crises and Resistance in the 21st-Century World-System,* edited by Wilma A. Dunaway. Westport, CT: Praeger. Background material.

———. 2004. "The Futures of Indigenous Peoples: 9/11 and the Trajectory of Indigenous Survival and Resistance." *Journal of World-Systems Research* 10, 1 (Winter): 153–197. Background material.

———. 2005. "Indigenous Peoples and Hegemonic Change: Threats to Sovereignty or Opportunities for Resistance?" Pp. 205–225 in *Hegemonic Decline: Present and Past,* edited by Jonathan Friedman and Christopher Chase-Dunn. Boulder, CO: Paradigm Publishers. Chapter 6.

———. 2008. "Indigenous Movements and Globalization: What Is Different? What Is the Same?" *Globalizations* 5, 1 (March): 1–11. Chapter 7 and elsewhere.

Index

Aboriginal(s), 53–55, 57; cultural destruction, 54; diversity of, 53; identity and, 53, 54; land and, 53; meaning of, 60n18; urban, 55

Acteal Massacre, 78–79

Adevasi: history of, 47–50; identity issues, 48–49; land and, 52, 57; origins, 40; population, 49, 51; resistance and revitalization strategies, 51–52; struggles of, 40; struggles with British colonialism/neocolonialism, 47–48; terminology, 48, 49. *See also* Gond; Warli

Africa: colonialism in South, 33; indigenous v. tribal, 148; peoples in, 32–34, 148–149; racial/tribal lines within, 33–34

African National Congress, 33

agriculture, conflicts in, 31

alcohol, abuse of, 8, 9

América Profunda in Mexico (2003), 22, 26, 82

American Civil War, 108; politics of, 113

"American Indian": academic representation of, 104; boarding schools, effects of, 124, 127; citizenship, 124; controlling and containing, 100; four analytical perspectives of, 91–92; identities/stereotypes, 91, 114, 127; status with United States/Canada, 92, 114. *See also* specific nations

American Indian Movement, 5, 6

American Southwest: colonization of, 106; guns, spread of, 108; shared identities and forced organization, 107–108; social organization in, 106; Spanish division of peoples, 106

Aotearoa, 39, 44

art, indigenous, 32–33

Arvol Looking Horse, 99

Australia, 53–55; arrival of humans in, 60n19; disease and colonization of, 53; genocide in, 53–54; race/racism in, 54–55, 61n22

autonomous rebel communities, 74

autonomy, 140; concerns over, 82; efforts, 35; globalization and, 11; maintenance, 145; in Mexico, 77; post apartheid, 33; rebuilding communities with, 31; unity and, 86

autoridad, 82

Awatere-Huata, Donna, 58n1

Aztec empire, 65, 71

Barta, Tony, 53

Bates, Crispin, 49

Battle of the Little Big Horn, on buffalo hide, 33 (photo)

Bear Butte, 101, 102 (photo); fasting and praying on, 102; gathers around, 30

Bechtel Corporation, 17n5

BIA. *See* Bureau of Indian Affairs

Bijoy, C. R., 48–49

Bill for the Recognition of Forest Rights, 52, 59–60n17

Biolsi, Thomas, 10

Black Hills, 99, 115, 144–145; control of, 9; initial extraction activities, 97; as symbol, 101. *See also* 1868 Fort Laramie Treaty

Bolivia, 87; Aymara in, 85; natural gas exploitation (2003), 3; protests in, 82; 2005 election, 3–4

Bonfil Batalla, Guillermo, 26, 67, 69, 84

Bureau of Indian Affairs (BIA), 109

California Indians, 111–112

Canada, 92, 114; apologies from, 155; "First Nations" in, 23, 57; Mohawk in, 130, 140; Navajo in, 105; recognition of indigenous groups, 141; supporting indigenous movements, 127

About the Authors

Thomas D. Hall is the Edward Myers Dolan Professor of Anthropology at DePauw University and coauthor, with Christopher Chase-Dunn, of *Rise and Demise: Comparing World Systems* (Westview 1997).

James V. Fenelon is Professor of Sociology at California State University–San Bernardino and author of *Culturicide, Resistance, and Survival of the Lakota (Sioux)* (Routledge 1998).